Portraits
of
Success

Compiled and Edited by
Hal Donaldson
Kenneth M. Dobson

Portraits of Success
Compiled and Edited by
Hal Donaldson and Kenneth M. Dobson

Printed in the United States of America
ISBN: 1-880689-03-0
Copyright 1994, Onward Books, Inc.

Cover design by Matt Key

The opinions contained herein do not necessarily represent the views of other participants.

Unless otherwise noted, Scripture quotations are taken from the *New International Version*. Copyright 1973, 1978, 1984, International Bible Society. Scripture quotations marked *NKJV* are taken from the *New King James Version*. Copyright 1979, 1980, 1982, Thomas Nelson, Inc., Publishers. Scripture quotations marked *KJV* are from the *King James Version* of the Bible. Scripture quotations marked *TLB* are taken from *The Living Bible,* copyright 1971 by Tyndale House Publishers, Wheaton, Illinois. Scripture quotations marked *NASB* are taken from the *New American Standard Bible,* copyright 1960, 1962, 1963, 1968, 1971, 1972, 1975, 1977, The Lockman Foundation. Scripture quotations marked *NEB* are taken from *The New English Bible*. Copyright The Delegates of the Oxford University Press and The Syndics of the Cambridge University Press 1961, 1970. Scripture quotations marked *Good News* are taken from the *Good News Old Testament* copyright 1976, American Bible Society.

Dedication

Dedicated to Jim and Barbara McGill, Ed Fortenberry, Bill and Louvada Davis, Bill and Berdeen Nelson, and Dick Vass.

Contents

Acknowledgments

Special thanks to Randy and Joanne Cole, Debra Petrosky, Sharon Souza, Matt Key, David Donaldson, and Bill Bolin.

Introduction

"Go, sell your possessions and give to the poor, and you will have treasures in heaven. Then come, follow me." Those were the terms Jesus offered the rich young man in Matthew 19:16-22. Certainly Jesus did not define success by one's bank account or mortgage payment. And, by His debates with the Pharisees, it is clear He also refused to define success by one's status, influence, or fame. Jesus' life and the principles He espoused unveil a portrait of success foreign to today's culture. He defined success by one's emptiness.

John the Baptist was not successful by human standards. He was homeless, ate insects, and possessed a wardrobe without name brands. Yet, he was successful because he understood the principle of emptiness. He said, "He [Jesus] must become greater; I must become less" (John 3:30). John the Baptist knew the more empty he was of fleshly desires—and the more dependent he was on God for his sustenance—the more pleasure he brought to the Father. For John, obedience to the Almighty required complete emptiness. That is not to suggest that obedience mandates a vow of poverty or living in obscurity. Emptiness has little to do with one's status or wealth; it has everything to do with the extent to which we will allow Jesus to fill us with His thoughts and ways.

Portraits of Success is a blueprint for serving Jesus and spiritual achievement, which, in turn, will lead to a more fulfilling and productive life. One principle pervades this book: "emptiness" is synonymous with success. By growing closer to Jesus, and allowing Him to govern and guide one's life, he or she is guaranteed significance and success.

In this age of self-servitude, greed, and temptation, the world's perception of success is being shaped by ungodly forces. Tragically, many Christians have allowed the world's view of success to dictate their actions and values. Jesus is merely waiting for individuals to invite Him to empty them of worldly, self-serving desires so He can refill them with spiritual possessions and newfound priorities. Emptying yields a greater degree of intimacy with Jesus. And, after all, what more can one want in life than to know and serve Jesus, Son of the living God?

Hal Donaldson

1

Is Your Tongue Sticking Out?

DR. GLEN D. COLE

The epistle of James is devoted to the subject of spiritual maturity. A great test of spiritual maturity is how one uses the tongue. James affirms that God gave man the gift of speech, but warns the gift can be used for building or for tearing down. We would much rather speak of the sins of thievery, adultery, murder, and covetousness than we would the sins of the tongue.

SEVEN THINGS THE LORD HATES

In my reading through Proverbs each month (one chapter per day according to the date), I discovered in Proverbs 6:16-19 seven things that the Lord hates. Three of those involve the use of the tongue: a lying tongue (vs. 17); a false witness who speaks lies (vs. 19); and one who sows discord among brethren (vs. 19).

Proverbs 13:3 pictures the double use of the tongue: "He who guards his mouth preserves his life, but he who opens wide his lips shall have destruction" (NKJV). When I come to Proverbs 18 in my monthly reading, I sit up straight and pay close attention to the dangers of a tongue that is sticking out: "Death and life are in the power of the tongue, and those who love it will eat its fruit" (Proverbs 18:21, NKJV).

I think it would be wise to note the words of Jesus regarding the use of the tongue:

> Therefore I say to you, every sin and blasphemy will be forgiven men, but the blasphemy against the Spirit will not be forgiven men. Anyone who speaks a word against the Son of Man, it will be forgiven him; but whoever speaks against the Holy Spirit, it will not be forgiven him, either in this age or in the age to come.
>
> Either make the tree good and its fruit good, or else make the tree bad and its fruit bad; for a tree is known by its fruit. Brood of vipers! How can you, being evil, speak good things? For out of the abundance of the heart the mouth speaks.
>
> A good man out of the good treasure of his heart brings forth good things, and an evil man out of the evil treasure brings forth evil things. But I say to you that for every idle word men may speak, they will give account of it in the day of judgment. For by your words you will be justified, and by your words you will be condemned—Matthew 12:31-37, NKJV.

THE UNRULY TONGUE

The apostle Paul made an evaluation of the sinner in Romans 3:9-18. He began with the fact that none are righteous and proceeded to describe our unrighteousness, beginning with the tongue: ". . . with their tongues they have practiced deceit; the poison of asps is under their lips" (Romans 3:13, NKJV). That evaluation agrees with James 1:26: "If anyone among you thinks he is religious, and does not bridle his tongue but deceives his own heart, this one's religion is useless" (NKJV).

The apostle Peter was the "big mouth" of the disciples, always ready to give his opinion. By the time he wrote his epistles he had matured tremendously. In writing to the infant church he quoted from Psalm 34:12-16 about how one should keep his "tongue from evil, and his lips from speaking guile" (1 Peter 3:10, NKJV).

Three of my favorite "sentence sermons" are found in *Quotable Quotations*, compiled by Lloyd Cory. They are all on the subject of the tongue: "A tongue three inches long can kill a man six feet tall" (Japanese Proverb); "A tongue doesn't weigh much, but many people have trouble holding one" (Grit); and "Sometimes I doubt whether there is divine justice. All parts of the human body get tired eventually—except the tongue. And I feel this is unjust" (Konrad Adenauer).[1]

THE TONGUE: A MIGHTY SWORD

I was intrigued to learn of an engraving on the United States Post Office in Washington, D.C., that defines the meaning of a letter:

> Messenger of Sympathy and Love
> Servant of Parted Friends
> Consoler of the Lonely
> Bond of the Scattered Family
> Enlarger of the Common Life
> Carrier of News and Knowledge
> Instrument of Trade and Industry
> Promoter of Mutual Acquaintance
> Of Peace and Good Will Among Nations.

One thing is left out of this declaration: the possibility of devastation through the words of a letter. We have all heard of the "Dear John" letter, but many letters have devastated their recipients because of their poison, wrath, lies, and evil intent.

We come back to James' letter to the church. After addressing the eagerness of many to speak in public without realizing the qualifications for and strict judgments upon a teacher, James pointed out three possibilities for the use of the tongue:

1. Power to direct. James referred to two observable items, the bit and the rudder, which have the ability to direct a horse and a ship, respectively. How often has something so small as a word directed a person into the wrong path, or even worse, into a life of destruction? Conversely, how often has a word brought hope, direction, and purpose into a life?

I recall a Sunday evening in my home church in Tacoma, Washington. At 17, I had just graduated from high school and planned to attend Washington State University with a music scholarship. My pastor's message was followed by a time of prayer around the front of the sanctuary. After waiting upon the Lord, I felt a strong sense of His presence, and I heard His still, small voice speak to me. The message was clear: "Go to Bible college and study for the ministry." I thought God had confused me with someone else. But the thought persisted: "Give up the scholarship; I will make a way for you."

Dorothy Kirschke, my pastor's wife, who was playing the piano nearby, sensed my struggle. I felt her hand on my shoulder and heard her say, "Glen, whatever God is saying to you, say yes." That was all she said. They were only a few short words, but they went right to my heart. I opened my mouth and said, "Yes, Lord." When I did, the struggle ended and freedom came. What a thrill to look back to that time in my life and realize that nine carefully chosen words sent me in a direction I would never have considered for myself.

Here is a significant revelation we can miss if we are not careful. The horse with the bit in its mouth needs someone to guide it. The ship's rudder is turned by the pilot of the vessel, sending it in the right direction. What a great influence exercised by so small an object—a bit and a rudder.

2. Power to destroy. "How great a forest a little fire kindles!" (James 3:5, NKJV). Many thousands of acres of timber are lost each year in our country because of careless campers or smokers. A small cigarette tossed indiscriminately can set an entire forest on fire, such as the blaze that went through Yellowstone Park in the 1980s. The application is not difficult. Lies, gossip, and heated words can destroy an individual, a family, or a congregation.

In Revelation 12:10 the devil is seen accusing the brethren "day and night" before God. How does he do this? By convincing us we are no good, worthless, and that we can never accomplish anything for God. Satan has convincingly accused us and has us right where he wants us.

He also accuses us through the rumor mill. Second Timothy 3 gives us a list of evils in the end-time. Slanderers—or gossips—are found with the brutal. But that isn't surprising, for you can destroy a person's reputation with the tongue. And, usually, the individual does not have a chance to defend himself. The tongue has done it again!

An interesting contrast to *tongues of destruction* is found in Acts 2. *Tongues of fire* rested on each one assembled in the upper room on the Day of Pentecost, empowering that early group of Christians to spread the gospel around the world. Their tongues were set on fire from heaven rather than hell. Creative power burst forth upon them to edify, build up, encourage, and to tear down the strongholds of the enemy.

If our tongues are not set on fire by the Holy Spirit, the rumor mill will grind on. Tale-bearers will function in great numbers. Whisperers and backbiters, with their tongues hanging out, will move about for the latest tidbits of gossip. They are referred to as "busybodies" in 2 Thessalonians 3:11 and 1 Timothy 5:13. "Every kind of beast and bird, of reptile and creature of the sea, is tamed and has been tamed by mankind. But no man can tame the tongue. It is an unruly evil, full of deadly poison" (James 3:7,8, NKJV).

One of the darkest times in my life came after I had been invited to be guest speaker in a church in one of the districts of our denomination. The invitation had been in my possession for a year, but five days before I was to speak I received a phone call canceling my appearance. One man had written a letter to the district officials that was filled with false rumors and innuendos. The district superintendent sent a letter to all the ministers on the roll stating that I was under charges—even though there was not an ounce of truth in the allegations.

What do you do in a situation like that? Fuss, fight, fume? That would be the natural response, but I decided to put it in God's hands, and I learned to trust Him in a greater way because of it. After all, how can you control the fallout of such an incident on your own? It is impossible. Jesus said, "Pray for those who spitefully use you and persecute you" (Matthew 5:44, NKJV). When you do, then you are able to let it go. Then God, who knows all and sees all, can work it out in His way, in His time. He does vindicate.

Someone captured the devastation of gossip in the following lines:

My name is Gossip.
I have no respect for justice.
I maim without killing.
I break hearts and ruin lives.
I am cunning and malicious,
and gather strength with age.
The more I am quoted the more I am believed.
My victims are helpless.
They cannot protect themselves against me
because I have no name and no face.
To track me down is impossible.
The harder you try,
the more elusive I become.

I am nobody's friend.
Once I tarnish a reputation, it is never the same.
I topple governments and wreck marriages.
I ruin careers and cause sleepless nights,
heartaches, and indigestion.
I make innocent people cry in their pillows.
Even my name hisses.
I am called Gossip.
I make headlines and headaches.
Before you repeat a story, ask yourself:
Is it true? Is it harmless? Is it necessary?
If it isn't, don't repeat it.[2]

As a member of the Rotary Club for a number of years, I was impressed with their four-way test. I believe James would have approved:

1. Is it the *truth*?
2. Is it *fair* to all concerned?
3. Will it build *goodwill* and *better friendships*?
4. Will it be *beneficial* to all concerned?

3. Power to delight. The last step in the evaluation of James is edification, or the power to bless. The writer points out the inconsistency of expecting a fountain to produce both fresh water and salt water. When compared to the tongue, the contrast is equally fitting. Should we use the tongue on Sunday to praise the Eternal God, then use the same tongue every other day of the week to abuse men who were created in His likeness? Should we sing praises to God in the sanctuary, then lambaste our brothers and sisters outside the doors of the church? Indeed, the tongue is very capable of inconsistency. If we do not harness the tongue, then our praises are tainted and worthless.

THE DELIGHT OF THE TONGUE

James said fresh water and good fruit are emblems of delight. I enjoy illustrating the delight of the tongue through a story about my youngest grandchild, Caitland. One Sunday when she was four years old, Caitland asked to come to our house following morning services. She thought it was really special having Grandma and Grandpa to herself since we have six other grandchildren. Following lunch, little Caitland took a nap, and she was still sound asleep when it came time to go back to church for the evening service. Her brothers and sister had run her ragged the day before and now she was catching up.

Finally, I had to wake her, and even though she hadn't finished her nap, she was pleasant. I put her dress back on, put her socks and shoes on the proper feet, then asked if she would like a banana. That suited her just fine. I offered to cut up an apple for her to take in a plastic bag. She liked that idea as well.

Caitland was in between Grandma and Grandpa in the car when she looked up at me (with the plastic bag neatly resting on her lap), and with a twinkle in her eye said, "Grandpa, you are a handsome prince!" Wow! I melted! She could have had half my kingdom! Her words were a delight, and I have feasted on them ever since. When others don't think I'm so great, all I have to do is look at Caitland's picture and hear those words, "Grandpa, you are a handsome prince!" I can go on.

The capstone of this subject is an observation made in Proverbs 15:4: "A wholesome tongue is a tree of life, but perverseness in it breaks the spirit" (NKJV). Think about it. Pray about it. Determine to keep your tongue from sticking out.

Dr. Glen D. Cole is senior pastor of Capital Christian Center in Sacramento, California. He serves as president of Capital Bible Institute and chairman of the board of Capital Christian School. The church has a series of radio broadcasts and has a weekly attendance of 5,000.

Dr. Cole serves on numerous boards, including the Executive Presbytery for the General Council of the Assemblies of God. A graduate of Central Bible College in Springfield, Missouri, he was awarded a Doctor of Divinity degree from Pacific Coast Bible College in Sacramento.

He and his wife Mary Ann have two sons, Randy and Rick, who are also ministers. The Coles have seven grandchildren.

2

It's Always Too Soon to Quit!

DR. GEORGE O. WOOD

Faith expresses itself two ways: an active belief for God to change our circumstances or an active trust in God when our circumstances remain the same.

What pressing load do you carry? Have you asked the Lord to lift it from you? If so, and the load is still there, then have you asked the Lord for strength to carry it?

Some falsely believe that faith has only the one element: God must remove the burden. But the Scriptures consistently teach us that faith is a two-sided coin. Just look at Hebrews 11:32-40 where the faith of some of God's heroes changed their circumstances by conquering kingdoms and shutting the mouths of lions, while the faith of God's other heroes brought no alteration in their circumstances—they were tortured and sawed in two. Yet both sets of heroes gain this good word: "These were *all* commended for their faith" (Hebrews 11:39, italics added).

I call the upper side of the "coin of faith" the miracle part; the New Testament calls the bottom side of the coin perseverance.

The underlying Greek word is *hupomene:* literally, a remaining under or behind. It carries the idea that when God does not remove the burden, He gives you the strength to carry it or to remain behind when others are running ahead. Our English translations of the Bible use terms such as patience, endurance, perseverance, or steadfastness to translate the one word *hupomene.*

Hupomene is an active word and not like the sentiments expressed in saying, "Hang in there, baby!" or "Pray for me that I'll hold out to the end." Such phrases describe a person who is barely holding on; *hupomene* describes the spirit of a winner who treats the present obstacle not as a disaster engulfing him but as a hurdle to overcome. The *hupomene* person is a fighter—with active and energetic resistance to hostile power. His endurance is not marked by complaining, weariness, despondency, or grumbling; it's inspired by a heroic will to remain firm. Such a person not only bears up with the burden, but contends with it!

When we ask the Lord to take away terrible or unwanted circumstances and He does not, we become disappointed. But God has not turned a deaf ear to us. His answer to our cry is the strength to carry the load; that's *hupomene:* perseverance!

DO I NEED PERSEVERANCE?

You need endurance only when obstacles, difficulties, and sorrows assail you. If you encounter no opposition to your well-being, health, finances, family, or service to Christ—then perseverance is not a high priority.

But this very day most of us have at least one problem for which there is no apparent human solution, and all of us will experience this dilemma sometime in our lives.

From where I sit at my office desk, I look up to a motto I have placed on the wall across from me: "It is not what happens to me, but what happens in me that counts." From a human point of view, I want only good things to happen *to* me, but God is more concerned that good things happen *in* me. Thus, perseverance is a quality, a fruit of the Spirit, which is necessary for the formation of our character as Christians.

Here is why we need *hupomene*.

1. Without perseverance, we will follow the Lord only when it is comfortable. Remember Jesus' story about the seed sown on the rocks?

> What was sown on rocky places is the man who hears the word and at once receives it with joy. But since he has no root, he lasts only a short time. When trouble or persecution comes because of the word, he quickly falls away—Matthew 13:20,21.

Some will follow Jesus only as long as there is no adversity—thus, their "discipleship" is only for a short time. How different for those with perseverance: they stay the course; they are in the race for the duration.

The book of Revelation was addressed to just such persons. The Saddam Hussein-like Roman Emperor, Domitian, was smashing his fist against the body of Christ at the end of the first century. The decade was marked by terrible persecution and martyrdom. Believers were being thrown into prison and killed with the sword. What counsel were they given by the Holy Spirit through God's Word? Simply: "This calls for patient endurance *[hupomene]* and faithfulness on the part of the saints" (Revelation 13:10)— relevant words for end-time tribulation saints, first century believers, or us today.

You need perseverance when it is not comfortable to follow Christ.

2. Without perseverance, we will miss being treated as God's children. The letter of Hebrews was addressed to Jewish believers who were having second thoughts about their faith in Jesus; some had already left the church to return to the synagogue. What counsel was given to wavering hearts? "Endure *[hupomene]* hardship as discipline; God is treating you as sons" (Hebrews 12:7).

The discipline referred to is not the discipline of punishment, but the discipline of conditioning. A disciplined Christian is like a disciplined athlete: neither are being punished, but their "workout" causes them to be in great shape for the event. Using the language of the gym weight room, trials or adversity are the pulleys, barbells, and bench presses of the soul.

When our children were smaller, I drove them to school. I overheard my daughter, then in the eighth grade, talking in the back seat with two of her friends. They were in a vigorous conversation analyzing the dislike they had for another girl in their class. They thought she was spoiled rotten. I smiled to myself when they arrived at the conclusion as to why she was spoiled: "She has been given everything she has wanted since the second grade!"

God does not give us everything we want because we are His children. No self-respecting parent honors all his or her child's requests. Why? Because it is not best for the child.

As much as we may pout or be disappointed when God does not answer us as we want, we must accept it as part of the discipline of being God's child. We must say, "God has not allowed this to make me bitter, but to make me better."

3. Without perseverance, we will falsely expect overnight solutions for complex problems. Do you face a problem for which there appears to be no solution? Do you sleep fretfully or lie awake at night worrying how a situation will turn out? Our dilemma is that we cannot see the end. We wish there were a simple way for extraction or resolution of this problem. But all we can do is pray, "Give us today our daily bread" (Matthew 6:11).

In those times when the fog of life has rolled in on our soul, our family, our personal situation—we long for simplistic answers. We wish there were a spiritual lottery where we could hit the jackpot, or a magic wand to make the physical or existential pain go away.

God designed *hupomene* as a grace implanted in our soul precisely for such times. The late Peter Marshall once opened a session of the United States Senate with this prayer:

> Our Father, when we long for life without trials and work, without difficulties, remind us that oaks grow strong in contrary winds and diamonds are made under pressure. With stout hearts may we see in every calamity an opportunity and not give way to

the pessimist that sees in every opportunity a calamity.

Yes, oaks and diamonds—and Christ-like character—take time to form! There are few simple solutions to anything! Perseverance is the quality that rivets us to our post when the gales of life seek to sweep us off the deck. Thus, the apostle Paul counseled believers to be "patient *[hupomene]* in affliction" (Romans 12:12).

4. Without perseverance, we could never handle injustice. The early Christians did not have an easy time of it. Peter wrote his first letter especially to encourage believers who were experiencing cruel injustice. These wonderful Christians had not done anything wrong; they were not charged by the Lord with a lack of faith or the presence of sin in their lives, or any other failure. Yet, they were suffering. What does Peter tell them to do?

> But how is it to your credit if you receive a beating for doing wrong and endure it? But if you suffer for doing good and you endure *[hupomene]* it, this is commendable before God—1 Peter 2:20.

Some missionary friends of mine experienced a terrible injustice. In the dead of night four intruders broke into their house. They savagely beat the husband while he attempted to defend his family, they raped the wife and adolescent daughter, and terrorized the young son. Leaving the husband for dead, they carried the wife off to their lair where they continued to abuse her.

The husband, stirred from his unconsciousness, was able to go for help. Within hours, the police had rescued the wife and brought her back to her home. She did not know at that moment if her husband was even alive. When she went back inside the house, she saw firsthand the evidence of the violent struggle that had taken place hours earlier. Her husband's blood was all over the walls and had commingled with the inches-deep water on the floors— water that had accumulated when the thugs had left the house with the taps running.

She returned to the police car, sat in the back seat, and suddenly found herself singing:

In moments like these, I sing out a song;
I sing out a love song to Jesus.
Saying I love You, Lord.

Amazed at her composure and song, the policemen asked her how she could do what she was doing. She responded, "The Lord gave me peace, and the enemy cannot take away what he has not given."

You see, the devil cannot give us peace—therefore, it is not his to take away. It is the Lord who gives us "a song . . . in the night" (Isaiah 30:29, NKJV).

The missionary husband later testified that he had a new understanding of Romans 8:28 as a result of that awful evening. He pointed out, "The apostle Paul wrote, 'We *know* that God works good in all things.' Paul didn't write, 'We *feel* that God works good in all things.' We must make a distinction, therefore, between our 'feelings' and our 'knowings.'"

How true! In trial and amidst burdens, our feelings deceive us. Our emotions shout with pain, depression, agony, and bewilderment. But, set against all that is our "knowing"! We know in whom we have believed! We know He is working for the good! We know Christ is risen and is seated at the right hand of God! We know there will come a day when all will be set straight! That "knowingness" on our part fuels our ability to persevere. We too shall overcome . . . some day!

5. Without perseverance, we will never finish. The Christian life is not a 100-yard dash. It is a marathon! Jesus Himself knew about the drop-outs, the ones who would not stay the course.

> Because of the increase of wickedness, the love of most will grow cold, but he who stands firm to the end *[hupomene]* will be saved—Matthew 24:12,13.

The writer of Hebrews also likens the Christian life to an endurance contest where the prize is eternal life.

> Remember those earlier days after you had received the light, when you stood your ground *[hupomene]* in a great contest in the face of suffering. Sometimes you were publicly exposed to insult and persecution; at other times you stood side by side with those who were so treated. You sympathized with those in prison and joyfully accepted the confiscation of your property, because you knew that you yourselves had better and lasting possessions.... You need to persevere *[hupomene]* so that when you have done the will of God, you will receive what he has promised—Hebrews 10:32-34,36.

What are we to make of all this? Simply that today's difficulty is not God's final word. The finish line is ahead.

Victory in this race is not for those who finish first, but for all those who simply finish. Persevere!

In his immortal novel, *War and Peace,* Tolstoy described a scene on the night before the great battle Russia fought with the French. Prince Andre studied the battle strategy for the coming day. The Czar listened and rearranged the maps. Andre asked, "Will we win the battle tomorrow?"

The Czar responded abruptly, "I think not."

The young prince was alarmed. His voice became frantic: "Lose the battle! But what if we *do* lose this battle? What will become of us?"

The answer of the monarch reflected his seasoned wisdom and perspective: "We don't count the battles. We only count the last battle. The last battle is the only one that really matters."

Remember that God alone holds the key to the final battle, and that is the battle that counts most! You may feel like this present sorrow is your Waterloo—but not yet! The Lord is coming with all His holy angels! Don't give up! Fight on!

Ralph Waldo Emerson said it well: "The hero is no braver than an ordinary man, but he is brave five minutes longer." The "five minutes longer" is what we call "perseverance!"

HOW CAN I GET PERSEVERANCE?

Granted, we need perseverance. But how do we get it? Sometimes we go about it much in the same way I once jumped into a jacuzzi and announced to my family, "I want to hurry up and relax."

Perseverance, like relaxation, cannot be hurried. As with most spiritual qualities, it is not gained in a spiritual microwave or at the push of a button. It is not obtained by telling God: "I want patience, and I want it *now!*"

1. Perseverance must become a desire of the heart. Paul told the suffering believers at Thessalonica: "May the Lord direct your hearts into God's love and Christ's perseverance [*hupomene*]" (2 Thessalonians 3:5).

What does it mean to be like Jesus? Perhaps you too have sung the chorus:

> To be like Jesus, to be like Jesus,
> All I ask, to be like Him.

A great part of being like Jesus is becoming a persevering person! Jesus did not live a life of comfort or convenience. He had no place to lay His head. His friends abandoned Him. A best friend betrayed Him. His enemies nailed Him to a tree. No one ever said of Jesus: "He had it easy."

We are to follow Jesus in running with perseverance the race set before us. In fact, we are to "fix our eyes on Jesus . . . who for the joy set before him endured [*hupomene*] the cross, scorning its shame, and sat down at the right hand of the throne of God" (Hebrews 12:2).

Let this be a constant prayer on our lips: "Lord, I want to be like You. I realize that You lived with great steadfastness. I want You to give me that same quality." To say that is to direct our hearts into Christ's perseverance.

We all like quick solutions, but the Bible points us toward desiring *hupomene!*

2. Perseverance must be acted upon. Desire is not enough! Action must follow. The apostle Paul encouraged

Timothy, "Pursue . . . endurance *[hupomene]*" (1 Timothy 6:11).

Is perseverance a goal you are pursuing? I have learned the difference between a wish and a goal. Over the past several years, I gained some weight. My problem? I liked food! Oh, I wasn't grossly overweight—just 30 pounds! I really wanted to lose weight. I wished it would happen. But I just kept eating—especially desserts!

One morning I looked at myself in the mirror. What had once been slim me looked like a blimp. My stomach hung over my belt. I did not like what I saw. At that moment I decided to lose weight.

I had been on diets where I lost weight and quickly regained it. I not only wanted to lose 30 pounds—I desired to keep it off. But I didn't want to give up the normal foods I liked just to lose weight. If I did, then sooner or later, I would return to eating my favorites.

What was my solution? Eat half! I experienced difficulties. My work is such that most of my food is eaten in restaurants. My Christian training had inculcated in me guilt for leaving food on my plate. But that is what I began to do. I cut the donut in half. I ate half the cheeseburger. I skipped the dessert. Now, four months later, I am 20 pounds lighter—heading for the final 10!

Why did it happen? I made weight loss more than a want or a wish. I made it a goal.

How does this relate to perseverance? You will not get it by hoping for it. Write it down as a goal. Do it. Strong people, men and women of faith, are not created instantaneously. They grow—because they desire to grow!

3. Realize that you have support. Gaining endurance is not simply a matter of gritting your teeth and doing it! You are not alone in your quest. Look at who and what is helping you.

■ **God Himself!**

The apostle Paul described God's role in endurance formation. He gives it! Scripture calls Him "the God who gives endurance" (Romans 15:5). We find ourselves "being strengthened with all power according to his glorious might so that [we] may have great endurance *[hupomene]* and patience" (Colossians 1:11).

Author Karl Heim compares God's help to that of the first flight of a baby eagle, pushed out of the nest by its parents and then discovering to its amazement that the invisible ocean of light in which it is dropping is capable of bearing it up. The presence of God which surrounds everyone is like this invisible ocean which bears us up more surely than do all the visible means of security. Indeed, it is part of our faith that "underneath are the everlasting arms!"

■ **Hope in Our Lord Jesus!**

The apostle Paul gave gratitude to God for persons whose "endurance *[hupomene]* [is] inspired by hope in our Lord Jesus" (1 Thessalonians 1:3).

It is hard, if not impossible, to hang on when we lose hope. What helps to keep alive prisoners of war? Hope that the long war will end and soon they will be in the arms of their loved ones.

But how sure is our hope? The word hope is used in all sorts of settings. Maybe you have said, "I hope someday I strike it rich." Others have said, "I hope I win the lottery." The chances of "striking it rich" or "winning the lottery" are slim indeed for most of us! Thus, the word "hope" seems very, very tenuous.

But what about the person who says, "I hope the sun will rise tomorrow." Well, that hope is rather fixed. The sun *will* rise—even if we don't see it because of clouds or fog.

Christian hope is that which is based on an event whose occurrence is a certainty. Jesus' presence and His return for us are not one-in-a-million shots. There are no odds given because the result is sure. Christ indeed is with us! Christ indeed is returning!

Thus, the admonition to put our hope in Jesus is like putting money in a bank that will never fail!

■ The Encircling Protection of Jesus!

Important people often need protection from their enemies. Just a few days ago I toured the Texas School Book Depository in Dallas. From a corner sixth floor window on November 22, 1963, Lee Harvey Oswald fired a bullet that ended the life of President John F. Kennedy. The President lost his life because his circle of Secret Service protection was not complete enough. There was a breakdown. He was not "encircled."

Hear what the Lord says to us through His words to the believers at Philadelphia: "Since you have kept my commandment to endure patiently [hupomene], I will also keep you . . ." (Revelation 3:10).

The Lord Himself promises to be the guardian of our souls. His circle of protection about us is impenetrable! In fact, there is a great image in Revelation 1 of Jesus holding the leaders of the church (code name: stars) in His right hand. The most significant thing about that picture is *not* that the leaders are holding Jesus, but that Jesus is holding them!

What applies to Christian leaders applies to all of us. Jesus has a stronger grip on us than we have on Him! He is not letting go of us in the fierce winds of life! He is helping us to hold on, to persevere!

■ **The Comfort and Example of Other Believers!**

Have you ever been strengthened by the testimony of another Christian who has persevered under great obstacles? I have. Their example fortifies me in my own hour of trial.

My uncle, Victor Plymire, was a pioneer missionary to China and Tibet. He went to that part of the world in 1908 and served 16 years before he won his first Tibetan convert! Most persons would have quit from discouragement—but he persevered. In his nineteenth year of missionary service, his wife and his only son died within one week of each other from smallpox. Because of anti-foreign feeling at the time, he had to make the coffins and dig the grave himself. It was the middle of winter in that bitter-cold part of the world, so he had only enough strength to dig one grave for the two of them.

Did he give up on his calling? Of course, he was disconsolate. Great periods of depression weighed upon his loneliness and grief. But, when spring came, he went out and sat by the graveside and wrote in his journal:

> Until the farthest nook and corner of Tibet has heard the call of God and the story of redemption

in Christ, my task is not complete. Until the last man has heard the gospel witness, my work is not done.

The next day he set out on a witnessing trek through Tibet. It took him nine months, during which he nearly lost his life on several occasions. He passed out 100,000 copies of the Gospel of John in the Tibetan language. He was the first person to ever walk through Tibet with the gospel.

When his journey was complete, he had not been back to America for seven years; but, instead of returning home, he headed from India back to China and returned to his post of service where he had buried his first wife and only child.

A hero? You better believe it! What was the quality that anchored him? Perseverance!

When I am tempted to quit, I think of my uncle Victor and I continue.

You probably have your own "Uncle Victor"—someone whom you look to as a shining example of triumph in adversity. God has put that person or persons in your life for the purpose of strengthening you to finish the course! If you don't have such a person to look at—find one; they are everywhere!

Therefore, since we are surrounded by such a great cloud of witnesses [Abel, Enoch, Noah, Abraham, Isaac, Jacob, Joseph, Moses, Invaders of Jericho, Rahab, Gideon, Barak, Samson, Jephthah, David, Samuel, the Prophets] . . . let us run with perseverance [hupomene] the race marked out for us— Hebrews 12:1.

■ **Love!**

The apostle Paul wrote that "love endures *[hupomene]* all things" (1 Corinthians 13:7, NKJV). Love puts up with a lot! If you do not love someone, you will not allow them much slack.

Someone saw a small boy carrying a handicapped boy on his back. The handicapped boy seemed almost as large as the lad bearing him. A stranger asked: "Isn't he heavy?" The young man replied, "He's not heavy; he's my brother."

Our adverse life situations are all the more bearable if we face them with honest love for Christ and for others.

WHAT DO I GAIN FROM PERSEVERANCE?

Business people call it the bottom line. It's the profit at the end. Is there any gain from perseverance? Yes!

1. Reward results from perseverance.

For the past number of years, Christians have been reluctant to talk about heaven. We were severely criticized for "being heavenly minded and no earthly good." So we have set about doing some good—and that is "good." But let's not lose sight that the day of the Lord is coming!

How we wish it were today! But if it is not today or tomorrow, we will need to persevere until He comes! And the New Testament tells us that such a day will be filled with reward.

By standing firm *[hupomene]* you will save your-selves—Luke 21:19.

All men will hate you because of me, but he who stands firm *[hupomene]* to the end will be saved— Matthew 10:22; Mark 13:13.

If we endure *[hupomene]*, we will also reign with him—2 Timothy 2:12.

You need to persevere *[hupomene]* so that when you have done the will of God, you will receive what he has promised—Hebrews 10:36.

Blessed is the man who perseveres *[hupomene]* under trial, because when he has stood the test, he will receive the crown of life that God has promised to those who love him—James 1:12.

These are God's wonderful and exceeding promises! They are ones He is sure to keep!

Life has been described in four ways: a journey, a battle, a pilgrimage, or a race. Select the metaphor you want, but the necessity of finishing is fundamental to each. If life is a journey, it must be completed. If life is a battle, it must be fought. If life is a pilgrimage, it must be concluded. And if life is a race, it must be won!

2. Character development.

The story is told of the cowboys who wanted to bring in the legendary wild steer who roamed the range. One day they saddled their horses and set off, leading a small burro. Days later they caught up with the massive steer and roped and tied him. Then they brought the burro alongside and tightly tied the two animals together around the neck. The legs of the steer were then loosened, and he arose with a bolt! That poor little burro! He was thrown every which way! The cowboys rode off. Many days later, a burro and a steer trotted their way into the coral back at the ranch. It was very much a domesticated steer by that time. Every time the steer had thrown the burro, he got back up and planted his feet in a very certain direction—one step closer to home. The burro, though far smaller and with seemingly less power, simply wore out the steer!

That's perseverance: a determination to get home, a determination so strong that it changes everything that gets in its way.

A favorite poem of mine says:

Plod on, plod on.
Plod on, plod on.
Plod on, plod on.
Plod on, plod on.

This poem has many stanzas, but only the same two words: plod on! How does this relate to the development of our Christian character? Do you remember the process the apostle Paul wrote about?

. . . but we also rejoice in our sufferings, because we know that suffering produces perseverance *[hupomene]*; perseverance, character; and character, hope —Romans 5:3,4.

Has it ever struck you as odd that Paul told us to rejoice in our suffering? What is he? A masochist?

The key to the passage is understanding the four-step process: first, there is the suffering itself; second, what the suffering produces—*hupomene* or staying power; third, what results from perseverance—character, what we really are; and finally, the end result: hope.

Notice that perseverance is the second step in a four-step process. It is needed only when the first stage, suffering or adversity, occurs. But perseverance is not an end; it leads to character development, the kind of person I am. Once we see that God is in the process of suffering-perseverance-character development, we get to hope—the end of the tunnel. You see, trials do not last forever. The fierce winds blow and then are gone. What's left at the end when we are through plodding? We see God was with us; we survived. We are better for what has happened. There is hope! That's why Paul said, "Rejoice." Rejoice—not because of the suffering—but rejoice because the suffering initiates a process which, in time, results in hope!

Yes, adversity forms character. The strong wind that uproots a tree also lifts an eagle. The opposing force becomes a lifting force if faced at the right angle!

James wrote much the same thing as Paul.

> Consider it pure joy, my brothers, whenever you face trials of many kinds, because you know that the testing of your faith develops perseverance [*hupomene*]. Perseverance must finish its work so that you may be mature and complete, not lacking any- thing—James 1:3,4.

What is the gain from all this perseverance? God is at work making something beautiful of our life!

The story is told of a king who owned a large, beautiful, pure diamond. The gem made the king's heart burst with pride! One day, the diamond sustained a deep scratch. The king called in the most skilled diamond cutters and offered them a great reward if they could remove the imperfection from the treasured jewel. None could repair the blemish. The king was greatly distressed. After some time, a gifted lapidary came to the king and promised to make the rare diamond even more beautiful than it had been before the mishap. The king was impressed by his confidence and entrusted his precious stone to his care. The man kept his word. With superb artistry he engraved a lovely rosebud around the imperfection and he used the scratch to make the stem.

This is what God does with our wounds—and what we are to do as well. When life bruises and hurts, even the scratches can be used to etch a portrait of beauty, memory, and love.

Don't lose heart in your trial! Arthur Matthews, missionary to China, wrote home sharing some of the difficulties he and his family were enduring:

> These trials of faith are to give us patience, for patience can only be worked as faith goes into the pressure chamber. To pull out because the pressure is laid on, and to start fretting, would be to lose all the good He has in it for us.

How true!

The southern tip of Africa used to be called "Cape of Tempests." Its swirling seas and continuously adverse weather conditions caused sailors great anxiety and took many lives.

But a certain Portuguese, determined to find a safer route through these seas to the renowned land of Cathay

(China), discovered a safer passage around this promontory. And the area was renamed the "Cape of Good Hope."

Have your difficulties seemed so insurmountable that you are considering dropping out? Don't! Rather than your adversity becoming a weight that sinks you, let God help you to make it a hope that lifts you! It's always too soon to quit! Persevere!

Dr. George Wood, general secretary of the Assemblies of God, is the son of missionary parents to China and Tibet. He holds a doctoral degree in pastoral theology from Fuller Theological Seminary, a juris doctorate from Western State University College of Law, and membership in the California State Bar. He is the author of five books, including Living Fully: The Successful Life *and a college text on the book of Acts.*

Dr. Wood formerly served as Assistant Superintendent for the Southern California District of the Assemblies of God and pastored 17 years at Newport-Mesa Christian Life Center in Costa Mesa, California.

Dr. Wood and his wife Jewel have two children: Evangeline and George Paul.

Reprinted from *Pleasing God, Pleasing You*, Onward Books, 1992.

3
Accepting Change

HULDAH BUNTAIN

The book of Esther has always been a favorite of mine, in that I have drawn from the life of Esther an example of great courage, strength, determination, dedication, and commitment.

Esther, a young Jewish woman, was made queen by King Xerxes and ultimately placed in the position of saving her people from destruction. She had to go before the king to intercede for her people, but to do so without an invitation could result in death. And, therefore, she called the Jews to a three-day fast, at the end of which she would take her petition before the king.

In studying the book of Esther I've discovered five steps that shaped her future and destiny—steps I can relate to, especially since the death of my husband Mark. When I reminisce over these past years I realize more than ever that God has taken me through these steps, and He has done so for a purpose.

Born of missionary parents in Tokyo, Japan, and brought up in a pastor's home, I saw the sacrifices my parents made. In my young heart I vowed that I would never follow in their footsteps.

As a teenager living on the coast in Vancouver, Canada, I often accompanied my parents to see missionaries leave for the Orient. The huge Empress Liners were gorgeous ships, but as I stood on the dock watching the streamers fly and listening to the band play, I thought in my heart how grateful I was to be on the dock and not on the boat. Once again I vowed that the life of a missionary was not for me.

God, however, changed the course of my life when I went to the altar during a youth revival. Little did I realize what the future held. I had no way of knowing that in October 1954, as a young wife and mother, I would be standing on the deck of a similar ship on my way to India. I am grateful God does not reveal everything to us at once, but leads us step by step. In this way He is able to work out His perfect plan for our lives; for if I had known the changes that were in store for me I would have said, "Impossible."

I am sure Esther never thought she would become queen of a great nation, but God had great things in mind for her. In order for Esther to accept the changes that would ultimately determine her future, she had to take the five steps that led her to a place in history.

FIVE STEPS TO ACCEPTING CHANGE

1. The Step of Courage. Esther felt incapable of the task that was before her, so she requested that there be fasting and prayer so that God would give her the courage she needed to carry out His plan for her people.

2. The Step of Strength. Esther knew she would have to ask God for supernatural strength to attempt such a critical plan.

3. The Step of Determination. She would also need determination to follow through with the plan—in spite of the danger.

4. The Step of Dedication. In the fourth chapter of Esther we read where Esther's uncle Mordecai told her of the king's decree to have her people destroyed. Then he said to her in verse 14: "And who knows but that you have come to royal position for such a time as this?" Her dedication to God and to her people had led her at a vital time to a vital place in the kingdom.

5. The Step of Commitment. Having sought God for courage, strength, determination, and dedication, Esther now had to be committed to the task at hand and to obey God's will, whatever it may be.

GOD'S WILL VS. SELF WILL

In my book, *Treasures in Heaven*,[1] I wrote that if I had designed my own life and not followed God's plan, it would have been very different. I can still visualize our arrival in Calcutta on the ship *City of Madras* six weeks after we had left New York harbor. It was quite a trip. I often smile when I recall our accommodations, for there was first class, second class, third class, and "missionary class"— which is as far down into the ship as you can get. It would be impossible to elaborate on every aspect of the journey;

suffice it to say it was long, hot, and difficult. We had to travel to what was then Ceylon (now Sri Lanka), and then wait to take another ship to Calcutta, only to arrive and find that our baggage had not been transferred to the second ship. I am sure you can imagine what a problem it was for a young family with a one-year-old child.

On that October day in 1954, I did not know if I had the courage, strength, determination, dedication, and commitment to face the changes in my life. Thirty-five years later, on June 3, 1989, when faced with another "impossible" situation, I again wondered if I had the courage, strength, determination, dedication, and commitment I would need to make a decision that would be harder than the one I had made so many years before.

ANOTHER CHANGE

I was preparing to leave India for the United States to help our daughter's family move from Columbia, Missouri to Salt Lake City, Utah, where our son-in-law had accepted a position with a medical heart program. I was to help them find suitable housing in Utah, then return to Missouri to help them pack and move.

When I said good-bye to Mark in Calcutta, he was perfectly well. I arrived in Bangkok two hours later and checked into my hotel room for the night. A note from dear missionary friends, Al and Lynette Johnson, was waiting at the desk: they invited me to join them for dinner later that evening. When I entered my room the telephone light was flashing. The operator told me to call my son-in-law immediately, for he had an urgent message. I could not believe the news. Ten minutes after I had left, Mark collapsed with a cerebral hemorrhage. Immediate surgery was scheduled. While still in Bangkok I received a call from Calcutta with the news that surgery had been successful. Al, Lynette, and I thanked God for His faithfulness, then we retired, encouraged that God had undertaken.

The next morning my world fell apart. Mark was dead. I could not believe it. I remember saying to Al, "What about the work?" I did not see how it could continue without Mark.

My thoughts went back to our first trip to Calcutta. We held our first meetings in a tent, then moved to an upstairs hall, and finally constructed and dedicated the first church built in Calcutta in 100 years. Our ministry was now responsible for numerous churches, a six-story hospital, and 21 schools within the seven states in East India. Was it to end all at once? It seemed "impossible" that I could carry on the work without Mark. Surely God would not require me to do so. After all, I had given faithfully and sacrificially the many years we had been in India. Wasn't that enough?

The hours after learning of Mark's death were a nightmare. I had to change my tickets, find my luggage, and get back to Calcutta. The Johnsons stayed with me until I went through immigration, then I was alone. My flight was delayed two hours, so I found a seat in the crowded airport, feeling as if my entire world had crashed in around me.

I couldn't concentrate to read, so I bowed my head, closed my eyes, and prayed. I confess I argued with God. Why had this happened? Why had He taken Mark? What did He expect of me? All of a sudden, I felt as if someone were standing next to me. I heard a distinct voice say, "Take it one day at a time, and I will help you." I looked around, but no one was there. Thinking I was hallucinating, I tried to pull myself together. But again, louder than before, I heard the words, "Take it one day at a time, and I will help you." I felt a strange warmth go through my body, and I knew it was God. I didn't have the answers to all the questions racing through my mind, but I knew God was with me, and that was enough.

As I walked through Calcutta customs, many of the men on duty had tears in their eyes. They had been Mark's friends and grieved at his passing. As expected, a large crowd met me at the airport, but because of God's faithfulness *I* was able to comfort *them*.

I was taken to the funeral home, and as I viewed the body of my husband I could not believe it was the same man I had left only a few hours before. I was reminded of the words Mark often quoted in his missionary messages. They were the words of Judson of Burma, but Mark inserted "India" for "Burma":

> Only one prayer I ask,
> Only one good I crave:
> To finish my task
> and then to lie
> Within an Indian grave.

Miraculously, government officials gave permission for Mark to be buried on the mission complex, where—only two days before his death—he had finalized plans for a new church and Bible college to be built. It was a sweltering June day with temperatures over the 100-degree mark. An estimated 20,000 persons, including family and friends, crowded in and around our complex for the funeral services. Many wept as the casket was lowered into the ground. Mark had his desire. But what about me? My heart cried out, "Dear God, how can I ever fill this man's shoes?" All of a sudden, the choir broke the silence with one of Mark's favorite songs:

Were the whole realm of nature mine,
And were a present far too small,
Love so amazing, so Divine,
Demands my soul, my life, my all.

Tears mixed with perspiration as I found my way to Mark's office. Plans for the new church and Bible college were still on his desk, just as he had left them. I knew we badly needed a larger church and a Bible college, but how could I undertake such a project? Then my eyes fell upon the message he had begun to prepare for the previous Sunday's service, which was to have been Faith Promise Sunday. Written in bold letters and circled in black felt pen were the words:

I GAVE, I GAVE MY LIFE FOR THEE,
WHAT HAST THOU GIVEN FOR ME?

I realized no dedication, no commitment, was too great for One who had given His all for us.

GOD'S FAITHFULNESS

In a further study of the life of Esther, I found she outlined a three-fold scheme that would help her fulfill her task:

1. She prayed.
2. She planned.
3. She acted.

Since Mark's death I've seen God fulfill the promise He gave me at the airport, as we have prayed, planned, and acted upon the direction God has given us. Young pastors fresh out of Bible school have picked up the torch, and God's work is going forward. Surely, Mark lives on in the lives he touched and trained.

On January 24, 1993, I again stood by Mark's grave, this time at the bottom of the cross of our new church. Dr. Raymond Carlson, general superintendent of the Assemblies of God, unveiled a plaque and dedicated the Mark Buntain Memorial Assembly of God Church. As we sang "To God be the glory, great things He hath done," I knew it had not been easy; the load had been heavy, and the responsibilities had been great; but God had been faithful to His promise. I had taken it one day at a time, and Mark's dream had been fulfilled.

It would not be possible to tell of the many miracles that took place during the past few years, but God has proven, "As thy days, so shall thy strength be" (Deuteronomy 33:25, KJV).

LINKS IN THE CHAIN

William Carey, the greatest missionary to India, said, "I am willing to go down to the pit if you will hold the ropes at home." Those are the ropes of prayer and support, and if the people at home will hold the ropes tightly, we will be able to accomplish the work God has placed before us.

Proverbs 3:27 says, "Withhold not good from them to whom it is due, when it is in the power of thine hand to do it" (KJV). We are all vital links in a great missionary chain, strengthening missions around the world, not allowing a single link to break. Together we will see God's plan and purpose fulfilled.

It is not ability—it is *avail*ability and *depend*ability that God wants. We will go down into the pit of darkness to win the lost for Christ—if you will hold the ropes at home.

Accepting change was not easy. In fact, it was extremely difficult. My new role was hard to accept, but I know God doesn't make mistakes. How thankful I am that He helped me—as He had promised—to take it one day at a time. I have been able to draw from God the courage, strength, determination, dedication, and commitment that I needed to follow His plan in the needy land of India.

Huldah Buntain accompanied her husband, Mark, to Calcutta, India in 1954. She has served faithfully as a missionary there. She pastors a large congregation and oversees a hospital, Bible college, numerous schools, feeding programs, and more. She also received an honorary doctorate from North Central Bible College.

She has one daughter, Bonnie.

4

For Men Only

DAVE ROEVER

As I tour the country's high schools sharing my story of tragedy-turned-triumph, I take time at the end of a presentation to visit with the kids one-on-one. I probe their minds trying to get a handle on what's causing this generation to wallow in a quagmire of hopelessness, despair, and turmoil. Whatever the topic of conversation, I ultimately come back to two basic questions: What about your home? What about your dad?

In answer to the first question, I occasionally hear, "Great . . . my parents are great." But to the second, all too often, the response is: "My dad left when I was little," or "My dad's hardly ever home," or "My dad lives outside the state, so I don't see him or talk to him much."

Another thing I've noticed as I tour the country is that our church congregations are made up of older people. Where are the children? The teenagers?

This isn't going to be another church-bashing session. I'm not blaming the church. In the past few years we've had all the church-bashing we can take; I'm not going to add to it. The difficulties we face in America today are not the fault of the church.

BETRAYED AND VIOLATED

After finishing a high school assembly in the northern United States, I opened the floor for questions and comments. A young lady stood in front of her 2,500 peers and said, "Mr. Roever, every night my father comes into my room and tries to sexually molest me. I have to run out of the house to get away from him." She hesitated a second, then in measured, calculated words, asked, "Mr. Roever, how can I get rid of my father?"

The most common statement made to me by girls in public schools is, "Mr. Roever, I wish you were my dad." My son and daughter are young adults now, but if either of them ever said to another man, *I wish you were my dad,* it would break my heart. Yet, I hear it every day, over and over again.

During an assembly in Michigan a few weeks later, I told the story of the girl who'd asked how to get rid of her father. When I finished my presentation, the kids lined up all the way to the back of the gym, waiting to speak to me. Most of them just wanted a hug—just wanted to hear somebody say *I love you.* At least a dozen times while doing an assembly, I tell the kids I love them, but that's not enough. They want me to look them in the eye and say it just to them.

This particular day, a little 17-year-old blonde sitting on the front row waited until everyone finished before she stepped up to me, grabbed my arm, and pulled me aside. "Mr. Roever, my name is Sasha," she said. Her eyes revealed a frantic young woman. When she spoke again, her words were barely audible, but desperate. "Please, Mr. Roever, what did you tell that girl?"

Taking Sasha's hand, I asked, "Do you have a problem at home?"

She nodded as tears filled her eyes. I knew if I asked her another question I would be involved, because if she answered it with a yes—and there wasn't the slightest doubt in my mind she would—I would break the law if I didn't report it. I plunged in. "Are you being sexually abused by your father?"

"Yes," she said, embarrassed and ashamed.

The details that followed defy comprehension by decent human beings. She said, "I was almost three years old when my dad left us. He was gone for nearly 10 years. When my mom begged him to come back, he said he would . . . on one condition . . . I wouldn't be a virgin when I turned 13." Sasha struggled to empty her soul of the awful story. "My mother said yes . . . and . . . and I've had to sleep with my dad for four years . . . and I hate it . . . and I want out."

I motioned for Danny, the youth pastor who had driven me to Sasha's school that day. "Danny," I said, "I need two counselors. I want Christian counselors, but they have to be state-approved. I need help and I need it now. Is there anyone you know?"

His eyes grew wide as he said, "You're not going to believe what happened! Early this morning I got a phone call from a couple in our church who work for the state as counselors! They said, 'We want to see Dave Roever in action in a public school. Can you get us into the assembly?' I called the school and got permission for them to come. They're waiting in the foyer right now."

Sasha never spent another night with her father. The counselors placed her with a good family, and that evening in our crusade she gave her heart to Jesus. Sasha faithfully attends church and is growing in the Lord, no longer tormented by fear of what her father might do next.

This story has a tragic twist to it. When Danny, his pastor and wife, and the counselors took Sasha to tell her parents what the state was doing and how the church was cooperating, they discovered the parents attended church regularly. After getting Sasha settled in her new home, Danny spoke with the parents' pastor. His comment? "You take Sasha for now. When you get her straightened out, bring her back to me and we'll take it from there."

Sasha found two more girls in her school who were in abusive situations. One had been abused by her father, the other by her high school coach. These men are sitting behind bars today and, as far as I'm concerned, they can throw away the keys.

EPIDEMIC PROPORTIONS

Statistics indicate that 25-40 percent of American women today have been sexually abused by a family member. And it doesn't occur only in families outside the church. All around us are individuals who have experienced sexual abuse. Many of them are angry and bitter and harbor a burning desire for revenge. Often the offender is dead and gone, but the wounds of the victims are still painful.

Many young people in America are living in hell on earth with no end in sight. The fastest growing cause of death among teens—next to drinking and driving—is suicide. Consumed with despair, they feel they have nothing to live for and suicide is their only way out. These are the kids I face regularly in the schools of our nation.

God save our children. Our greatest natural resource, if you can call it that, is our kids. It's not oil; it's not technology; it's our children. And what's being done to many of them is incomprehensible.

A CHALLENGE FOR FATHERS

By now, you've probably figured out where I'm heading. This is a gut-wrenching subject, and one that's difficult to discuss, but I challenge you to keep reading. The problem in America is not the government; it's not the schools; it's not the church. The problem is Dad. So when we're through blaming the government, the schools, and the church, we finally have to admit the responsibility lies with us.

Some of the last words of the Old Testament say it clearly: "Behold, I will send you Elijah the prophet before the coming of the great and dreadful day of the Lord. And He will turn the hearts of the fathers to the children" (Malachi 4:5,6, NKJV). That means fathers' hearts have not been where they should be. And now, just before it's too late, just in the nick of time, the heart of the father must be turned to his children, and the hearts of the children to the father. Why? "Lest I come and strike the earth with a curse" (Malachi 4:6, NKJV). I hate threats, but I love a challenge. Challenge me and I'll go the last mile; I'll go miles past the last mile; I'll overrun the objective in my eagerness to accept a challenge because I believe in challenges. *Lest I come and strike the earth with a curse* can be taken as a threat or challenge. If it's a threat, it may be too late. If it's a challenge, we have an opportunity to prevent it from coming to pass. I prefer to take it as a challenge.

PRIEST AND PROVIDER

Every husband/father is called to be the priest and provider of his home. If you think you're a good provider, but you're a lousy priest, you're kidding yourself. There's no such thing as a good provider who is not a good priest. Nor is there a good priest who is not a good provider. A good priest will always provide for his family; that's an automatic. But I caution you, Dad, if you give your kids Izod shirts and Air-Jordan shoes every day of their lives but don't have the love of God in your home, you're a lousy provider.

You may say, "I'm a good priest, Dave. I pray for my family." When was the last time your kids heard you call their names before the throne of God? It's not too late to start. Pray for your children. Intercede for them. Let them hear you. If they can't hear you when you pray, then pray by the air-conditioning vent. Pray for the sins they thought you didn't know about, and let them experience a few sleepless nights wondering how in the world you found out. All over America I deal with kids whose lives are shattered. I'm convinced it wouldn't be so if they regularly heard their fathers pray.

Mothers, I'm not ignoring you. I know many of you have carried the load and been the priestesses of your households because your husbands have ignored their God-given responsibility. Thank you for being godly women, but it's time for men to assume spiritual leadership of their homes.

SHOW AND TELL

Many fathers have never said the words "I love you" to their children. You may be one of them. You think they *know* you love them, but if you don't tell them they can't be sure. Tell your kids you love them, then show it by sharing your life with them. Dad, turn your heart to your children. Don't let anything take precedence over them. If your company offers you a 10-times-your-regular-pay raise to do a job that would send you to Timbuktu when your little girl is being smooth-talked by some boy in school and she's about to give away her virginity because she thinks she's giving him her love, don't take the job! Stay with your daughter. I'd lose my job, pick up aluminum cans, and sell them to feed my family—for the rest of my life if necessary—before I'd put my daughter on the altar of sacrifice for my personal success.

Lose your job, but don't lose your children.

Take your boy fishing and hunting. I'd rather go hunting *with* my son today than go hunting *for* him tomorrow.

HEROES

I'm tired of seeing our children turn to the rock-and-roll gods of this generation in search of heroes. They have posters all over their walls, and they bow down before their gods at rock concerts. They ought to have better role models than rock stars who do drugs then say, "Don't do drugs." The kids see through it; they know most of the rock stars are just trying to appease irate parents. So, in essence, they're setting two examples for today's youth: one of lying, the other of drug abuse.

I think Dad ought to be the hero in the family. What's this nonsense of turning silly little *teenage neutered midget turtles* into heroes? I thank God my kids had more to look up to than neutered turtles living in a sewer! There's got to be more for our children. Give them a dad to look up to, and when someone asks who their hero is, they'll say, "Dad's my hero."

How do you become a hero? Be a man of your word. When you make a promise, live by it. If you break a promise, go to your children and explain why you can't do what you said you'd do. And make sure your reason for not doing what you promised is more important than doing it. The integrity of a father's word is a standard for the lives of his children. Unfortunately, for many of America's kids today, no standard exists. There's no dad to be a hero.

Believe it or not, you can be a hero by saying no. Your kids may be saying, "Aw, Dad!" on the outside, but inside they're saying, *Thank you! You gave me a reason to say no when I didn't have the courage to say it on my own.*

Another way to be a hero to your kids is to treat their mother with love and respect. Call her *honey*, not *heifer*. Tell her you love her everyday—right in front of the kids. Tell her three, four, five times a day. They need to hear you say it. Send your wife flowers; not just for her but for your kids as well. When they come home from school and see them, they'll say, "Oooo, Mom, where did the flowers come from?" The look on her face when she says, "Your dad sent them" will speak volumes to your kids. They find great security in knowing that Mom and Dad love each other.

Be a gentleman. It may seem old-fashioned to open a door for your wife, or help her on with her coat, but some things never go out of style. Besides that, it's scriptural. Ephesians 5:25 says to love your wife like Jesus loves the church and treat your wife like Jesus treats the church. He gives the church gifts; He opens the door; He shows His goodness and kindness, and He says "I love you." We ought to do the same. Don't be so busy you don't have time for a little kindness along the way.

I may not be the best at chivalry, but I had the best teacher a man could want. My daddy treated my mama with respect. He walked into the kitchen every morning, bent down and kissed the back of her neck right in front of us kids, and said, "Lois, darling, I love you." We thought it was funny and we'd snicker and say, "Daddy's kissing Mama!" But he taught me how to treat my wife by the example he set.

Not long ago Dad stepped into a room in his three-piece suit and walked up to Mama's casket. He bent down, brushed the hair from her ear and said, "Lois, darling, I love you." My dad kept his vows unto death. That's why he's my hero.

A friend named Lee Williams lost his wife and two daughters when a drunk driver sped down the wrong side of an interstate highway and killed 27 passengers on a church bus.[1] Lee's wife and two daughters were his entire family. Two years after the tragedy, I asked Lee how he was doing.

"Pretty good, Dave. . . . I just came from the cemetery. I don't get there often, but I had a promise to keep. Kristen would have been 16 this week, and I promised her 16 roses on her 16th birthday, so I made a trip up to Missouri and put them on her grave. You know, Dave, a dad's got to keep his word." He continued, "Robin's grave is right beside Kristen's. The color of her phone is kinda faded now. . . . I promised her a phone of her own on her 14th birthday. A man has to keep his promises."

You say, "Dave, the kids are dead. You don't keep vows to dead people." You're right. Lee was keeping vows to *himself.*

Dad, if you're going to turn your heart to your children, you have a few promises to keep—to yourself and to them. There are things you said you would do that you haven't done. It's time to do them. For your kids' sake, give them a hero.

RESPONSIBILITY: A TWO-WAY STREET

Every kid living at home has a responsibility, too. Not only does that verse say the fathers should turn their hearts to their children, but the children should turn their hearts to their fathers. Kids may ask, "How can I turn my heart to my father?" Start by telling him you love him. "But I don't love him. In fact, I think I hate him," you may say. Tell him you love him anyway. You may be as surprised as he is to find out you really do.

Keep *your* promises to your parents. Do your homework. Clean your room. Honor your father and mother. You have an obligation and a responsibility before God to do so. If you call yourself a Christian, you should behave as a child of God. If you don't, you're in double jeopardy.

Every child should make this pledge: "I solemnly vow I will clean my room. I will obey my father and mother. I will do my homework. I will be a child of God who accepts responsibility. And I will serve You, Lord Jesus, so help me God."

THE AWFUL TRUTH

When I spoke at a prayer breakfast in Alaska, the governor handed me a paper. The message on it has changed my life. It said:

Today in America . . .
2,795 teenagers will get pregnant
1,106 teenagers will have abortions
372 teenagers will have miscarriages
1,027 babies will be born to mothers addicted to cocaine
67 babies will die before they are 30 days old
105 babies will die before they are a year old
211 children will be arrested for drug abuse
437 children will be arrested for drinking and driving
10 children will die from gunshot wounds
30 children will be wounded by gunfire
135,000 children will take guns to school
1,512 teenagers will drop out of school
1,849 children will be abused or neglected
6 teenagers will commit suicide
3,288 children will run away from home
1,629 children are in adult jails
7,742 teens will become sexually active
623 teenagers will contract gonorrhea or syphilis[2]

Tomorrow in America it starts all over again. . . .

Dad, turn your heart to your children. Turn your heart to God. Don't be so proud or so arrogant as to think you're too big for correction. Don't be so senseless as to think you're too big to respond to the tug in your spirit. For the sake of your children, for your own sake, Dad, turn your heart to your kids.

When you stand before God on Judgment Day, the only thing you can take with you is your wife and children. You can't take your job. You can't take that gold watch signifying 40 years of service. You can't take any of the things you thought were so important. The only thing you can take is your family. That's it. You can have all the gold watches that were ever made, but I'm sure you'd trade them in a New York second for the daughter who won't make it to heaven because you were too busy earning watches.

Dad, God loves you and so do I. I want God to do a miracle in your life today. Follow me in this simple prayer. Pray it only if you mean it. Let it come from your heart. This is an act of the priest; the responsibility of the priest; the duty, the performance—not the put-on. Speak it out like the man you are. I want God to hear you, and I want the devil to hear you, too:

> Lord Jesus, thank You. Thank You for Your love, Your patience, Your life, Your death, and Your resurrection. You are my High Priest; You intercede for me; You shed Your blood for me because You loved me. God, in those areas where I'm wrong— and You know them as well as I—please forgive me. Cleanse me of all filthiness of the flesh, mind, and spirit as I commit myself to You. As I study Your Word, I pray Your characteristics will become mine. Jesus, help me to be a man of my word. Help me to stand for what is right regardless of what the rest of the world may do. Give me the strength of the Holy Spirit to be the witness a dad ought to be. Thank You for my children. Thank You for my wife. Make me a holy priest, a godly priest, a priest filled with integrity. And now, as priest of my household, I hold my family before You and I intercede for them. I will not let go of them. Dear God, save my family, cleanse them, preserve their souls, and let us all stand in an unbroken circle around the throne of God.

Satan, you're a liar. You've lied to me for years, but Jesus has set me free. The blood of Jesus cleanses and keeps my family. Satan, you no longer have any part in my family. You are finished; you are history. Jesus is Lord of my family and we will stand before Him in peace and love. In the name of Jesus Christ, Amen.

The Reverend Dave Roever, horribly burned when a white-phosphorus grenade exploded inches from his face in Vietnam, inspires thousands across the nation with his enthusiasm for life. Credentialed with the Assemblies of God for 30 years, and speaking for public high schools, television, business conventions, crusades, and churches, he crisscrosses America bringing a message of hope.

Dave attended Southwestern Assemblies of God College and currently serves as president for the Roever Evangelistic Association, Inc. and the Roever Educational Assistance Program, Inc.

He and his wife Brenda are the parents of son Matthew and daughter Kimberly Roever Chapin.

Reprinted from *Parenting*, Onward Books, Inc., 1993.

5

The Believer's Balance Beam

JOHN M. PALMER

A vacationer on a hurried tour of Europe stopped in front of a great cathedral and called to his wife, "You take the inside, I'll take the outside, and I'll meet you out here in five minutes."

That's not the way to tour Europe, or the way to live a balanced life. Yet, because we are so pressured and rushed, daily life becomes much like trying to do back-handsprings on a balance beam: it's possible, but it's not easy. It takes a great deal of practice and focus, and it requires commitment and energy. Lest they tumble off, Christians must keep their eyes on the Lord, just as gymnasts must keep their eyes on the beam.

Early in His ministry, Christ explained to the disciples, "My food . . . is to do the will of him who sent me and to finish his work" (John 4:34). Just before He went to the cross, Jesus prayed to the Father, "I have brought you glory on earth by completing the work you gave me to do" (John 17:4).

Had Jesus visited everywhere on earth? Had He healed all who were sick? Had He raised everyone who had died? Was He a personal teacher to everyone in the world? No. Yet He could make the claim of John 17:4 because He had done the will of His Father and finished the work that God had given Him to do.

You and I can't do everything. Some things are outside the realm of possibility for us, and we simply don't have the time to do all we would like. Therefore, it is important that we live well-balanced lives so we can fulfill the work God planned for us.

The Sermon on the Mount provides powerful teaching for a balanced life. Matthew 5 reveals the *principles* of the balanced life; Matthew 6, the *priorities* of the balanced life; and Matthew 7, the *Person* who exemplifies the balanced life: our Lord Jesus Christ.

PRINCIPLES OF A BALANCED LIFE

1. Happiness comes by being, not by having. In Matthew 5:3-11, Jesus repeatedly used the word "blessed." In the Greek, "blessed" means having an inner joy that cannot be taken away. It goes beyond the happiness that comes from good circumstances.

Jesus taught the key to happiness is not found in *having,* but in *being.* Our society places so much emphasis on having: having a good job, a good income, lots of friends, a nice car, a beautiful home, fashionable clothing, etc. When we buy into that mind-set and embrace the philosophy of "when I have, I'll be happy," we exert an inordinate amount of energy in the pursuit of things, and that puts our life out of balance.

What can we learn from the Beatitudes in Matthew 5? When Jesus said, "Blessed are the poor in spirit . . ." (vs. 3), He taught us the importance of acknowledging our own spiritual impoverishment. When He said, "Blessed are those who mourn . . ." (vs. 4), He taught us to be broken. When He said, "Blessed are the meek . . ." (vs. 5), He taught us to be humble. When He said, "Blessed are those who hunger and thirst for righteousness . . ." (vs. 6), He taught us to hunger for spiritual food. When He said, "Blessed are the merciful . . ." (vs. 7), He taught us to be compassionate. When He said, "Blessed are the pure in heart . . ." (vs. 8), He taught us the importance of keeping our motives and actions holy. When He said, "Blessed are the peacemakers . . ." (vs. 9), He taught us to be healers and those who bring people together. When He said, "Blessed are those who are persecuted because of righteousness . . ." (vs. 10), He reminded us that we are to be righteous, no matter the cost.

Many of us are like the prodigal son who said, "Father, give me . . ." (Luke 15:12) because he thought happiness would come from the things he possessed. When he discovered the emptiness found in possessions, he said, "Father . . . make me . . ." (Luke 15:18,19). He understood the difference between having and being. The person who strives to take on the characteristics of the Beatitudes is the one who will find true happiness. Wealth, fame, popularity, position, power, and prestige can't be substitutes for what we ought to be as Christians. You can't substitute *having* for *being*.

I learned the hard way that hair spray doesn't make a good deodorant. A can of each stands in front of the mirrors at my health club. One day, while in a hurry to get back to the church after a workout, I failed to read the cans and sprayed hair spray under my arms and deodorant on my hair. My hair smelled great, but my underarms were sticky until I could get to a shower. Some things have no substitute. You have to reach for the right can. Happiness lies in being, not in having.

Why is it that some people work from dawn to dusk in an effort to make a living, build a fortune, advance in the company, yet spend little time with their families and give little attention to spiritual matters? It's because, like the prodigal, they expect to find happiness in *having* rather than *being*.

2. Fulfillment comes by being true to who we are. Jesus said, "You are the salt of the earth. But if the salt loses its saltiness, how can it be made salty again? It is no longer good for anything, except to be thrown out and trampled by men" (Matthew 5:13). If we are the salt, let's be salt—not sugar, not pepper; but salt. That's what God called us to be.

Our lives get out of balance when we seek to be somebody we aren't, when we seek to do things not within our character and nature, when we seek to be all things to all people. We have to accept our role, our place, and who we are in Christ.

Jesus also said:

> You are the light of the world. A city on a hill cannot be hidden. Neither do people light a lamp and put it under a bowl. Instead they put it on its stand, and it gives light to everyone in the house. In the same way, let your light shine before men, that

they may see your good deeds and praise your
Father in heaven—Matthew 5:14-16.

If we are the light, let's be light. Don't be ashamed of
who you are, and don't be embarrassed by your priorities.
Because God has called you to be a light in the world, your
priorities will differ from those of other people in the world.
When we recognize God has called us to make a difference
in the world, and that fulfillment comes from being true to
His call, then we go to work or school not just to make
money or get a degree, but we go with an understanding
that our environment is our mission field.

A long time ago I heard a story about William Carey, a
shoemaker by trade who longed to be a missionary. Everyone who came into his shoe shop heard about Jesus Christ.
One day his friend took him aside and said, "William, all
this talk about Jesus is ruining your business."

Carey responded, "My business? My business is to
extend the kingdom of God. I only fix shoes to meet
expenses. My business is to be a light. I'm only doing this
to pay the bills because God called me to be a light in the
world."

When our lives are in balance, God is glorified.

3. Greatness comes by being what we believe. Jesus
said, "But whoever practices and teaches these commands
will be called great in the kingdom of heaven" (Matthew
5:19). According to Scripture, our relationship with God is
the most important in our lives. Then comes our relationship with spouse and children, followed by commitment to
our work, and our local church and its ministry. When we
keep these priorities in order, we successfully walk the
balance beam.

Unfortunately, many of us get up in the morning and leave for work or school without talking to God or spending some time in His Word. We go the entire day without devoting time to the Lord, yet say our relationship with Him is the most important. If we who are married spent as much time with our spouse as some of us do with God, we would not have much of a relationship. If God truly holds the most important place in our lives, then our schedules must reflect that. Greatness does not come by being popular, rich, or famous. Greatness, Jesus said, comes when we practice what we believe. God honors obedience to His commands.

4. Growth comes by being committed to a higher standard. Matthew 5:21-48 provides six instances in which Jesus illustrates the difference between the law of the Old Testament and the love of the New Testament.

The law says, "As long as you don't physically kill anyone, you're okay. You can hurt them, you can say nasty things about them, you can embarrass them, you can verbally assault them, and you're still okay" (Palmer translation). In contrast, love says, "We must deal with any hurt in a relationship." We must be reconciled to those with whom we have had differences. When there is a problem, we need to settle matters quickly.

The law says you can't have sexual relations with someone who is not your spouse. Love goes beyond that. It says sin begins in the heart. Jesus taught, "Anyone who looks at a woman lustfully has already committed adultery with her in his heart" (Matthew 5:28).

The law says, "Anyone who divorces his wife must give her a certificate of divorce." In other words, marriage only lasts as long as you want it to. When you get tired of your wife, divorce her; just be sure to do it legally. Love teaches that marriage is built on mutual faithfulness and trust, and it is meant to last a lifetime. So, as we seek to walk life's balance beam, our commitment to a marriage built on faithfulness and trust will help us make good decisions about the time we spend with our spouse.

The law says, "Keep your promises." Love says, "Be a person of your word so you won't have to swear on your oath." Jesus said, "Be a person of your word so when you say 'yes,' that's all you have to say. When you say 'no,' that's all you need to say."

The law says, "Do unto others as they do unto you. You've heard it said, 'an eye for an eye and a tooth for a tooth.'" If somebody socks you in the nose, sock them back. If they steal your coat, steal theirs in return. Love says, "Do better than you are expected to do. If someone strikes you on the right cheek, turn to him the left one. If someone sues you and takes your tunic, give him your cloak too. If someone forces you to go one mile, go with him two."

The law says, "Love your friends and hate your enemies." Love says, "Love your enemies, then you certainly can love your friends." Jesus said, "Anybody can like and love somebody that likes and loves them. I want you to take it a step further."

In every instance love was the higher standard. That's the standard Christ exemplified, and the one He has called us to.

PRIORITIES OF THE BALANCED LIFE

In Matthew 6, Jesus taught one central thought, and the key verse upon which this teaching hinges is Matthew 6:33:

"But seek first his kingdom and his righteousness, and all these things will be given to you as well." The secret of living a balanced life is to *seek God*.

   1. Seek God by helping the poor. Jesus instructed:

> Be careful not to do your "acts of righteousness" before men, to be seen by them. If you do, you will have no reward from your Father in heaven. So when you give to the needy, do not announce it with trumpets, as the hypocrites do in the synagogues and on the streets, to be honored by men. I tell you the truth, they have received their reward in full.
>
> But when you give to the needy, do not let your left hand know what your right hand is doing, so that your giving may be in secret. Then your Father, who sees what is done in secret, will reward you— Matthew 6:1-4.

Proverbs 19:17 teaches, "He who is kind to the poor lends to the Lord, and he will reward him for what he has done." Jesus later explained why:

> Then the King will say to those on his right, "Come, you who are blessed by my Father; take your inheritance, the kingdom prepared for you since the creation of the world. For I was hungry and you gave me something to eat, I was thirsty and you gave me something to drink, I was a stranger and you invited me in, I needed clothes and you clothed me, I was sick and you looked after me, I was in prison and you came to visit me."

Then the righteous will answer him, "Lord, when did we see you hungry and feed you, or thirsty and give you something to drink? When did we see you a stranger and invite you in, or needing clothes and clothe you? When did we see you sick or in prison and go to visit you?"

The King will reply, "I tell you the truth, whatever you did for one of the least of these brothers of mine, you did it for me"—Matthew 25:34-40.

Jesus makes it very clear that seeking Him involves reaching out to all His children, including the poor. When we do so, we are doing it as unto Him.

2. Seek God through prayer. Seeking God through prayer is vital. It is during prayer, as we wait on God, that He lets us know what aspects of our lives are out of balance. Jesus provides instruction on the nature of our prayers. First, our prayers must be sincere:

And when you pray, do not be like the hypocrites, for they love to pray standing in the synagogues and on the street corners to be seen by men. I tell you the truth, they have received their reward in full. But when you pray, go into your room, close the door and pray to your Father, who is unseen. Then your Father, who sees what is done in secret, will reward you—Matthew 6:5,6.

Some have mistakenly taken this to mean we are not to be involved in corporate prayer because of Jesus' instructions in these verses. Jesus wasn't addressing the *method;* He was addressing the *motive.* The motive of the Pharisees was wrong. They were not sincere in their praying. They were praying so people would see them and say, "What spiritual people they are!" Jesus denounced them as hypocritical because their motives were not pure.

Second, our prayers must be thoughtful:

And when you pray, do not keep on babbling like pagans, for they think they will be heard because of their many words. Do not be like them, for your Father knows what you need before you ask him— Matthew 6:7,8.

We do not pray to be heard by men or to impress them by our phraseology. Our prayers, directed to the Father above, need to be thoughtful and consistent with the Word of God.

Third, our prayers must be focused:

Our Father in heaven, hallowed be Your name [we focus on God's character].

Your kingdom come. Your will be done on earth as it is in heaven [we focus on God's will].

Give us this day our daily bread [we focus on our needs].

And forgive us our debts, as we forgive our debtors [we focus on relationships].

And do not lead us into temptation, but deliver us from the evil one [we focus on overcoming Satan]—Matthew 6:9-13, NKJV, with author additions.

Only one line in the Lord's prayer focuses on the temporal: "Give us this day our daily bread" (NKJV). Everything else focuses on the spiritual. Yet, when we pray, most of us over-emphasize temporal needs.

Fourth, our prayers must be accompanied with forgiveness:

> For if you forgive men when they sin against you, your heavenly Father will also forgive you. But if you do not forgive men their sins, your Father will not forgive your sins—Matthew 6:14,15.

All of us have been hurt, wronged, or disappointed, but Jesus taught us that prayer must be accompanied by forgiveness. "If you do not forgive . . . your Father will not forgive . . ." If we are not forgiven, our prayers will not be answered because the Lord will not hear us if there is iniquity in our hearts. That is why Jesus said:

> Therefore, if you are offering your gift at the altar and there remember that your brother has something against you, leave your gift there in front of the altar. First go and be reconciled to your brother; then come and offer your gift—Matthew 5:23,24.

The Lord placed great importance on maintaining balance in our earthly (horizontal) relationships, as well as strengthening the spiritual (vertical) relationship between ourselves and God through prayer.

Fifth, our prayers must be accompanied by fasting. Jesus did not say "*if* you fast," but "*when* you fast." Accordingly, fasting ought to be a part of every Christian's life. That might mean giving up food for one meal or giving up food for one day. It could even include a modified fast if a dietary problem is involved, but when you fast, give that time to serving the Lord or to prayer.

Jesus cautioned:

> When you fast, do not look somber as the hypocrites do, for they disfigure their faces to show men they are fasting. I tell you the truth, they have received their reward in full. But when you fast, put oil on your head and wash your face, so that it will not be obvious to men that you are fasting, but only to your Father, who is unseen; and your Father, who sees what is done in secret, will reward you— Matthew 6:16-18.

The ladies weren't putting on their make-up and the men weren't shaving. When people asked them what was wrong, they replied, "Oh, nothing. I'm just fasting." Jesus said, in effect, "Put on make-up, shave, comb your hair, and don't make it obvious to other people that you are fasting. It's between you and God."

It should also be between you and your spouse if your spouse is doing the cooking! On a few occasions I have fasted without telling my wife; then I have a problem to work out at home! Being considerate by letting your family know you won't be eating a meal is not the same as fasting to be seen by men.

3. Seek God by investing in eternity.

> Do not store up for yourselves treasures on earth, where moth and rust destroy, and where thieves break in and steal. But store up for yourselves treasures in heaven, where moth and rust do not destroy, and where thieves do not break in and steal.

For where your treasure is, there your heart will be also.

The eye is the lamp of the body. If your eyes are good, your whole body will be full of light. But if your eyes are bad, your whole body will be full of darkness. If then the light within you is darkness, how great is that darkness!

No one can serve two masters. Either he will hate the one and love the other, or he will be devoted to the one and despise the other. You cannot serve both God and Money—Matthew 6:19-24.

We are bombarded at every turn with persuasive suggestions to invest in the future. There is nothing wrong with that, to a point. Stewardship involves preparing for the future so that we can adequately take care of those for whom we are responsible. However, it is important that we invest in treasures that are eternal, as well. Jesus said, "Where your treasure is, there your heart will also be."

The apostle Paul addressed this issue in 2 Corinthians 4:16-18:

Therefore we do not lose heart. Though outwardly we are wasting away, yet inwardly we are being renewed day by day. For our light and momentary troubles are achieving for us an eternal glory that far outweighs them all. So we fix our eyes not on what is seen, but on what is unseen. For what is seen is temporary, but what is unseen is eternal.

Where our eyes are focused determines the spiritual quality of our lives.

We need to invest ourselves in eternity. That is one reason we teach the importance of tithing (giving 10 percent of our income to the Lord) and giving in freewill offerings. It is important to invest in the kingdom of God, not just for the sake of furthering the work of the Lord, but for investing in the eternal. For where your treasure is, there your heart will be. Christians who stop tithing over a period of time will become lukewarm in their faith because they've redirected where their treasure is. That is generally the first step in falling away from the Lord.

4. Seek God by doing His will first and foremost. "But seek first his [God's] kingdom and his righteousness, and all these things will be given to you as well" (Matthew 6:33).

When we seek the Lord, He will provide all we need and desire. How does He reward us as we seek Him? He rewards us with wisdom so we know how to order our lives. He rewards us with peace so we can handle the disappointments of life. He rewards us with joy so we can have strength through our trials. He rewards us with steadfastness so we can stand in good times and bad times. He rewards us materially by meeting our needs and giving us extra to meet the needs of others.

PRACTICING THE BALANCED LIFE

To live a balanced life we are called to practice specific attitudes and actions.

1. Do not judge. Balanced Christians look at themselves before looking at others. Jesus said:

Do not judge, or you too will be judged. For in the same way you judge others, you will be judged, and with the measure you use, it will be measured to you.

Why do you look at the speck of sawdust in your brother's eye and pay no attention to the plank in your own eye? How can you say to your brother, "Let me take the speck out of your eye," when all the time there is a plank in your own eye? You hypocrite, first take the plank out of your own eye, and then you will see clearly to remove the speck from your brother's eye—Matthew 7:1-5.

Jesus taught about the importance of examining ourselves before we examine others, and He called those who look at others first "hypocrites." The apostle Paul warned, "But if we judged ourselves, we would not come under judgment" (1 Corinthians 11:31).

If we are to be balanced Christians, we must examine our own faults and weaknesses before we examine the faults of others. We must deal with our own sin before we seek to deal with the sin of our brothers and sisters. When we do look at others, it should be to help rather than to judge.

2. Look to the Lord in every situation.

Ask and it will be given to you; seek and you will find; knock and the door will be opened to you. For everyone who asks receives; he who seeks finds; and to him who knocks, the door will be opened.

Which of you, if his son asks for bread, will give him a stone? Or if he asks for a fish, will give him a snake? If you, then, though you are evil, know how to give good gifts to your children, how much more will your Father in heaven give good gifts to those who ask him! So in everything, do to others what you would have them do to you, for this sums up the Law and the Prophets—Matthew 7:7-12.

If we look to the Lord in every situation of life, we will stay balanced and humble before Him: balanced because of the direction He gives, humble because we can't look to Him with pride in our hearts.

In the above passage Jesus said, in essence, "Keep on asking and it will be given to you. Keep on seeking and you will find. Keep on knocking and the door will be opened." Don't give up. If circumstances have not yet worked out in accordance with God's will, continue to hold on in faith; continue to stand on the promises of God. "In all your ways acknowledge him, and he will make your paths straight" (Proverbs 3:6).

3. Don't take the easy road—take the right one.

Enter through the narrow gate. For wide is the gate and broad is the road that leads to destruction, and many enter through it. But small is the gate and narrow the road that leads to life, and only a few find it—Matthew 7:13,14.

Jesus spoke about the narrow road that leads to eternal life, as opposed to the wide road that leads to destruction.

He said, "I am the door of the sheep. All who came before Me are thieves and robbers" (John 10:7,8, NAS). The balanced Christian walking the path of the Lord does not take the easy road; he takes the right one—the one Jesus described as narrow.

When Lillian Trasher was 19 years of age and engaged to be married, God called her to be a missionary. She went home and phoned her fiance. "I am so excited!" She announced, "God has called me to be a missionary!"

Her fiance, a dedicated Christian who planned to enter the pastoral ministry, responded, "God has not called me to be a missionary."

Lillian told her fiance, "I will not marry you unless you also sense a call to be a missionary," and she prayed that God would direct him accordingly. Either God did not call him to be a missionary, or he rejected the specific call, so Lillian broke their engagement. She went to Egypt where she spent more than 50 years and built one of the largest Christian orphanages in the world. Lillian never married. At one time she had hoped to have 12 children of her own; instead, she provided a home to more than 12,000 orphans from Cairo and surrounding areas who came to know Jesus Christ as their Savior. Lillian Trasher took the right road— even though it was the hard road.[1]

Jesus didn't promise that everything would turn out the way we expect it, but Scripture does promise that God has a plan for our lives. Proverbs 19:21 says, "Many are the plans in a man's heart, but it is the Lord's purpose that prevails." God wants to allow His purpose to prevail in our lives, but it will only happen when we take the right road, not necessarily the easy one.

4. Do more, talk less. In verses 15-21, Jesus taught that our lives are measured more by the fruit we bear than by the words we share.

> Watch out for false prophets. They come to you in sheep's clothing, but inwardly they are ferocious wolves. By their fruit you will recognize them. Do people pick grapes from thornbushes, or figs from thistles? Likewise every good tree bears good fruit, but a bad tree bears bad fruit. A good tree cannot bear bad fruit, and a bad tree cannot bear good fruit. Every tree that does not bear good fruit is cut down and thrown into the fire. Thus, by their fruit you will recognize them.
>
> Not everyone who says to me, "Lord, Lord," will enter the kingdom of heaven, but only he who does the will of my Father who is in heaven. Many will say to me on that day, "Lord, Lord, did we not prophesy in your name, and in your name drive out demons and perform many miracles?" Then I will tell them plainly, "I never knew you. Away from me, you evil-doers!"
>
> Therefore everyone who hears these words of mine and puts them into practice is like a wise man who built his house on the rock. The rain came down, the streams rose, and the winds blew and beat against that house; yet it did not fall, because it had its foundation on the rock. But everyone who hears these words of mine and does not put them into practice is like a foolish man who built his house on sand. The rain came down, the streams rose, and the winds blew and

beat against that house, and it fell with a great crash—Matthew 7:15-27.

Notice that Jesus said, "Not everyone who *says* . . . but only he who *does* . . ." (vs. 21). He taught that the greatest impact we make lies not in our words but in our lives. The words of Martin Luther King, Jr., in his immortal "I have a dream" speech, would have been forgotten had Dr. King not lived what he said. He marched the streets of the South; he stood for what he believed; he did what he said; and his life made a difference.

False prophets often say the right words, but their actions reveal them to be wolves in sheep's clothing. They say one thing, but do another. Likewise, those who call themselves Christians, who talk the talk but don't walk the talk, will find that Christ rejects them because of it. Our actions must line up with our words.

Jesus taught that our reward is based on doing the will of the Father, not just doing good deeds. The ones He criticized were doing good things—prophesying in His name, driving out demons, performing miracles. He said, "You can do those things, but if you do not do the will of My Father who is in heaven, you will not enter the kingdom of God."

Further, Jesus says our ability to stand in times of trial depends on how well we have put God's Word into practice. Jesus used the analogy that "everyone who hears these words of mine and puts them into practice is like a wise man who built his house on the rock" (Matthew 7:24). The house built on the rock withstood the storm; the house built on sand did not.

Some Christians withstand every kind of storm that comes their way. They're like rocks, unmoved, their faith firmly established. The apostle Paul was just such a man. He suffered far more than most Christians, yet we consider him to be one of the strongest and most spiritual men of all time. Why was he able to stand? Because he put Christ's words into practice.

James taught us to be "doers of the Word and not merely hearers" (James 1:22, NAS). The word *do* is the biggest little word in the Bible, and it spells the difference between spiritual success and failure, between standing or collapsing under the weight of the trial. God calls us to pray, not just talk about it; to give, not just talk about it; to witness, not just talk about it; to study the Bible, not just talk about it; to love, not just talk about it. These are things we can *do* to practice the balanced life.

If you are stalled in your spiritual life, it's not because Jesus doesn't love you. It's not because you don't love Him. It may be because you are not *do*ing what God has called you to *do*.

The successful gymnast must keep both eyes on the beam regardless of whatever else is happening. The same is true for the Christian who wants to live a balanced, fruitful life: keep your eye on the beam—none other than our Lord Jesus Christ, the Author and Finisher of our faith. A balanced life will bring glory to God and yield rich benefits and blessings for the child of God.

The Reverend John M. Palmer, a graduate of Central Bible College in Springfield, Missouri, pioneered his first church in Athens, Ohio, where he pastored for 11 years. He currently is senior pastor of First Assembly of God in Des Moines, Iowa.

The author of a Sunday school training manual entitled, Equipping for Ministry, *the Reverend Palmer serves on the Board of Directors at Central Bible College; the National Harvest Task Force for the Decade of Harvest; and as Director of the North Central Region, Decade of Harvest.*

He and his wife Debbie have three children: Amy, Jonathan, and Bethany.

6

Leisure Time in a Busy World

JOHN N. VERTEFEUILLE

Are you doing more but enjoying it less? It seems to be a common complaint today. Ask someone how he is doing and you are likely to hear one of these responses: "I'm exhausted!" "I'm just trying to stay afloat." "There's too much to do!" "I'm burnt out!"

We spend most of our conversational time comparing how tired and weary we are. Do any of the following conversations sound familiar?

"Boy, I've got so much work to do I'm going to be up until midnight."

"Well, at least you'll get to go to bed."

"That's only because I was up all night last night."

or

"I haven't had a day off in two weeks."

"I haven't had one off in two years!"

"I was talking about my second job."

Our days are no longer lived—they are lamented; our lives no longer enjoyed, but endured.

Certainly, we all feel driven by the unrelenting pressure of the fast-paced life in which we must keep up or get run over. One of the ironies of our society is that while technology has made more hours available through time-saving devices, we have filled those hours with more time-consuming commitments. And, at every turn, something is expected of us. The boss expects us to work harder; the church expects us to be more committed; the school expects us to support the PTA, help out in the classroom, and make props for the school play; the doctor directs us to exercise more; the dentist tells us to floss every night; the community encourages us to coach little league and support an endless array of causes; and our family asks for a little of our time and energy. I tend to agree with Flip Wilson, who said, "If I had to live my life all over again, I don't think I'd have the strength."

NO TIME TO REST

We talk about how busy and tired we are, but we don't seem willing to rest. If anything, we want more hours! Peruse the shelves of your local bookstore (if you have time) and see how many titles deal with the time crunch. The "How-Tos" range from adding extra hours to your day to surviving a busy schedule. One title offers to help us relax without feeling guilty, but it is difficult to break away from our sense of being driven.

Why are we so driven? Why do we find it so difficult to relax? Perhaps at the heart of the matter is our own insecurity. There is the insidious belief that our acceptance by others is based on our ability to perform. We will be liked based on *what we do,* not *who we are.* Because we want people to like us, we keep doing more. We struggle with saying no, and before we know it, we are overextended. We become "human doings" instead of "human beings."

Our insecurities cause us to compare ourselves with others, which often leaves us with a feeling of inadequacy. Pick up almost any Christian book and read the biography of the author. It may read something like this: Author, popular conference speaker, pastor, husband, and father of three. We think we could never measure up to all that—but, oh, how we try.

The paradox is that we find ourselves doing more and feeling tired, stressed, and burned out as a result; meanwhile, we live in the most leisure-oriented society in the world. The American leisure industry spends billions of dollars encouraging us to play harder. The problem is that we are as intense about leisure as we are about work.

Leisure does not equate with rest. How many go on vacation every year only to come home exhausted? We almost need a vacation to recover from our vacation! We rush from place to place at a frantic pace and forget to enjoy ourselves. Our unspoken motto is: Hurry up and relax!

SPIRITUALLY EXHAUSTED

For many, life is so full of stress that even sleep does not provide the needed rest. While I was going through seminary, I worked a high-pressure job where performance was measured by speed. After an eight-hour shift, I drove home, went to bed, and dreamed all through the night that

I was on the job. I woke up in the morning physically and emotionally exhausted. It was as if I had worked a double shift.

Our malady isn't limited to being physically tired; we are tired in spirit as well. Gordon MacDonald shares an insightful account from Lettie Cowman's wonderful book, *Springs in the Valley*, where she recalls the following tale from her missionary experience in colonial Africa:

> In the deep jungles of Africa, a traveler was making a long trek. Coolies had been engaged from a tribe to carry the loads. The first day they marched rapidly and went far. The traveler had high hopes of a speedy journey. But the second morning these jungle tribesmen refused to move. For some strange reason they just sat and rested. On inquiry as to the reason for this strange behavior, the traveler was informed that they had gone too fast the first day, and they were now waiting for their souls to catch up with their bodies.

She concluded:

> This whirling rushing life which so many of us live does for us what that first march did for those poor jungle tribesmen. The difference: they knew what they needed to restore life's balance; too often we do not.[1]

Isn't that true! We are so busy *doing*, and it seems we are making good progress, but our souls are often left behind in the process. The same can be said of our spirits. It is easy to think that our stock with God rises or falls on our ability to perform. We can be so busy doing things *for* God that we have less time to spend *with* Him. Because we have not been renewed by God's presence, our spiritual lives become dried up and we are thirsty and panting for something to refresh us within.

SPIRITUAL SINKHOLES

A sinkhole is a geological condition that occurs when underground streams drain away, leaving the ground at the surface with no underlying support. Without warning, large areas of the surface collapse, pulling cars—even houses—into the resulting hole. On the surface everything appears normal until, suddenly, everything begins to cave in. The same thing can happen to us, spiritually speaking. When the streams of our soul dry up, when the inner support is gone, everything on the surface is in danger of collapsing.

When we begin to dry out, we often start to work harder. Instead of slowing down to replenish ourselves, we tend to speed up. Life is characterized by action without heart, work without spirit, and doctrine without love; and dominated by shoulds, ought tos, and musts. We become irritable, critical, and impatient. As the streams of the inner spirit dry out and the world around us speeds up, the turbulence rises until it all caves in.

A PLACE OF REST

So what is the solution? How can we be successful while resisting the temptation to succumb to all of life's demands? How do we remain productive without becoming compulsive? How do we keep from becoming burned out, dried up, and caved in? By accepting an invitation from our Lord: "Come with me by yourselves to a quiet place and get some rest" (Mark 6:31).

Jesus was not unfamiliar with the demands of an active schedule. He lived a life of purpose, but it was not with the frantic fury that seems to characterize so many of us. His disciples, on the other hand, had been so busy doing things for their master they had not even taken time to eat. They were touching lives by the thousands, but they were not replenishing themselves. That's when Jesus extended the invitation.

There is an ordering to the verse in Mark 6 that diminishes the busyness of life and allows us to enter the place of rest. First, Jesus says, "Come with me . . ." Come with the One who carries every demand and every burden. Come with the One who can give you rest. Come with the One who knows how badly you need it. He tells us in Isaiah 30:15, "In repentance and rest is your salvation, in quietness and trust is your strength."

Sadly, we usually resist the Lord's invitation. I know fellow ministers who go on vacation—richly deserved and long overdue—and forsake worship, prayer, and the study of the Word of God. They refresh the body, while the spirit craves renewal, and they usually return as tired and weary as when they left. Why? Because true rest is found by coming to the Lord, not moving away from Him.

Second, Jesus invites us to come *by ourselves.* He doesn't want us to bring the demands of life with us. Just as the disciples left the crowds they were ministering to, we must leave everything that demands our time, our strength, and our energy and get alone with God.

Third, we are invited to a quiet place. There are no noisy demands in the presence of Jesus. His grace subdues the voices that say, "You haven't done enough." We need to learn to sit at the feet of Jesus and listen to His voice of renewal.

In Luke 10:38-42, we find Jesus in the home of two sisters:

> As Jesus and his disciples were on their way, he came to a village where a woman named Martha opened her home to him. She had a sister called Mary, who sat at the Lord's feet listening to what he said. But Martha was distracted by all the preparations that had to be made. She came to him and asked, "Lord, don't you care that my sister has left me to do the work by myself? Tell her to help me!"
>
> "Martha, Martha," the Lord answered, "you are worried and upset about many things, but only one thing is needed. Mary has chosen what is better, and it will not be taken away from her."

While Martha was busy with work and activity, her spirit was distracted, critical, and resentful. Her sister sat at Jesus' feet, listening to His words, which Jesus described as choosing what was better. The strength she gained would "not be taken away from her," but was the result of spending time with the Lord.

Finally, Jesus said, "get some rest." Rest could well be defined as *the refreshing power of grace.* It is gracious because it comes to us through Christ, and because it allows us to cease from the stress and strife of life for a time.

Rest has always been a part of God's provision for our lives. He set the example for us Himself. Following six days of creation, God rested. The Law reestablishes the provision for rest when it commands us to honor the sabbath. Sadly, it has turned into another day of activity—even for Christians. The writer of Hebrews reminds us:

> There remains, then, a Sabbath-rest for the people of God; for anyone who enters God's rest also rests from his own work, just as God did from his. Let us, therefore, make every effort to enter that rest—Hebrews 4:9-11.

3 R's OF REFRESHMENT

There are three components of rest that I call the 3 R's of refreshment.

1. Remembering. David faced his own sinkhole condition in Psalm 63. He described his life as a dry and weary land where there was no water. He found a way to bring water to his thirsty soul and replenish his weary spirit: by remembering. "On my bed I remember you; I think of you through the watches of the night" (vs. 6). Remembering brings perspective. David recalled the faithfulness and lovingkindness of God, and it renewed his trust in God. We, too, can be reminded of the One who is at work in our lives to accomplish His good purpose in us.

Remembering also helps us reestablish our priorities. When we remember to put God first, we can release to Him those things that cause us worry and stress. When we remember to seek first His kingdom (see Matthew 6:33), He provides for all our needs. When we forget God's goodness and lovingkindness, we lose perspective on life. We want to seize control and find ourselves once again buried in stress.

2. Restoring. Restoring has to do with securing those areas of life that are prone to get loose. An old garage door on my house faces the sun and is exposed to all kinds of weather. The more it goes up and down, and the more severe the weather to which it is exposed, the more the nails tend to work loose. Occasionally, I need to pound them back in so they remain snug and the door stays in place. That garage door is a picture of my life. Through the constant ups and downs, and the storms and stresses of life, some areas have a tendency to get loose. If left unattended, it is only a matter of time until I "fall off my hinges."

Rest is essentially taking time to anchor the loose places of life to the Word of God. It allows the presence of Christ to restore and renew us.

3. Releasing. Refreshing comes when I release myself fully to Jesus. In His presence, in that quiet place with Him, I can release whatever drives me and find rest for my soul. First Peter 5:7 exhorts us to cast all our cares on Him, because He cares for us. Verse 10 says, "And the God of all grace, who called you to his eternal glory in Christ . . . will himself restore [refresh] you and make you strong, firm and steadfast."

Are you doing more, but enjoying it less? Listen one more time to the words of Jesus:

"Come with me . . . by yourself . . . to a quiet place . . . and get some rest."

John N. Vertefeuille is senior pastor of Faith Chapel in the San Diego, California area. He served as associate pastor for seven years before accepting his current position. He has also pastored in Oregon, Washington, and Burbank, California.

He received his Bachelor of Arts degree at Northwest College in Kirkland, Washington, and graduated summa cum laude from Fuller Theological Seminary in Pasadena, California.

John's experience includes teaching, counseling, Christian education, and retreat and conference speaking on a national and international level. He is author of Sexual Chaos, *published by Crossway Books, and is a regular contributor to* Youthworker *and* YouthLeader.

He and his wife Cindie have been married 18 years and have three children: Ali, Andy, and Peter.

7

Hold on to Hope

ALTON GARRISON

Jesus stood by the hot, dusty road. The cooling foam of the sea behind Him did not relieve the searing heat of the day. Sweat tinged His brow as He scanned the multitude before Him. Incredible. Throngs of bodies pushed and shoved against one another, reaching and grasping to touch the Master, waiting for Jesus to arrive from the other side. They had come with their children, with the elderly, with those on crutches. Some crawled on the ground to reach Him. Some came because of their need; others came to observe, particularly the religious scribes.

News spread throughout the land that Jesus, the great teacher from Nazareth, was also a healer and miracle-worker. Just the mention of His name sent multitudes running for a glimpse.

On this occasion, Jesus had come from the country of the Gadarenes. He dramatically delivered a madman there, casting out a legion of demons. As the little ship drew near the shore, Jesus' heart must have melted as He looked upon the people crying out in need . . . sheep without a shepherd. The boat docked, and the disciples, dreading what awaited them, looked at one another and nodded in mutual support. They formed a tight circle around Jesus and escorted Him through the mass of bodies as the crowd shouted His name. "Jesus! Jesus, help me . . . have mercy on me . . . Jesus!"

Jairus, a man who held a position in the Jewish synagogue, was there that day. Being a man of prestige, he was able to chisel his way through the wall of bodies. As he got near the front, he was pushed into the disciples' arena. Realizing he stood before the Master, he fell at Jesus' feet and pleaded, "My little daughter is dying. Please come and put your hands on her so that she will be healed and live" (Mark 5:23). Jesus consented, and the people followed, pressing upon Him to such a degree that He was nearly suffocated.

Hundreds of heart-rending conditions were represented by that crowd, but only two were mentioned: Jairus' daughter, and a woman who suffered with a chronic bleeding condition. For 12 long years she had gone to physician after physician—to no avail. She spent all she had and had only grown worse. Death awaited her. Nothing remained except the determination only hope could produce. She had heard about the great miracles Jesus performed and believed He could heal her . . . if only He would.

Suddenly, the press of people thickened. Jesus was coming closer. *There He is! I can see Him! He's walking my way . . . but He's not looking at me. He's going past me.*

As she saw the Lord walking behind His disciples, hope began to rise in her heart. If she could just touch Him, she would be healed. She knew it. Somehow, she pressed through that suffocating mass, and as Jesus passed by, she reached out to touch Him. With all her strength she reached for Him . . . until she touched the hem of His garment. *What is happening? Life is coming into my body. Strength is flowing through me. I feel strong. There is no pain! The bleeding* . . . She gasped. *There is no blood! The bleeding has stopped! I am whole! I am whole!*

"Who touched Me?" Jesus turned and surveyed the crowd.

The disciples looked at Him in disbelief. Jesus expected them to know many things, but this was too much. They were nearly crushed by the crowd, and He wanted to know who touched Him?

"It was I," the woman said, quivering. "It was I." She fell at His feet, trembling, as the power of God continued to work in her body. Fear vanished as she looked into His eyes and told Him she had been healed when she touched His garment.

Meanwhile, Jairus shifted from one leg to another. Why didn't Jesus come with him? His daughter was near death; she could be dying this very moment. Didn't Jesus know how urgent it was that He come right away? Why did He take so long with this woman? She had bled for 12 years already . . . what was a little longer when death was imminent for one he loved so dearly?

The words of Jesus interrupted his thoughts. "Daughter, your faith . . . your trust and confidence in Me . . . has restored you to health. Go in . . . peace, and be continually healed and free from your . . . disease" (Mark 5:34, Amplified).

While Jesus spoke, a group of men found Jairus. "Your daughter has died; come with us now. Why bother and distress the Teacher any further?" *Your daughter has died . . . your daughter has died . . . your daughter has died . . .*

Before Jairus could say a word, Jesus turned to him. "Do not be seized with alarm and have no fear, only keep on believing" (Mark 5:36, Amplified).

HOPE DELAYED

Have you ever been in a desperate situation: doubting whether your marriage would last; wondering if you should continue to believe for healing; fearing you would never overcome financial difficulties? Have you felt there was no cure, no help, no hope? Have you wrestled with despondency to such a degree that you wondered if God was still there?

In the small town of Bethany, right outside Jerusalem, lived a family Jesus dearly loved. Mary, Martha, and Lazarus had traveled extensively with Him. The sisters had often gone before the Master, making the next town ready for His arrival. They had seen Him perform many miracles and were present when the multitude was fed and when He turned the water into wine. Often, they sat late into the night, listening to the profound teachings of Christ, the Son of God, their dearest friend.

And then tragedy struck. Lazarus was deathly ill.

"Martha, send word to the Master," Mary said. "I know He will come right away, and when He does our brother will recover and be healed." She was convinced of it. After all, she had seen Jesus heal persons He had never met. Surely, as dearly as He loved Lazarus, He would stop everything and come to his bedside. "There is no need to be concerned.... Jesus will come. He will be here by nightfall."

She glanced toward her brother, who was already unconscious. *Everything will be fine. He will come. Soon Lazarus will be talking and laughing with us as before.*

Martha, wanting to remain at Lazarus' side with Mary, sent trustworthy friends to Jerusalem to find Jesus. They left before dawn for the two-mile journey. They would find Jesus and tell him about Lazarus. Soon this sickness would be forgotten.

Dawn turned into morning; morning eased into afternoon, but there was no sign of the Master. Mary paced before the window of Lazarus' room. *Where is He? Why doesn't He come? Can't they find Him? It's okay. Relax. He will be here soon.*

But the afternoon passed with no word from Him.

Suddenly, a knock at the door startled the sisters. They jumped up and ran to open the door. Expecting to welcome the Lord, their hearts sank at what they saw. Their friends had returned . . . but where was Jesus?

"We found the Master and His disciples," they said. "We told Him of Lazarus and of your desire for Him to come heal him. Jesus said to us, 'This sickness is not to end in death . . . but to glorify God.'"

Mary spoke first. "But where is He? Why isn't He here?"

The friends exchanged a glance. "He remained in Jerusalem with the disciples. He didn't come back with us."

Three days later, at the entrance of their brother's tomb, Mary and Martha stood in a whirlwind of emotions. Doubt, anger, and fear fought to control them. *Why didn't He come? Have we not served Him since the day He found us? Did we not give our lives for Him? Why would He heal those who never knew Him; those who had not given all to Him? Was our belief in vain? If only He had come, our brother would not have died. Why did He let us down when we needed Him the most?* Mary looked around at the temple leaders who had come to offer support. *Even those who do not believe have come. They have shown us greater support than the One we gave our lives to . . . .*

In time of despair it is often said, "Their faith has been destroyed." We bundle everything together as "faith," forgetting the other ingredients that must be in operation as well. Faith is imperative. "Without faith it is impossible to please God . . ." (Hebrews 11:6). But what about *hope?* Without it, faith cannot produce the desired results. Faith and hope are not the same; one cannot exist without the other. If we want to move forward, if we are to stand victorious in adverse situations, faith and hope must operate together in our lives.

Faith deals with details; hope deals with Deity. Faith finds its foundation in the Word; hope is a mental attitude. Faith is the activator and the channel for the miracles of Jesus; hope is the motivator that brings us to Jesus in the first place.

The story of the woman with the issue of blood, as told in Mark 5, is a classic example. She had faith, but hope put her on the road to health.

What does the Bible say about hope? "For whatsoever things were written aforetime were written for our learning, that we through patience and comfort of the scriptures might have hope" (Romans 15:4, KJV). In other words, the Word produces hope, which causes faith to rise, which brings results.

Hope is defined as "the feeling that what is wanted can be had or that events will turn out well; to believe, desire, or trust." Faith is the dynamite that explodes truth and brings us from doubt into belief; from defeat into victory; from the unseen to the seen. Hope is the fuse that sets it off. Without a fuse, dynamite is worthless.

HOPE EMBRACED

The town of Shunem had been good for them. Her husband was influential in the city, and they had prospered far above the average person. They were hard workers who served people and respected God. The prophet Elisha passed through their city.

I would like to find him, introduce him to my husband, and invite him to my home, the Shunammite woman thought. *I think I will serve him a meal. I hear this is a true man of God, but I want to know for myself. If by chance it is true, I want to serve him and meet his needs while he's in my city.*

That is exactly what she did. She found Elisha and offered him a generous meal at her home. Elisha enjoyed the company of the Shunammite woman and her husband, and he made it a practice to visit each time he was in their city. (See 2 Kings 4:8-17.)

"I perceive this is truly a holy man of God," she said to her husband. "Why don't we make a bedroom for him to sleep in when he comes to Shunem? He blesses us with his presence; I think we should bless him also."

As Elisha rested in the room they had prepared for him, the Spirit of God prodded his heart. God wanted to bless the woman and her husband, but Elisha did not yet understand how. He was prodded again by the Spirit as he considered the matter. *Yes, Lord . . . the Shunammite woman . . . what is it You would have me do?* The answer was clear.

"Gehazi," he called to his servant, "run and get the Shunammite woman, and bring her before me."

When she arrived, he began to speak to her. "You have always gone out of your way to see all my needs are met. You have provided this resting place for me, and the company of you and your husband refreshes my spirit.

Would you like a position in government? You would serve the nation well. Knowing your character, I would be glad to recommend you to the king."

"I am happy in my own city, serving this small group of people. I ministered to you and your servant because I desired to know more of God. I need no favors."

The subject appeared closed, but once again the Lord prodded Elisha. The Spirit wanted to bless this couple.

"Tell me, Gehazi, have you observed anything about this couple?" Elisha asked. "Is there something they don't have? Something they need?"

"She has never said a word," Gehazi replied, "but they have no children, and her husband is getting old."

"Call her," Elisha said. Again the Shunammite woman stood before the prophet. "At this season next year you shall hold a son from your husband."

Excitement overwhelmed her. "I dare not believe it. You are a man of God. Why would you say such a thing to me and bring to the surface the thing I desire most?"

As Elisha had prophesied, she conceived and brought forth a child.

My, how our son has grown. I remember when he was a baby . . . those tiny hands I'll never hold again . . . but I'll always hold this gift of God in my heart. Now he is strong and so diligent to work with his father in the fields. What a blessing he is to me. God has made sure I will be protected when my husband is gone. My son will take care of our household. How wonderful You are, God. Thank You for blessing me with this boy.

A commotion outside the house interrupted her thoughts. Her servants ran toward her—carrying her son! "There is trouble . . . there is trouble . . . the boy is sick!"

She held him close to her, as she had done when he was a child. As he cried in pain, she felt the limpness of his body, the shallowness of his breathing. Suddenly, the breathing stopped. Without a word, she carried him up the stairs, past her bedroom, past his room, and into the room they had built for Elisha. She laid him on the bed, shut the door, and turned to her servants. "Get me a donkey. I will go quickly to the man of God and come back again."

From a distance, Elisha could see the dust. "Look, Gehazi, there is the Shunammite woman. Run to meet her and ask if all is well."

Gehazi hurried to meet her as she slid off the donkey, her face staunch and unflinching. "Is all well with your husband and son?" Gehazi asked.

"All is well," she replied, walking past him toward Elisha.

HOPE REWARDED

Why had she responded so? Because the hope inside her refused to give up. She knew God, and hope sent her straight to His prophet for a miracle.

Satan's attack may not be against our faith so much as our hope, for he knows hope is what takes us to faith. It is easier for him to discourage us emotionally than spiritually. But he cannot alter the Word of God. If we cling to His promises we need not be defeated by our circumstances.

Despite such devastating events, the Shunammite woman refused to lose hope. After she told Elisha about the death of her son, Elisha sent Gehazi to raise him from the dead. It didn't work. Still she did not give up. Then Elisha came and shut himself up with the woman's son. He did not come out of the room until the boy was restored to life. Warmth returned to his body; he sneezed seven times and opened his eyes. Hope in God's Word had produced the desired miracle.

What about the woman with the issue of blood? The doctors had only bad news for her. Her pain intensified daily. Yet she fought through a crowd to reach the One who could help—because of hope.

TIME OF TESTING

Many persons around the world have believed God for a particular need, then, when the answer didn't come right away, they gave up. They lost hope. God not only wants to inspire our faith; He wants to rekindle our hope. Faith says, "He is able." Hope says, "He is willing."

God *is* willing to meet our needs. The Bible says that "through endurance and the encouragement of the Scriptures we might have hope" (Romans 15:4). Often, there is a time lapse between the giving and fulfillment of God's promise. During that time, we are tested. Imagine how Jairus felt. He made his way through the crowd, got Jesus' attention, and found Him willing to help. But they were pressed for time. Jairus' daughter was near death. The woman with the issue of blood had a need, but his daughter was dying! Then the news came; it was too late. Jesus had taken too much time with the woman.

Jairus was between the promise and the fulfillment of the promise. He was in the time of testing. Jesus helped him and said, "Don't be afraid. Only believe."

Fear robs our hope. It is a thief that paralyzes our faith. That is why Jesus addressed the fear issue first. "Fear not," He said, then added, "only believe." Jairus chose to do just that. He took the Son of God into his daughter's room and watched life come into her again.

What about Mary and Martha? Of course, they were disappointed that Jesus didn't come when they thought He should. After all, their brother's life was on the line. As Martha met Jesus, she grabbed His hand. She looked into His eyes, and all doubt disappeared. Every distressing thought was gone. She did not understand it, but she spoke the truth when she said, "Master, if You had been here, my brother would not have died." In spite of the negative thoughts that assailed her, she remained faithful to the One she had served.

She ran back inside the house to tell Mary the Master wanted her. Mary ran so quickly the Jewish leaders thought she was running to the tomb to mourn. They followed, not knowing they were about to see the greatest miracle of their lives.

Jesus, the Life-Giver, walked up to the opening of the cold, dark tomb. "Take away the stone," He commanded. He lifted His eyes and addressed His Father, then with a loud voice He declared, "Lazarus, come forth!" Immediately, Lazarus arose and walked into the daylight, still bound head and foot in grave clothes. Mary and Martha received their miracle, and many observers became believers.

It doesn't matter what the doctor says. It doesn't matter what the checkbook says. It doesn't matter how dismal the situation appears. God is willing to bring a miracle when it is needed. When He gives a promise, He will perform. He is the One who "calls things that are not as though they were" (Romans 4:17).

DESTROYERS OF HOPE

There are three things that destroy hope. The first is *when we believe what we see.* When the devil succeeds in making the circumstance seem bigger than the Creator, hope is lost. He brings fear, paralyzing our ability to

believe. He lies to us; and his subtle ways make us vulnerable—if we take our eyes off Jesus. We must remember Jesus
promised trouble would come our way. But He also promised never to leave us or forsake us.

Hope is also destroyed *when we battle God's promise.* What
did Abraham think when God promised him a son—when
God said his offspring would be as the sands of the sea?
After all, Abraham was 75 years old, and his wife 65. There
was nothing visible to produce hope. The situation looked
impossible. When Sarah first heard, she laughed. But
Abraham knew God had the ability to do what He had
promised, no matter how impossible it seemed. And, just
as God had said, Sarah conceived a son.

Abraham did not have the written Word to offer
strength, faith, and hope. He did not have fellowship with
other believers. All he had was the promise of God. Every
day he had to battle the lies of the enemy. "It's impossible!
There is no way! Everyone is going to think you are a fool!"

Unlike Abraham, we have both the written Word of God
and the fellowship of the saints. We have Christian television and radio. We also have the same enemy that
tempted Abraham to doubt. He still tries to convince us
God's promises are not true. But we must remember,
circumstances are not greater than the power of our God.

Third, hope is destroyed *when we become our own answer.*
When we think we must bring forth the promise, hope is
destroyed. Waiting is the hardest thing to do, including
waiting on God. We devise ways to bring about what God
said *He* would do and get ahead of Him. That is when the
trouble comes.

The world promotes the philosophy that we must do
something. "Don't just sit there. Do something!" it says.

Often, we should reverse that saying when it comes to the promises of God: "Don't do anything. Just sit there!"

Impatience leads to erratic behavior. We try one thing and it doesn't work; we do another and it doesn't work. Consequently, we become confused and wonder if God really spoke to us in the first place. The further we venture out on our own, the deeper the trouble becomes.

Abraham and Sarah fell into the trap of impatience and decided to "help God" fulfill His promise. Under Sarah's instruction, Abraham went to her servant and conceived a son by her. When Sarah finally conceived the son of promise, she became jealous and demanded the woman and her son be sent away. God reprimanded Abraham for not waiting on God, but promised to care for the child. Abraham knew he had to send Ishmael and his mother away, but he missed his son and grieved over him. That grief remained with him the rest of his life because he and Sarah tried to fulfill the promise of God instead of waiting for Him to do it in His own time. Like Abraham, when we attempt to solve problems in our own strength, we create "Ishmaels."

SOURCE OF HOPE

God has set the date for performing what He has promised. We have to wait for His time. Reading and believing the Word of God will produce hope and help us hold on while we wait on God, for God is the source of hope. "Now the *God of hope* fill you with all joy and peace in believing, that ye may abound in hope, through the power of the Holy Ghost" (Romans 15:13, KJV). Hope is only as good as its source. If God is the God of hope, we have nothing to worry about. God is in control; He is immutable. It doesn't matter what man says—only what God says.

When a man's health is gone, he is handicapped. When his wealth is gone, he is hindered. When his hope is gone, he is paralyzed. But no adversity can triumph over a hope-filled believer. There is no circumstance too great, no tragedy too heart-breaking, no affliction too devastating to conquer hope. Romans 8:31 says, "If God is for us, who can be against us?" What greater way can hope be quickened in us, than to know the Source of all good things is on our side?

Having served as an evangelist for 19 years, the Reverend Alton Garrison presently serves as pastor of the First Assembly of God, North Little Rock, Arkansas. During his tenure there, the church has experienced tremendous growth, necessitating construction of a new facility and relocation.

Garrison has served on the Foreign Missions Board for the Assemblies of God in Springfield, Missouri, and is an Executive Presbyter for the Arkansas District. He serves on the Board of Regents of Southwestern Assemblies of God College, Waxahachie, Texas; the Board of Hillcrest Children's Home, Hot Springs, Arkansas; and is President of Christian Civic Foundation of Arkansas.

His wife has published Tangled Destinies, *an account of her family's hardships through the Nazi holocaust, an Indonesian Revolution, and subsequent immigration to the United States. They have one daughter, Lizette.*

8

Defeating Procrastination

DR. JAMES BRADFORD

I have put off writing this chapter, even though the topic is procrastination. As a husband, the father of two pre-schoolers, and the pastor of a very active church, reasons for procrastinating have been easy to find.

Life for me is a constant battle, waged in the arena of choices. I'm continually making value judgments, pitting one priority against another, and dealing with unplanned emergencies. If I get tired or behind, some of the good choices begin to feel out of reach. Then I escape into the myth that somehow, magically, there will be more time tomorrow or next week. So, things get put off.

Some things need to be put off. They simply are not as important as other things. "Things which matter most must never be at the mercy of things which matter least," said Goethe.[1] But what if "putting off" has become a habit, affecting the truly important areas of life?

PROCRASTINATION DEFINED

The Latin word for procrastination is *procrastinatus*. The prefix *pro* means "for" or "forward." The root *crastinus* means "belonging to the morrow," taken from the Latin word *cras*. Procrastination is the tendency to put things forward into tomorrow. Deadlines are always pushed, projects are avoided, and good intentions begin to pile up. At more serious stages behavioral paralysis sets in and an acute sense of powerlessness develops. As one friend put it, "I just can't seem to make myself do it."

The biblical paradigm for the chronic procrastinator is the sluggard. Though not flattering, the characterization yields some fascinating insight. Part of the sluggard's problem is, of course, laziness. "As a door turns on its hinge, so a sluggard turns on his bed. The sluggard buries his hand in the dish; he is too lazy to bring it back to his mouth" (Proverbs 26:14,15). His life is marked by patterns of passive sensuality and a work ethic that is far from adequate. He is a man without a plan, and motivationally he is a mess.

But something else is going on here. The previous verse makes a penetrating observation: "The sluggard says, 'There is a lion in the road, a fierce lion roaming the streets!'" (Proverbs 26:13). Note the rationalization. Conflicts rage inside him that run deeper than laziness or poor time management. He is paralyzed by fear and self-deception. The "fierce lions" are merely imagined excuses to stay in bed and put off the day's responsibilities.

CAUSES OF PROCRASTINATION

What are some of the lions that control the procrastinator?

1. Emotional patterns. Learned over many years, these are sensual (feeling) responses repeatedly given priority over volitional (will) responses, which control the procrastinator. The procrastinator believes, "I cannot make myself do what I do not feel like doing." That, of course, is a lie, but it makes for a convenient excuse. Learning to act in accordance with the *will* rather than *emotions* may be difficult at first, but the old habits can be broken with God's power. An important part of Christian freedom is the ability to follow through on the choice to do right. ". . . clothe yourselves with the Lord Jesus Christ, and do not think about how to gratify the desires of the sinful nature" (Romans 13:14).

2. Fear of failure. Fueled by an inappropriate sense of perfectionism or low self-esteem, this creates paralysis in the procrastinator. The rationalization goes, "I cannot live with myself unless I perform perfectly, but if I leave it to the last minute I can avoid that issue for the sake of just getting it done." Imperfection is excused by the fact that there was not adequate time to do a perfect job, and procrastination has served its purpose. The root problem, however, is in how we view who we are. "For by the grace given me I say to every one of you: Do not think of yourself more highly than you ought, but rather think of yourself with sober judgment, in accordance with the measure of faith God has given you" (Romans 12:3).

3. Fear of success. The responsibilities that go with achievement can be as paralyzing as fear of failure. So, too, will a family system that berates ability, leaving the individual with the feeling that he'll "never amount to anything."

Either way, the procrastinator begins to rationalize, "I will put off responsibility to avoid the consequences of doing well, or to prove to myself that I really can't do anything well anyway." God promises us fruitfulness with an ability to embrace it graciously. "You did not choose me, but I chose you and appointed you to go and bear fruit—fruit that will last. Then the Father will give you whatever you ask in my name" (John 15:16).

4. A rebellious spirit. This is another cause of procrastination. The procrastinator delays because of defiance. "No one is going to tell me what to do!" The task remains to be done, but it is resented and every stall tactic is employed. This is one of the most willful causes of procrastination, bordering on all-out refusal. Saying no is an important skill, but not for the wrong reasons. "Submit to one another out of reverence for Christ" (Ephesians 5:21).

5. Lack of motivation. This cause of procrastination is related to discouragement, lack of personal direction and/or reinforcement, and, possibly, fatigue. The result is a sense of inner resignation. The procrastinator lives on the edge of depletion and often concludes, "I can't be responsible any more, and why should I?" Responsibilities pile up, but they are met with indifference. At the root is the need for renewal of spirit and purpose, and perhaps rest. "For it is God who works in you to will and to act according to his good purpose" (Philippians 2:13).

6. Aversion to discomfort or difficulty. This often prevents some from beginning a task. The reward simply is not worth the cost. Difficulties may be encountered that take effort to work through. Present comfort and personal gratification must be deferred, but that is not easy. "Too much like work—I just don't feel like it," the procrastinator concludes. Tomorrow becomes a seductively appealing option. Such is the temptation the procrastinator must learn to overcome. "The lazy man does not roast his game, but the diligent man prizes his possessions" (Proverbs 12:27).

These are some of the "lions" in the procrastinator's life. Some are obvious, others are not. They all involve inner rationalizations that serve to paralyze us when we should be taking action. They need to be confronted, especially if procrastination has become habitual.

WISDOM IN A SMALL PACKAGE

The antithesis of the sluggard, according to Scripture, is the ant. "Go to the ant, you sluggard; consider its ways and be wise" (Proverbs 6:6). The ant is the consummate picture of diligence. "Ants are creatures of little strength, yet they store up their food in the summer" (Proverbs 30:25). Though small in size, they dwarf the sluggard with their wisdom. In fact, their diligence is their wisdom being lived out in practical ways. They do what is needed, when it is needed, so they will have what they need when they need it.

The ant is an example of responsibility and faithfulness, traits that are found at the heart of the diligent person's character. Responsibility and faithfulness are antidotes to procrastination. Together they constitute the New Testament concept of stewardship. Here are some suggestions for managing procrastination by nurturing a lifestyle of responsibility and faithfulness.

MANAGING PROCRASTINATION

1. Have a vision for your life. Know where you are going. A vision focuses priorities, motivates action, inspires sacrifice, and counteracts discouragement. Ask God to share His dreams for your life with you, then write them down. Ask yourself who God has made you to be, and what you feel destined to do. Complete the sentences, "If I had . . . , then I would . . . ," or "At my funeral, I want people to remember me as . . ." Make an inventory of your primary roles in life: spouse, parent, employer, employee, friend, neighbor, ministry volunteer, community activity coordinator, primary care person for a parent, etc., then seek the Lord for His direction in each of them. Look for scriptures that enhance your understanding of each role and help you to perform them according to God's will. Then make your vision a matter of continued prayer.

2. Plan ahead with that vision in mind. Procrastination is easier when you have no plan in mind or no direction in which to move. Four times a year take time to plan the next three months of your life in light of what you want to accomplish. Then plan, week by week, in line with your three-month plan. Schedule in the important, leave room for the urgent, and give yourself time for balance and rest. If your pattern is to put off important things, then share your plans with prayer partners who will promise to follow up with you.

3. Be decisive in starting projects. Don't cave in to the myth that "it can wait" or "there will be more time tomorrow." Train yourself to hear red-alert danger signals going off in your head whenever you start to think that way. The future usually has no more time than the present unless you plan for it. The hardest part is getting started. That is where the most energy is required. Learn the habit of beginning *now,* even if you have to finish later. That decision will be won or lost in only a few seconds. It is the trigger point that makes all the difference in what is accomplished or forgotten.

4. Do the hardest things first. When I was a child and had to eat something I didn't like, I ate it first and saved the best for last. With the worst part behind me, the best was even better. Most of us avoid what is unpleasant or distasteful. Instead we should put the hardest task first, then follow up with a reward. Explore ways in which to make unpleasant responsibilities more enjoyable, either in the way you do them or in the attitude you choose while doing them. We all do better when we have something to look forward to. That is why hope is so central to positive motivation.

5. Break projects into manageable units. In addition to conflicting priorities, another reason I put off writing this chapter was that I was waiting for a block of several hours to become available so I could get off to a great start. Unfortunately, large blocks of discretionary time don't often "show up" at this stage of my life. I would have been better off spacing the project over a longer period of time, taking an hour every day to write. Most of the big achievements of life are the sum of many little achievements.

6. Surround yourself with as much order as possible. Order tends to reinforce order. Conversely, disorder in one area of life tends to spill over into other areas, multiplying like compound interest. To interrupt that spiral and get things moving in the right direction, choose one thing initially to work on. Avoid tackling too much all at once. Let one victory lead to another. Get excited and motivated with the process. It will make a difference.

7. Monitor your vital signs. Remember that self-neglect is very different from self-denial. Self-denial is a conscious choice to defer gratification for a greater cause than the gratification itself. Self-neglect, however, is a violation of the biblical principle of stewardship. We are responsible to faithfully preserve and manage the resources of our lives. Monitor your mental, physical, and emotional fatigue levels and make sure that rest, exercise, stimulating reading, and fellowship are regular features of your day. Eat properly, fast periodically, and pace your schedule. Know what depletes you and what restores you. Most of all, stay in fellowship with God by spending time in His Word, time in prayer, and time in service to Him. Let the spiritual disciplines be a part of your spiritual journey. Pray daily to be filled with the Holy Spirit and make it the most important prayer you pray. When body, heart, and soul are strong, there is energy for life. The more energy there is, the easier it is to get things done.

VICTORIOUS IN CHRIST

Scripture tells us that, as Christians, we are "in Christ" (Romans 8:1; 1 Corinthians 1:30; 2 Corinthians 5:17). Being "in Christ" has many privileges. In Christ our sins are forgiven and our identity is secured. Apart from Him that cannot be true. In Christ we do not need to fear others or ourselves. In Christ we are loved and have been given the many promises of God. In Christ our lives are rebuilt by the Carpenter of Nazareth. In Christ we have the power of the Holy Spirit. In Christ our actions can be guided by our values rather than external forces. "I can do everything through him who gives me strength" (Philippians 4:13). That includes defeating procrastination.

Begin with renewed commitment, not to tasks, but to Christ. With repentance and faith, invite the Lordship of Christ into every area of your life. Make intimacy with Christ the central pursuit of your life. Allow the Holy Spirit to reveal weak areas of your life, then confess your sins and trust the Lord to give you the strength you need to live a life that is pleasing to Him. Memorize those scriptures that most directly refute the lies involving your "lions" and meditate on them daily. Let root issues be resolved and watch freedom and faithfulness begin to blossom in you.

Robert Thornton Henderson once said, "There are few ideal and leisurely settings for the disciplines of growth." You can defeat procrastination. Let who you are in Christ confront the lions that keep you from being all you can be, then embrace the disciplines of responsibility and faithfulness with joy. Make it a lifelong adventure for God's glory. Don't wait until it's easy. Don't wait for someone to do it for you. And don't wait until it's too late.

Dr. James Bradford is the senior pastor of Newport-Mesa Christian Center, located in Costa Mesa, California. Dr. Bradford has a Ph.D. in aerospace engineering from the University of Minnesota. He has also taught Bible and campus ministry classes at North Central Bible College.

Presently, he serves on the board of directors of Southern California College and the presbytery of the Southern California District of the Assemblies of God. The author of numerous articles and training manuals, he is a frequent speaker at retreats, conferences, and leadership gatherings.

He and his wife Sandi have two daughters: Meredith and Angeline.

9

Living with Integrity

RICK COLE

Integrity is defined as *adherence to a code of values; utter sincerity, honesty, and candor.* As the 1990s have ushered in a valueless society, integrity has become a rare commodity. Our country is eroding because of a lack of biblical values. Businesses are suffering from a cutthroat mentality that has rewritten the code of ethics in an effort to stay ahead of competitors. The time-honored tradition of sportsmanship in athletics has gone by the wayside, replaced by a win-at-all-cost attitude. Marriages are failing as vows made before God no longer mean anything. Families are disintegrating as parents view their children as burdens rather than blessings from the hand of God. Topping all these violations of integrity is the most horrifying of all: the departure from integrity in the pulpits of America's churches. As the church goes, so goes society.

REVIVAL OF INTEGRITY

Two proverbs speak of the contrast we see around us: "He who walks with integrity walks securely, but he who perverts his ways will become known" (Proverbs 10:9, NKJV). "The integrity of the upright will guide them, but the perversity of the unfaithful will destroy them" (Proverbs 11:3, NKJV). We stand in desperate need of a revival of integrity in our land. We can regain the glory of the Lord if we return to His Word and rediscover the foundation that we need for success in every aspect of life. While many are being destroyed, it is time for the people of God to walk in integrity.

INTEGRITY AND GOD

Jesus said, "He who has My commandments and keeps them, it is he who loves Me. And he who loves Me will be loved by My Father, and I will love him and manifest Myself to him" (John 14:21, NKJV). Those who claim to love God and willfully disobey His commands are liars without integrity. "Now by this we know that we know Him, if we keep His commandments. He who says, 'I know Him,' and does not keep His commandments, is a liar, and the truth is not in him" (1 John 2:3,4, NKJV). The litmus test for determining the truth of our love for God is whether or not we are living by the standards He has established.

There are churches filled with people who come on Sunday and lift their voices and hands to God in praise, who would do just as well to go outside and spit in the wind. God will not receive praise from people who refuse to follow His commands the rest of the week. Sunday morning church does not make up for lying and cheating, swearing at the kids, and drinking a few beers with the boys after work. Praise to God must flow out of a pure and repentant heart that is submitted to the lordship of Christ in every aspect of life.

As a Christian leader I am constantly haunted by the words of Jesus in Matthew 7:

> Enter by the narrow gate; for wide is the gate and broad is the way that leads to destruction, and there are *many* who go in by it. Because narrow is the gate and difficult is the way which leads to life, and there are *few* who find it....
>
> Not everyone who says to Me, "Lord, Lord," shall enter the kingdom of heaven, but he who does the will of My Father in heaven. Many will say to Me in that day, "Lord, Lord, have we not prophesied in Your name, cast out demons in Your name, and done many wonders in Your name?" And then I will declare to them, "I never knew you; depart from Me, you who practice lawlessness!"—Matthew 7:13,14,21-23, NKJV.

How many professing Christians today practice lawlessness? The devil wants to convince us that God does not really require holiness from us. We must not succumb to his lies. Those who love Jesus and are truly His disciples must strive with every ounce of energy to ensure that their lives line up with their profession of faith.

Integrity in our relationship with God demands that we call sin what it is. We dare not rename it. There are those who want to call adultery an "affair." It is entirely too nice a word for what God calls sin. Some wish to call lies, "white lies" or "fibs." Regardless of what it is called, lying separates a person from God. Pornography is not glorifying God's creation; it is a demon of lust that clouds the soul and chokes the life of God out of you. Unforgiveness is not justified because of the offense against you; it is a torturing spirit that will keep you from having your own sins forgiven. Swearing is not something I can do to be accepted by those I work with; it is profanity and an offense against God's holy name. Sin is sin. Disobedience to God's commands is rebellion, and it will cause you to lose fellowship with Him.

Evangelist Eddie Rentz preached a sermon in our church recently on the subject of obedience. The first principle he taught was that *obedience brings blessing.* Scripture declares:

> "Come now, and let us reason together," says the Lord. "Though your sins are like scarlet, they shall be as white as snow; though they are red like crimson, they shall be as wool. If you are willing and obedient, you shall eat the good of the land; but if you refuse and rebel, you shall be devoured by the sword"; for the mouth of the Lord has spoken—Isaiah 1:18-20, NKJV.

God is faithful to show us the blessings of obedience and the destruction of disobedience:

> Do not be deceived, God is not mocked; for whatever a man sows, that he will also reap. For he who sows to his flesh will of the flesh reap corruption, but he who sows to the Spirit will of the Spirit reap

everlasting life. And let us not grow weary while doing good, for in due season we shall reap if we do not lose heart—Galatians 6:7-9, NKJV.

You cannot fool God. He knows what is in your heart, and He will not tolerate a deceitful attitude in your relationship with Him.

The second principle he taught was that *obedience brings authority in prayer:* "And whatever we ask we receive from Him, because we keep His commandments and do those things that are pleasing in His sight" (1 John 3:22, NKJV). When we live a life of integrity in our relationship to God, our prayers become powerful. The lack of power in the church today and in our individual lives is directly related to our lack of obedience in following the Lord's commands. Our authority is connected to our integrity.

The third principle he taught was that *obedience brings favor:*

Now therefore, if you will indeed obey My voice and keep My covenant, then you shall be a special treasure to Me above all people; for all the earth is Mine—Exodus 19:5, NKJV.

So if you walk in My ways, to keep My statutes and My commandments, as your father David walked, then I will lengthen your days—1 Kings 3:14, NKJV.

If you keep My commandments, you will abide in My love, just as I have kept My Father's commandments and abide in His love—John 15:10, NKJV.

The simple lessons of obedience are difficult to learn. As children, if we disobeyed our parents, a swat or spanking was guaranteed. Disobedience brought pain. If we obeyed their directives, blessings resulted and life went smoothly. How simple, yet how profound. The problem is that the flesh rises up and wants to submit to no one. When we allow the flesh to rule our thinking, we lose our integrity in our relationship to God.

INTEGRITY AND THE FAMILY

Many children and teenagers today are in rebellion to God and those in authority because of the hypocrisy they have witnessed at home. Dad looks good at church on Sunday, but acts like an angry monster at home the rest of the week. Mom goes off to the prayer meeting, but exercises a bitter and contentious spirit toward her husband for the lack of affirmation and love he shows her. The children are told not to listen to worldly rock music, but the parents are tuned in to the country western station all day. Saying one thing while doing another rips apart our homes.

The Christian family is America's hope for the future. We must regain integrity in our homes in order to keep our dreams alive. Proper discipline of children is a starting place, but in many families discipline fails because of inconsistency.

My parents were visiting us in Omaha recently, and we had taken a family trip to the local shopping mall. As we sat down in the food court area for lunch, a classic example of the breakdown of the family occurred right in front of us. A child about three years of age went into a tirade at the table next to ours. The mother spoke sweetly to the child, hoping to quiet her. It became obvious right away who was in charge: the child! She continued to throw her tantrum while the lunch crowd looked on. My dad looked squarely in the child's eyes and said, "It looks like you need a spanking." She quieted down for just a moment, wondering if he might administer one to her. Then, sensing she was safe, she broke into another fit as the mother dragged her away without dealing with the problem.

How will children ever learn the difference between right and wrong unless they are taught *consistently* by their parents? That same child will grow up to be a menace to her teachers at school, the husband she will eventually marry, and society in general. Unfortunately, this is not an isolated incident. It is happening in thousands of households.

I have heard countless encounters of parents with unruly children who have said, "If you don't stop that, I'm going to spank you." When the child continues the bad behavior they say it again: "If you don't stop that, I'm going to spank you." At that moment integrity has been lost. The child did not stop the rebellious behavior, and the parent did not follow through with what she said she would do. The child is now in charge. It is as simple as that.

Some parents use a counting method in disciplining their children. "I'll give you to the count of 10 to put that down! One, two, three, four, five, six, seven, eight, nine . . ." At the count of 10 the child may or may not obey, depending on what happened to them the last time they reached that number. If discipline occurs one time and not another, the child will become confused and never know quite what to expect.

We have adopted what we call "the one-time rule" in our family. Our children are given one chance to correct improper behavior. If they test the limits looking for a second chance, they lose. When discipline is administered after the count of one, obedience will be attained quickly and calmly. The children will know what to expect every time. Order is maintained and integrity is in place. This produces children of integrity as well. When a teacher at school corrects a student who immediately responds with obedience, you have produced a spirit of integrity.

Children can become disillusioned, not only by inconsistent discipline, but also by broken promises. When a father says we'll go to the park on Saturday then plays golf with his buddies instead, integrity has been lost. There may be a time when a legitimate conflict arises. In that case, explain what happened and set another time to replace the lost opportunity. Integrity will still be maintained. Unless it is truly unavoidable, if we tell our children or spouse that we are going to do something with them we need to follow through. To change our plans for our own benefit is a subtle form of lying and a blatant form of selfishness borne out of a lack of character.

One hot summer day my wife and I took our three children to the local swimming pool. While playing with our kids, a boy we had never met entered into our little games. He climbed on my back and begged me to throw him in the air like I was doing with the others. For at least an hour the boy participated in our family fun. Not surprisingly, I did not see the boy's parents one time in all our trips to the pool. I wonder how many broken promises he had received. He was starved for attention and was a prime target for the devil.

Marriage is taking a major hit in our generation because of a "me-centered" philosophy—a doctrine that says "I owe it to myself to make myself happy." What we really owe is a life of giving and sacrifice to God and others. "Or do you not know that your body is the temple of the Holy Spirit who is in you, whom you have from God, and you are not your own? For you were bought at a price; therefore glorify God in your body and in your spirit, which are God's" (1 Corinthians 6:19,20, NKJV). We belong to God because He bought us with His precious blood on Calvary. And, therefore, we should find every way possible to please God in all our relationships.

At the marriage altar we make a vow, a covenant with God and our marriage partner. It has become normal—almost expected—to break our vows and go back on our word. Such action reveals a lack of integrity. Whatever happened to: "I take you to be my wedded wife, to have and to hold, from this day forward, for better or for worse, for richer or for poorer, in sickness and in health, to love and to cherish, until death do us part"? Have we forgotten our vows, or is it no longer important to keep our word?

Integrity begins to break down in marriage when we become more concerned with our own needs than the needs of our spouse. We open the door for the enemy to come in and make matters even worse than they are. We begin to welcome advances from members of the opposite sex who will show us a little kindness, attention, and respect. We did not set out to break our vows in the beginning. It was a subtle process that beguiled us before we realized what had happened. It is imperative we recognize the devices of the enemy and hold on to our integrity, not allowing the devil the smallest foothold.

Men should avoid praying with women at the altar. Men and women should avoid lunching together without their spouses. When couples get together for fellowship, they should be careful to avoid a nurturing relationship with the opposite spouse. Be aware of the potential to fall into compromising situations. Acknowledge the fact that flirtatious relationships can happen to anyone—including you. Such an awareness will allow you to keep your guard up against such temptations.

When a woman is unhappy with her husband and then spends hours each week reading romantic novels, she sets herself up for trouble. No man will ever fulfill the fantasy dreams portrayed in such materials. They are designed to leave one feeling trapped in a boring relationship with no possible fulfillment in sight. These novels should not be a part of our reading matter. We need to fill our homes with God's Word and other materials rich in godly wisdom.

Since your body and spirit belong to God, find the joy of using them to make a difference in the lives of those God has given you to love. It is time for the church of the living God to stop moaning about what we don't have and start giving what we do have. We will then discover the reality of reciprocity. Give and it will be given back to you. Sow and you will reap.

Men need to get their eyes off pornography. It is an evil that destroys the integrity of men. If you have cable television and find yourself scanning the channels in search of some form of nudity, it is time to cancel the cable subscription. You can do without ESPN, CNN, or TBN for the sake of your own spiritual health and integrity. There is much to be done to build God's eternal kingdom, but an inordinate amount of time is wasted in front of television screens. The time wasted is of great concern, and the material consumed erodes the fiber of our character.

My wife and I decided about a year ago to cancel our cable subscription. It has resulted in less time spent watching television and more time spent in constructive relationship-building with our children. We do not regret our decision, and neither do our children. It has helped us maintain integrity as a family.

INTEGRITY AND FINANCES

Contrary to popular belief, money is not evil. It is the *love* of money that leads to every kind of evil. "For the love of money is a root of all sorts of evil, and some by longing for it have wandered away from the faith, and pierced themselves with many a pang" (1 Timothy 6:10, NAS). What we do with the money God supplies is a strong indication of what is in our hearts. Luke 12:34 tells us, "Where your treasure is, there your heart will be also" (NKJV). You will discover what is in your heart by examining what you do with your money.

What do you do at the amusement park when the price for children under 12 is $8.95, the price for 12 and up is $14.95, and you are in line with a child who just turned 12? You can rationalize all you want to justify paying the "children under 12 price." You may even say you are just trying to be a good steward of God's money. The truth is that paying the lower price is lying and stealing.

In my relationship with other ministers I have discovered reasons for concern in the area of financial integrity. When a church leader is motivated by money, he becomes incapable of making godly decisions. When a pastor refuses to deal with a rebellious member of his church because that member contributes a significant amount of money, he has lost his integrity. I have seen pastors attend denominational conferences who skip the business sessions to play golf or lounge by the pool. They were sent as representatives of their churches to have a voice in the business and spiritual affairs of the organization, not to enjoy an all-expenses-paid vacation. To neglect the business sessions for personal pleasure is a violation of financial integrity.

I know of a man who went on vacation with his wife and three other couples. All were pastors of churches. They enjoyed three days of golf and leisure at a comfortable resort. Upon returning home, the minister in question turned in the receipts from the hotel and meals for reimbursement. He called the vacation a business trip because he had been with three other ministers and expected the church to pay for it. As if that were not enough, some of the receipts were for meals consumed and paid for by the other couples. The minister not only had his own expenses covered, but he made money in the process. This is nothing short of stealing.

Integrity in finances must include a biblical work ethic. Christian workers ought to have the best reputation in every business. An employee should give eight hours work for eight hours pay. Working hard is critical to upholding our witness for Christ. Laziness and irresponsibility are not to be tolerated according to God's Word. The apostle Paul says, "In the name of the Lord Jesus Christ, we command you, brothers, to keep away from every brother who is idle and does not live according to the teaching you received from us" (2 Thessalonians 3:6). Verse 10 goes on to say, "If anyone will not work, neither shall he eat" (NKJV).

It is an embarrassment to the cause of Christ when an individual attempts to witness, but is unwilling to work hard. It is a violation of integrity to spend time witnessing when we are being paid to work. We can find time to witness at lunch, on breaks, or before and after work. But while on duty we should put all our effort into the task for which our employer is paying us.

I have arrived at a simple seven-step process for myself and my family to walk in victory in the area of finance:

1. Tithe.
2. Give offerings to foreign and home missions.
3. Limit credit buying. (Tear up the credit cards if they cannot be controlled.)
4. Develop a plan for paying off all debt (including home mortgage).
5. Pay all bills on time.
6. Live by a written budget.
7. Teach your children the proper attitude toward the use of money.

INTEGRITY BEGINS IN THE LITTLE THINGS

Integrity begins with the little decisions of life. If we are faithful in the little things, we will be faithful in the big ones. If we cast off restraint in the little decisions, it will not be long before we are deceptive with the big ones. Do not consider any violation of integrity to be a small issue. They are all big in God's eyes.

Examine yourself regularly to see if you have allowed compromise to creep into your life. Humble yourself before God and He will lift you up. Exalt yourself and you will have a great fall.

To summarize integrity: "Do what you said you would do when you said you would do it."

Proverbs 20:7 says, "The righteous man walks in his integrity; his children are blessed after him" (NKJV). I would like to dedicate this chapter to my father, Glen D. Cole, who has left a legacy of integrity for me to walk in. There are few role models in our world today from whom we can learn integrity. Thank you, Dad, for your commitment to God and truth-telling in every aspect of life.

Rick Cole attended Northwest Bible College in Kirkland, Washington, and graduated from Bethany Bible College in Santa Cruz, California, with a Bachelor of Science degree in Ministerial Studies.

He served as youth pastor at Church on the Hill in Vallejo, California; Evangelistic Temple in Houston, Texas; and Bethel Church in San Jose, California. He served as senior pastor at Glad Tidings Church in Omaha, Nebraska, and currently is senior associate at Capital Christian Center in Sacramento, California.

Rick and his wife Cathy are frequent speakers for men's and women's conferences, and marriage and family seminars. They have three children: Nathan, Laine, and Travis.

10

Planning for Success

RICH GUERRA

What is success? As a pastor I have struggled with this question. Webster defines it as "a favorable result, or the gaining of wealth, fame, etc."[1] Somehow, I don't believe that is God's definition.

I heard a pastor share that ministers often define success by "The Three N's: Noise, Numbers, and Nickels!" At district and general councils we recognize those who give the most, have the most, and make the most noise. That is not necessarily wrong. I also admire those who are highly esteemed in our fellowship. But I don't believe the "Three N's" are God's measure for success. I believe, instead, God measures success by our faithfulness, as evidenced by this account:

> Now Jesus sat opposite the treasury and saw how the people put money into the treasury. And many who were rich put in much. Then one poor widow

came and threw in two mites, which makes a quadrans. So He called His disciples to Him and said to them, "Assuredly, I say to you that this poor widow has put in more than all those who have given to the treasury; for they all put in out of their abundance, but she out of her poverty put in all that she had, her whole livelihood"—Mark 12:41-44, NKJV.

By giving "all that she had" she demonstrated her faithfulness to the Lord, and the Lord counted it success.

One of the amazing truths I see in the parable of the talents in Matthew 25:14-30 is that Servant No. 1 and Servant No. 2 received the same reward from the master. Servant No. 1 doubled his talents from five to ten; Servant No. 2 doubled his from two to four. Yet, the master rewarded them equally. To both servants the master said, "Well done, good and faithful servant; you were faithful over a few things, I will make you ruler over many things. Enter into the joy of your lord" (Matthew 25:21, NKJV). What separated the first two servants from the third? They were faithful with what the Lord had given them. Servant No. 3 hid his talent and was condemned.

I have had the joy of ministering to groups, both small and large, and have felt successful in both cases. In situations where I know I didn't do my very best, I felt like a failure. So, for me, the important questions are:

1. Did I do all that I could?
2. Have I been a good and faithful servant?

You might have your own formula for planning for success. I would like to give you an easy and practical guide that has helped me throughout my ministry. It involves success in the areas of life, ministry, and the church.

SUCCESS FOR LIFE

In America today success is big business. In the 1960s, concern about success was considered passe. In the 1990s, people want to know who is successful and how they got that way. The most popular books sold today deal with how to be successful. Image consultants charge $400 to teach us how to dress for success. It is big business.

A Northwestern University sociologist said, "Success in America is one-third family, one-third ability, and one-third luck." Isn't it a tragedy that even those in full-time pastoral ministry can get so caught up in the secular approach to success that we forget God's approach? That could be the reason we have seen so many ministers and ministries fail during the past several years.

The March 1991 issue of *Omni* magazine included an article about the success syndrome. Its victims suffer from the three A's: aloneness, adventure-seeking, and adultery. The article noted that the successful person snaps his Midas fingers and people jump. Yet, when a person seems to have it all, the castle comes crashing down and everything he or she touches turns to trash.

If the three A's entrap those in the secular world, what about believers and those in the ministry? I believe we are just as vulnerable. I have many books on success in my library that supply tremendous insight, but I don't want to become so success-oriented that I don't learn the greater lessons God wants me to learn.

The lessons I have found life-changing have not come from books. Rather, the principles were shared or modeled by faithful servants who have been in the ministry for many years. I have condensed them into seven foundational principles.

1. Build upon your strengths. We cannot all be "five talent" servants. It is easy to look at those who are more talented and feel you can't do anything worthwhile for God. But the parable of the talents teaches us to judge success by what we have, not what we don't have. We must discover our strengths and build upon them. We must also discover areas in which we are weak, then surround ourselves with individuals who are talented in those areas.

God has given me the talent to make people laugh and cry. If I use my talent for the glory of God, I will see Him touch hearts and lives. If I continue to build upon my strengths, I will become an effective leader.

2. "To be" is more important than "to do." All my life I have tried to do the right thing. As I mature in the Lord I recognize God is more concerned that I "be" the man of God He wants me to be, rather than "do" the things I think He wants me to do.

When Jesus healed a demoniac, the man was so grateful he wanted to stay with the Lord. Instead, Jesus said, "Go home to your friends, and tell them what great things the Lord has done for you, and how He has had compassion on you" (Mark 5:19, NKJV). The man wanted to be a disciple; Jesus wanted him to be a witness.

In the Sermon on the Mount (see Matthew 5:3-10), Christ lists the qualities needed to be a disciple. Those qualities make it evident God is more concerned about character than performance. The qualifications for a minister given in 1 Timothy 3:2-7 and Titus 1:7-9 also deal with character.

Character is more important than reputation—and there is a difference. Reputation is what you're supposed to be; character is what you are. Reputation is the photo; character is the face. Reputation grows from without; character grows from within. Reputation is what you have when you're first introduced; character is what you have when you leave. Reputation is learned in an hour; character might come about in a year. Reputation is made in a moment; character is made in a lifetime. Reputation makes you rich or poor; character makes you happy. Reputation makes you grow like a mushroom; character makes you grow like an oak. Reputation is what men say about you on your tombstone; character is what angels say about you before the throne of God.

3. Be the best you can be. For a minister the battle is not necessarily between good and evil, but between "good enough" and the best. My parents always challenged me to be the best I could be. Jesus, speaking to Martha, said, "Mary has chosen what is better, and it will not be taken away from her" (Luke 10:42).

The difference between good enough and best is like going to church versus being committed to God. I don't want to be a minister and just get by; I want to be the best I can be. I don't want to preach half-hearted sermons. I don't want to minister in a half-hearted manner. I want to give my all for Christ—who gave His all for me.

4. What happens *in* me is more important than what happens *to* me. Most of us in the ministry have gone through difficult times. We usually pray for a change of circumstances when God wants to bring about a change of character. You cannot remain neutral in a crisis. You either become bitter or better. The apostle Paul calls on us to "rejoice in our sufferings, because . . . suffering produces perseverance; perseverance, character; and character, hope" (Romans 5:3,4).

5. It is always too soon to quit. The word *perseverance* comes from the Greek word *hupomene,* a compound word which means "to remain under" in the presence of pressure. A diamond is a stone that has been under pressure for a long period of time. As Christians, you and I are molded into the image of Christ because of the pressures of life. In light of that, realize it is always too soon to quit.

Runners face times when they feel they can't go on. They call it "hitting the wall." Those who give in to the urge to quit never build their endurance to its greatest potential. Those who continue find new strength to carry on and reach a new plateau in their endurance. If we as Christians quit every time we "hit a wall," we will never learn the lessons God wants us to learn, and our endurance will be underdeveloped.

6. Follow a formula for success. If you want to fail, look at the size of the obstacle and take your eyes off the Lord. If you want to succeed, keep your eyes on the Lord and don't worry about the size of the obstacle.

What are your eyes on today? The 12 spies who went to search out the land of Canaan came back with different reports. Two of them said, "We should go up and take possession of the land, for we can certainly do it" (Numbers 13:30). The other 10 saw it differently. They said, "We can't attack those people; they are stronger than we are" (Numbers 13:31). They looked at the size of the obstacles and took their eyes off the Lord. David was able to defeat

Goliath because he knew his God was bigger than Goliath. David kept his eyes on God and not on the size of the obstacle.

7. Were you faithful? The Lord is not going to ask if I was successful in the work He gave me to do. He will ask, "Were you faithful?" In the parable of the talents the master commended his two faithful servants. "Well done . . . you were faithful over a few things, I will make you ruler over many things. Enter into the joy of your lord" (Matthew 25:21, NKJV). They were given a responsibility and were faithful to perform it.

Have you been faithful with the responsibilities God has given you? That's a question I often ask myself, because I know that is what God requires of me. A fellow minister who recently celebrated his eighty-second birthday is on my pastoral staff. We pray for each other during staff meetings, and when I asked what his greatest prayer need was, he replied, "That I might know more of Jesus." What an example of faithfulness. It's the kind of example I want to follow.

Success in life may not always show outwardly. If we look at Christ on Calvary, He appeared to be an ignominious failure. It was said of Him, "He saved others; Himself He cannot save" (Matthew 27:42, NKJV). Inwardly He was able to say, "It is finished." He was faithful to the end—a success in the eyes of the Father. Success doesn't get any better than that.

SUCCESS FOR MINISTRY

Success in ministry and the Christian life doesn't just happen. It is a result of faithfulness, discipline, and planning. We've already talked about faithfulness, and we know there is no substitute for spiritual discipline (i.e., spending time in prayer and in the Word of God), but many ministers fail to recognize the importance of planning.

Proverbs 29:18 declares, "Where there is no vision, the people perish" (KJV). Many in ministry dream of something great happening, but a vision is different. A vision begins with an image of something the person or group would like to see happen, and, like a dream, excites all the emotions. But a vision goes beyond a dream to "capture" the person. A person may *have* a wish or a dream—a vision *has* the person. He will pay any price to bring the vision into full reality.

Scripture repeatedly illustrates the tremendous effect of a vision upon a person. A vision always results in action. When a minister or ministry lacks vision, the minister or people perish. That is why we need God to supply us with the vision, then we need to develop a plan to see it happen.

In *Let My People Go: Empowering Laity for Ministry,* Lindgren and Shawchuck wrote:

> Planning is like navigation. If you know where you are and where you want to go, navigation is not so difficult. It's when you don't know the two points that navigating the right course becomes difficult. To illustrate the logic, let's use a comparison. Assume you board a luxury ocean liner, its engines running in preparation to leave port. You go into the chart room and ask the captain to show you your present location, what his next port-of-call will be, your final destination, and the route he will take to get

there. He answers, "I don't know any of that, I just pay attention to keeping the ship moving." Would you want to be a passenger on his ship?

Should you not use intelligence in planning the future course of your church as you would expect the captain to? There has never been a church that planned to fail, but there have been many who failed to plan. Unfortunately the results are about the same.[2]

Navigation requires that you know where you are, where you want to go, and the route you will take to get there. This information is necessary whether you are navigating a ship or a church. One of the most helpful tools I have discovered is found in the book, *Revitalizing the 20th Century Church,* by Lloyd M. Perry and Norman Shawchuck. In it they use a diagram called "The Vision Cycle." I have used this model in every area of ministry in which I have served. It has become a vital tool in planning for success in my ministry.

The Vision Cycle begins with *mission clarification.* It asks the question, "What is God calling us to be and do?" The answer to this question is your purpose or mission statement. The mission statement must be based on God's Word, and you must feel that God is speaking to you personally about your purpose in ministry. What is God calling you to be? What is God calling you to do?

Once you develop the mission statement you can go to *congregational assessment.* It asks the question, "Where are we now?" Before you can plan for the future, you have to know where you are in the present. To help you assess that, you need to ask yourself three questions:

1. What are the strengths of my church or ministry?
2. What are the weaknesses of my church or ministry?
3. What are the hopes and dreams of my church or ministry?

Once you have assessed where your church or ministry is, then you can capitalize on the strengths, reduce the weaknesses, and realize your hopes and dreams for the future.

Now you are able to move into the planning stage, which is called *goal setting*. It asks the question, "Where do we want to be?" Proverbs 11:14 says, "For want of skilful strategy an army is lost; victory is the fruit of long planning" (New English Bible). Goals move a ministry or congregation in the direction it wants to go. Perry and Shawchuck suggested a goal should meet as many as possible of the following tests:

1. *Is it mission directed?* It can be clearly seen as a help toward achieving the church's mission.

2. *Is it desirable?* It grows out of congregational interests and needs that have been expressed, or represents conviction about its need for a more healthy and effective church organization.

3. *Is it conceivable?* It can be expressed in clearly understandable words.

4. *Is it assignable?* Persons asked to achieve it can see their tasks clearly.

5. *Is it believable?* It is entirely possible.

6. *Is it achievable?* The existing resources—or those that can be secured—of time, skill, materials, facilities, persons, and dollars are sufficient to do the task.

7. *Is it measurable?* It is possible to tell when it has been accomplished, and some judgment can be made as to whether the effort was worthwhile.

8. *Is it controllable?* It produces a minimum of unintended consequences; persons and groups are not involved unintentionally or without their permission.[3]

The next stage in the Vision Cycle is called *implementation*. It asks the question, "How do we plan to get there?" Lindgren and Shawchuck described the components of a good implementation plan. They said:

> Good implementation begins with developing a good plan. This plan needs to be written and comprehensive enough to serve as a road map to achieving the goals. A road map that is so incomplete as to leave out important information is no good, and one that is cluttered with unimportant and confusing material is also no good.[4]

A good implementation plan will give information regarding the following:

- Strategizing: *What* activities will we do to reach our goal?
- Scheduling: *When* will each activity take place?
- Recruiting and assigning: *Who* is responsible to see that it happens?
- Resourcing: *What* are the equipment, space, money, and worker needs to carry out the activity?
- Monitoring: *How* will we check up to be sure the plan functions properly and on time?[5]

Now you have a plan for action. You have answered the questions "What is God calling us to be and do?" "Where are we now?" "Where do we want to be?" "How do we plan to get there?"

At the end of the year, perhaps at a staff retreat, you can discuss the final stage of the Vision Cycle. It is called *evaluation*. It asks the question, "How close did we come to our destination?" Evaluation is the missing link in most church planning activities. Evaluation not only helps you to see if you accomplished your goals, but it also helps you reevaluate your mission statement. Then you can go through the whole cycle again.

I make it a point to go through the Vision Cycle with my staff every year. It has been a useful guide to help me plan for success. Proverbs 16:3 says, "Commit to the Lord whatever you do, and your plans will succeed." You need a plan for your personal life, ministry, and church.

SUCCESS FOR YOUR CHURCH

As I stated earlier, success is big business—even in the church. I am flooded with advertisements for church growth seminars, church growth books and tapes, and church growth consultants. I have benefited tremendously from much of the material that is available to help grow a church. Yet, despite the fact that there is more material on church growth available than ever before, the church in America is not growing. The problem is not the material; the problem is the focus. The church is a living organism, not just an organization. A living organism produces life; an organization just exists. Along with organizational helps that church growth experts can supply, there needs to be steps taken to ensure that your church is a living organism.

Jesus said, "And I also say to you that you are Peter, and on this rock I will build My church, and the gates of Hades shall not prevail against it" (Matthew 16:18, NKJV). The building up of the church is the primary interest of God today. He wants to build up your church, and His great building process has not changed since the first church. I call it "The Secrets of the Growing Church."

We can read about the early church in the Book of Acts. Notice three vital elements of a growing church:

> And they continued steadfastly in the apostles' doctrine and fellowship, in the breaking of bread, and in prayers. Then fear came upon every soul, and many wonders and signs were done through the apostles. Now all who believed were together, and had all things in common, and sold their possessions and goods, and divided them among all, as anyone had need.
>
> So continuing daily with one accord in the temple, and breaking bread from house to house, they ate their food with gladness and simplicity of heart, praising God and having favor with all people. And the Lord added to the church daily those who were being saved—Acts 2:42-47, NKJV.

1. Prayer. The early church was devoted to prayer. How important is prayer in the life of your church? It should be vital. Church history tells us that every major revival was a result of prayer. We need to devote ourselves to prayer if we want to see our churches grow.

2. Power. The early church leaders were characterized by power. A mistake many churches make is neglecting the supernatural manifestation of the power of the Holy Spirit. A wise pastor once told me, "If you get just the Word, you'll dry up. If you get just the Spirit, you'll blow up. But if you get the balance of both, you'll grow up!" Let us not neglect the power of the Holy Spirit in the life of our churches. Invite people not only to receive Jesus Christ as their Lord and Savior, but to experience the baptism of the Holy Spirit with the evidence of speaking in other tongues. The result will be healings and deliverance from the bondage of sin.

The early church was a church of power. We still need this power for effective evangelism. In Acts 3, we read about Peter and John who went to the temple to pray. A lame man sat at the gate asking alms. Peter said, "Silver or gold I do not have, but what I do have I give you: In the name of Jesus Christ of Nazareth, rise up and walk" (Acts 3:6, NKJV). He was immediately healed and he entered the temple with Peter and John, "walking and jumping, and praising God" (vs. 8). Now notice verses 9 and 10: "And all the people saw him walking and praising God. Then they knew that it was he who sat begging alms at the Beautiful Gate of the temple; and they were filled with wonder and amazement at what had happened to him" (NKJV). The manifestation of the power of God is an effective evangelism program. Is it happening in your church? If not, it should be.

3. People. In Acts 2:44-46, there was spontaneous and voluntary benevolence as a result of prayer, power, and God's love. We need to be committed to people in order to see our churches grow. Commitment to facilities or programs won't grow a church, but a commitment to people will. From the early church we can see three areas of commitment that are essential: they loved one another; they gave financial support; they gave of their time to serve God.

What was the result of having people who were committed to prayer, committed to power, and committed to people? "And the Lord added to the church daily those who were being saved" (Acts 2:47, NKJV). The Lord wants His church to grow. Is your church growing? At times it is tempting to find a quick, popular, successful plan for church growth. But if it is not based on these three biblical truths—prayer, power, and people—your growth won't be lasting or rewarding.

When I was in Bible college I had an opportunity to minister with a well-known evangelist. I remember standing beside him one Sunday evening in a packed church. I had never seen so many people in church before, and I was impressed. He told me, "Never be impressed with big crowds, because even the circus can draw a big crowd."

Those words have stayed with me all these years. Our goal must not be to attract great crowds; our goal must be to build great churches. With all the church growth materials that are available today, we still need the message of Acts 2:47: "And the Lord added to the church daily those who were being saved" (NKJV). The Lord is still in the church building business—and I want Him to build my church.

SUCCESS TAKES TIME

Pastoring in Las Vegas, Nevada, has been an amazing experience. I've seen people from around the world come to "make it big." They are hoping for one lucky roll of the dice, deal of the cards, or pull of the slot machine. The vast majority go home discouraged, depressed, and broke. There's an important parallel that can be drawn here. Don't be persuaded that there is a get-rich-quick formula to success, whether it is for your life, your ministry, or your church. Success takes discipline and time.

A fisherman was lying on a New England river bank, lazily casting his line into the water. Now and then he caught a silvery salmon. As he was hauling in a fish, a well-dressed, prosperous businessman from a nearby town strolled over.

"Don't you realize," he asked the fisherman, "that you could catch more fish if you put several lines into the water at the same time?"

"Why would I want more fish?" asked the fisherman.

"Well, if you had more fish, you would have more to sell, and you would make more money. And, if you made more money, you could buy a big fishing boat. Then you could open up a store and sell your fish to the whole town. After you opened one store, you could open a second, and then a third. You would have many people working for you. Eventually you could open a large wholesale fish market, shipping fish all over America. You could become a very rich man."

The fisherman looked unconvinced. "And then what would I do?" he asked the industrialist.

"Why, then you would be successful, and you'd have all the time in the world to do whatever you most enjoyed doing. You could just lie on your back, relax, and go fishing!"

The fisherman looked up at him and smiled. "But that's what I'm doing now."

If you have answered Jesus' call to be a fisher of men, you are a success. One day we will hear the Master say, "Well done, good and faithful servant; you were faithful over a few things, I will make you ruler over many things. Enter into the joy of your Lord."

Rich Guerra is the senior pastor of Trinity Life Center in Las Vegas, Nevada. He is a graduate of Southern California College, where he received his Bachelor's degree in Biblical Studies and his Master's degree in Church Leadership.

He formerly served as singles pastor at Capital Christian Center in Sacramento, California. The Reverend Guerra at one time also held the position as Youth Ministries Director for the Southern California District of the Assemblies of God.

He and his wife Coni have three children: Ryan, Andrew, and Lindsay.

11

Pursuing Excellence

KAREN BENNETT

The pursuit of excellence has become the buzz phrase of the 1990s. It is something we face in our society—including the church—every day. The pursuit of excellence in our careers, our relationships, our families, our health, and our appearance has become a national obsession and a multi-million dollar industry. Seminars are held throughout the country to teach us how to achieve excellence. Entire stores are devoted to the merchandising of excellence.

All these methods are used to inspire and help us climb the ladder of success. But is the excellence we hear so much about today the type we should pursue? More importantly, is it the excellence Christ would have us pursue?

Excellence can be defined as fame, fortune, and success; it can mean "to stand out, to surpass, to be stronger." It is pursued by many who don't realize countless hurts can be accumulated on the way to the top.

This pursuit of excellence has crept into the church and destroyed the hearts of innocent believers. It has camouflaged itself as humility, only later to be exposed as deceit in once-sincere Christian leaders. It may begin as a desire to be one's best for Christ, but somewhere the intentions change. What may have started as a desire to be like the disciple who laid his head on Jesus' chest, turned into a quest for a few pieces of silver and a fleeting moment of fame, and ended as a tragedy to the one who lost his own soul and perhaps his only friend.

There is another type of excellence spoken of in John 3:22-30. John the Baptist was baptizing people in the Jordan River. Some of his followers came to him and said, "Rabbi, that man who was with you on the other side of the Jordan—the one you testified about—well, he is baptizing, and everyone is going to him" (John 3:26).

John's followers loved their master and were jealous of the success of Jesus. Through the innocence of caring individuals, the devil attempted to change a sincere desire to serve into a selfish desire to succeed. Unlike many, John the Baptist did not respond jealously, but in humility—the most important quality in the pursuit of excellence.

John the Baptist turned to his followers and said, "The friend who attends the bridegroom waits and listens for him, and is *full of joy* when he hears the bridegroom's voice. That joy is mine, and it is now complete. *He must become greater; I must become less*" (John 3:29,30).

The pursuit of excellence is losing everything we are so we can be everything Christ wants us to be. This is excellence—more of Jesus, less of me! It is giving ourselves for a higher purpose and a just cause, the cause of Christ. It is a willingness to lose one's life so it can be found again with a new purpose in Christ.

THE ENEMY'S DISGUISE

Throughout our lives we learn from our experiences, through the friendships we make, and through the vast amount of information that comes our way. Growing up in a single parent home, with a mother who worked hard to provide for her two children, I learned values for which I am eternally grateful. Our family did not attend church, but there were strong morals and ethics we were taught to live by.

Our neighborhood was made up of hardworking people, including a family whose father was a convicted felon. Occasionally, he escaped from prison and returned to hide out in his home. When the police came to apprehend him our neighborhood turned into a live movie set, and my friends and I had front-row seats.

Despite some of the unusual circumstances we faced, I always knew my mom wanted the best for us. I remember the day she introduced my sister and me to Bill, a man she had been dating. I don't so much remember meeting Bill as I do seeing his car as he drove into our neighborhood. It left a great impression on me.

Our neighborhood was not affluent. Driveways were lined with old station wagons, oil spots, or pieces of cars strewn about the yard. Amazingly, our family was the proud owner of a brand new, bright yellow Dodge Dart with black vinyl upholstery. This was quite a step up from the station wagon we had previously owned, which had two large holes in the floor boards as part of its standard features. It didn't look too good, but we could throw our trash away without ever leaving the car.

We were proud of our new yellow Dodge, but it was no comparison to what pulled into our driveway the day we met Bill. As I was sitting outside waiting to meet what may be a prospective step-father, I saw a long, elegant car drive into our neighborhood. I had never seen a car quite so big or beautiful. I expected it to pass by and go down to the house where the fugitive lived, but to my surprise it pulled into our driveway. My eyes got as big as golf balls when the car door swung open and a distinguished-looking gentleman stepped out. Mom came out to meet him and introduced us. We tried to be polite, but our eyes were fixed on his beautiful car.

We made friends with Bill right away, especially since he let us sit in his car. My friends came over to see if they could play in the car with me; they had never been so close to such a magnificent car, either. It was a baby blue Lincoln Continental Mark IV, with soft velour interior that didn't burn your legs when you sat down. It had air conditioning—unlike our Dodge Dart—and remote control seats, which I charged my friends a nickel to play with. It was the greatest car I had ever seen.

Mom and Bill became serious, and eventually they were married. We moved from our small home to an eight-bedroom mansion in the ritzy part of town. Life took on a new meaning, with new experiences and new desires. We went from being K-Mart shoppers to millionaires overnight.

In our old house we shared one black and white television set; now we each had our own color set—with remote control. Mom and Bill often took trips to places such as Lake Tahoe, the Bahamas, and Switzerland. Whatever we asked for, almost assuredly we got.

At first, this new fortune and success was wonderful, but as I learned, if it is not the excellence Jesus has for us, it will leave us empty-handed. It appeared that our family had achieved excellence, but it was only a clever disguise.

My step-father had been a successful builder, but in the 1970s the construction industry hit bottom. Properties were not selling, and many builders went bankrupt. I could see the anxiety on Bill's face as he feared he would lose everything he had spent a lifetime working for. Losing money daily and having no hope in sight, he turned to alcohol. His drinking became excessive and soon he lost the ability to control his company. Before long, he was forced into bankruptcy.

I remember the day he lost everything. After the bank had taken control of his properties, Bill came home staggering drunk. His face showed the emptiness he felt inside— emptiness that comes when a person realizes his life was built on empty success. He could barely walk but managed to make it to the stairway, where he collapsed and fell down a flight of stairs. My mom and I ran to help, but he did not want us around. I sat on the stairway looking at this once-successful pillar of the community, now curled up like a frightened child. He had spent a lifetime pursuing an excellence that brought temporary joy. I wish he had spent a lifetime pursuing an excellence that gave eternal joy.

As my mom and I sat on the stairs, my heart felt broken. I told her how much I missed going to K-Mart, and her telling me I could not get anything that day—maybe later. How quickly those precious moments lose their importance when the devil flashes his camouflaged version of excellence in our face. That day, sitting on those stairs, I would have much rather been back in my old neighborhood with our yellow Dodge Dart. We had bought the devil's lie—and we had paid dearly.

Excellence is not the amount of money we have in our bank accounts, the number of people who attend our church, the type of car we drive, the positions and awards we obtain, or the brand of clothes we wear. Excellence is a way of life that reflects the humility of Jesus Christ. Pursuing excellence is pursuing Christ and giving Him ownership of our lives—lives that are full of joy.

Bill had been a successful and prominent builder, but he failed to build his own life on the sure and solid foundation: the excellency of Jesus Christ. He became an alcoholic, and eventually he and my mother divorced. Even so, they remained close friends until his death in 1991.

GOOD INTENTIONS

Recently, I was reading about Neil Armstrong, the first man to walk on the moon. When someone asked if he was nervous pondering his trip into space, he said, "Who wouldn't be? There I was sitting on top of 9,999 parts and bits—each of which had been made by the lowest bidder!"[1] This is the place in which many of us find ourselves: starting out with good intentions, yet allowing cheaply made bits and pieces to ruin our lives. This is the place Judas Iscariot found himself—and he sold himself short.

Like many of us, Judas started out with noble intentions. After all, he forsook everything to follow Jesus. Not only did this indicate his potential, but the fact that Jesus prayed extensively the night before choosing the 12 disciples gives credibility to his call. (See Luke 6:12-16.) Judas was chosen as treasurer of the group and was obviously trusted by the others. But somewhere along the way his understanding of excellence changed. He traded those precious, intimate moments with Jesus for cheap bits and pieces of greed and ambition.

Judas began to slip, and the values he had learned from Jesus over three years lost their meaning. Unlike John the

Baptist, Judas gave way to jealousy and began to covet fame, fortune, and power. It was at this point that his heart began to harden. Greed and pride replaced humility. Jesus saw what was happening and on numerous occasions warned Judas concerning his life, yet Judas did not respond. This is an example to us that even when we are off course and our actions go against Christ, He reaches out His hand of grace to pull us in. All we have to do is reach back and take hold of it.

Humility is the most important quality in the pursuit of excellence, because it enables us to respond to Jesus. Will we be like Judas and allow pride and selfishness to keep us from responding? Or will we be like John the Baptist and in all humility say, "He must become greater; I must become less"? For all of us, including Judas, one thing is certain: timing is everything. One day the hand of Jesus may not be there; we may have turned Him away one too many times. On that day we will understand the nervousness Neil Armstrong felt when he said, "There I was sitting on 9,999 parts and bits—each of which had been made by the lowest bidder!"

THE ROAD TO EXCELLENCE

After Bill and Mom divorced, our family struggled once again. I went to work at the age of 13 to help make ends meet. I enjoyed working and have always been a dreamer. The desire to succeed has always been a part of my life. I just didn't know what to succeed in since my understanding of excellence wasn't based on Christ. Consequently, I found myself in dangerous territory, nearly destroying my life at times.

My curiosity and desire to succeed and feel important led me to drugs. What began as an experiment ended as an addiction. I was doing thousands of dollars worth of cocaine, thinking I was important and going somewhere significant; but in actuality I was completely lost. If it were not for the consistent love of my father, I would not be writing this chapter today.

My father left my family when I was four years old. He wasn't a great father. He didn't come see us much; he had abused my mother on several occasions, and he did almost nothing to care for our needs. Despite his many downfalls, Jesus reached out His hand of grace and, thankfully, my dad reached back. When I was 13 years old, my dad called to tell me he had gotten saved. God totally changed his life. There was a night-and-day difference. My dad was a new man. Immediately, he tried to make up for all the wrong he had done, and I could sense a genuine love from him. Unfortunately, by then our lives were going in two different directions and we had little in common.

As I grew older, I was honest with my dad concerning my involvement with drugs. Something about being around a Christian brings out the truth in a person. No matter what I told him, Dad never got mad at me. He believed in me and told me there was a special purpose for my life. Every time I talked to him, he would say, "Sis, God has a better way for you. He has a better way." Even the night I had to call him from jail and ask him to bail me out, Dad walked me to my car, looked at me, and said, "Sis, God has a better way for you. He has a better way."

For six years Dad witnessed to me without ever getting mad or giving up. When you travel the road to excellence, others will want to travel with you one day. At 19, I made my decision to follow Christ and travel that road with my dad.

Regardless of my past, Jesus reached out His hand of grace as He had to my father. I, too, reached out and took hold of it. At my mom's house, not knowing exactly what to do, I knelt beside her sofa and said, "God, if You'll just get me out of Atlanta and away from these drugs, I promise I'll never leave You." That day I gave my heart to the Lord and was forever changed.

Through a high school friend I learned about Lee College in Cleveland, Tennessee. I knew I had to leave Atlanta and the drugs in order to change my life. I called the college and, much to my surprise, it was a Bible/Liberal Arts school. The tuition was more than I could pay, and classes began in three days. It didn't look as if I would be able to attend, but Dad told me not to give up. He said, "The devil doesn't want you to have the things God wants you to have."

With these words in my heart, I kept trying to get the necessary funds. The day before classes were to begin, my mom's boss, Mr. Cowart, called and asked me to come see him at his office. I had no idea what he wanted to see me about, but I went. He said, "I heard you want to go to college." I said, "Yes, sir, I do." He offered to pay my way to a community college, but I explained that I had been saved two days earlier and needed to be around Christians to help get my life straightened out. A few minutes later, Mr. Cowart pulled out his checkbook and wrote me a check for $2,000 so I could go to college. This man, an elder at the first church I attended, paid my entire way through Bible college.

I thought this was the greatest thing that had ever happened to me, but an even greater thing was that Lee

College was located only 30 minutes from my dad's house. I went from seeing Dad a few times a year to seeing him every day. God has every step of our lives planned; all we need to do is follow Him. When our hearts are pure and our motives sincere, God will help us pursue excellence. The first step is learning to respond when Jesus reaches out His hand of grace to us.

Every day after class I drove to my dad's house to spend time with him. Every night we sat at the kitchen table and had Bible study together. Our Bible studies were very exciting because Dad was an independent fundamental Baptist, and I was attending a pentecostal Bible college. It was the greatest time of my life. We became as close as a father and daughter could be.

That time together was a special gift from God. But it was a chance that came only once—a time I would have missed had I not responded to the outstretched hand of Jesus. Six months after I arrived at Lee College, my dad and step-mother were tragically killed.

PRECIOUS MEMORIES

As I look back, I realize how close I came to never knowing the love my dad had for me. We never would have shared our relationship with Jesus; never would have prayed together; never would have had Bible studies together. I would not have the memories of the greatest dad God ever created had I not responded to Christ that fateful day. I wonder how things might have been for Judas if he had responded to Christ in humility, seeking forgiveness. I am thankful I don't have to wonder about myself; I only have to close my eyes and thank God for the memories.

The loss of my father still brings pain; I miss him more than words can describe, but he lives on in my thoughts everyday. His every word and action, his humility, and his uncanny ability to know what I needed even before I asked, are ingrained in my heart. I think about him every-day, and with every remembrance comes an abundance of joy and love. He was the most caring, unselfish person I have ever known.

Few individuals have had such a powerful impact on my life. You see, a life based on true excellence lives on in the hearts of those it touches. What will you be remembered for? Will you be remembered as a traitor? Will you be remembered at all? Jesus' hand is reaching out. He wants us to respond and commit our lives to the pursuit of excellence. How will you respond?

TRUE EXCELLENCE

After the death of my father and step-mother, I felt my life had come to an end. I was all alone. I had spent every available moment with my dad and had spent no time building relationships with other Christians. For several months I barely came out of my room at school, and my prayers became repeated cries for help.

During this time of loneliness and sorrow, I experienced a new relationship with Christ. During my time of suffer-ing, I went from liking the Lord to falling in love with Him. All I wanted was more of Jesus in my life.

Throughout college that relationship continued to grow. I wanted desperately to serve Him, but feared He might not call me into the ministry. The devil played on my insecurities, but my desire for God ran much deeper. All I desired was the Lord's will in my life, and with each passing day that hunger grew.

I started going to the prayer room during the day to spend time with God. I could sense a history of prayer and an inviting presence of the Lord in the old auditorium where the prayer room was located. It wasn't uncommon for my friends and me to sacrifice meals so we could spend more time in prayer. Anticipation grew in my heart; a burden for the lost caused a heaviness to weigh on me. During that time of total devotion the Lord began to teach me the meaning of true excellence.

During an evening chapel service at school I responded to an altar call. The power of God was so strong that hundreds of students could not even make it to the altar. As they entered the aisles, they knelt or fell on their faces, crying out to the Lord. I managed to find a small corner all to myself. I tried to pray, but all I could do was cry. I felt totally surrendered to the Lord that night, giving Him every area of my life. A reverence in that auditorium filled our lives as it filled that building.

While I was at the altar, I felt the Lord touch my life in a new way. He put a dream in my heart and confirmed His call on my life, and I knew without question the direction in which He would take me. My main prayer then and now is for the Lord to use me to touch lives the way my father touched mine. That's my sole desire—more of Jesus and less of me!

While still in Bible college, I began a children's ministry in Cleveland, Tennessee, which grew to 400 youngsters in three short years. Out of this effort I founded a clowning ministry to reach children. My staff and I left for Chicago to begin an inner-city work for children. Within eight weeks, over 300 children were being bused to "Saturday Sunday School," one of our unique ministry concepts to reach kids. In 1989 God opened a door for me to carry my dream back to the streets of Atlanta, my home town.

THE PRICE OF EXCELLENCE

Four years after that altar call, the Lord began to make the dream of my heart a reality. My staff and I went from a kids club to a national children's ministry; from a church of 20 to being on staff at a church of 10,000; from living a comfortable life to a life of sacrifice that enables dreams to be fulfilled; from living in nice apartments to living in an old warehouse with no heat, no air conditioning, and 17-inch sewer rats; from ministering to 15 children to ministering to 3,000 children weekly; from a small adult Bible study to a congregation of 200; from faith for one school bus to faith for 12; and from young people with a dream to young ministers fulfilling a purpose—all in a very short period of time.

Our young ages, the focus of our ministry (an inner city church primarily for children), and the fact that I am a female pastor, generates a great deal of interest in our work. The Lord began to give us favor, and word spread about our quick success. Several articles were published on our ministry, and I began to be featured on Christian radio and television programs. Persons of influence began to support us and believe in what we were doing. The Lord blessed our efforts in ways we never imagined and provided through means that man never could.

Some rejoiced with our success; others became jealous and tried to destroy our efforts. The devil will use any means necessary to harden hearts, including fame, jealousy, greed, and bitterness. He targets our weakness and blinds us to the warnings Jesus sends our way. He brings distractions that can harm us and those in our care. We must understand the pursuit of excellence is not easy; there is a price to be paid, sufferings to be endured, and lessons to be learned. True excellence costs us something; something few are willing to pay.

Never was this more clear to me than when I met a young man named Tim Hunter. He was a 28-year-old homosexual drug addict who lived in a cardboard and plywood hut under a bridge in Atlanta. It was not long before Tim agreed to attend one of our services, where he gave his heart to the Lord. He began to attend services regularly and volunteered to help around the church. Tim did not care whether he was cleaning bathrooms or participating in the service. He was just glad to be at church.

The children took to him right away, and the adults loved him as well. Eventually, Tim became my twelfth full-time staff member. Then, without warning, Tim came to me and said he had to leave the church. I asked why, but he wouldn't tell me. I tried to stay in touch with him, but he refused all contact with me and the church. Finally, one of his friends told me Tim left because he was diagnosed HIV positive. I told his friend this did not change the way we felt about Tim, but despite our efforts we could not get through to him.

Several months passed when I received a call from Tim asking me to come visit. I got directions to his home and left immediately. I knocked on his door and waited for him to answer. When the door opened I could not see very well because the lights were off. As my eyes adjusted to the dimness, I saw that Tim had gone from a healthy 150 pounds to less than 80. He had full-blown AIDS. Sores covered his arms and face, and it took every ounce of strength within me to hold back the tears.

I stayed with Tim for several hours. His thoughts wandered because of the massive doses of pain killer he was taking. It was late when I started back to the church. Before I left, Tim said, "You know, Pastor Karen, I never dreamed it would end this way, but at least you gave me the chance to know where I'm going." Three months later, while ministering in Florida, I received a call from my staff telling me Tim had passed away.

While making arrangements for his funeral, I had occasion to speak with his hospice worker. For several weeks she had been telling him he needed to make arrangements for his funeral and that she would be glad to help. Tim never responded, but moments before he died, she asked him one more time. Finally he looked up and said, "I'm not worried. Pastor Karen will take care of me."

Two days later I did my first funeral for a very special friend. I could barely speak, but I did take care of him.

The business of life and the pressure to succeed can cause us to lose sight of true excellence. Pursuing excellence is allowing the humility of Christ to rule our lives and cause us to respond when He reaches out to us. It is allowing Christ to become greater while we become less. A life based on true excellence is made obvious because it lives on in the hearts of those it touches. We all have the opportunity to pursue excellence. Jesus is reaching out His hand of grace today. Will you accept it? Or will you sell yourself short for 30 pieces of silver?

Karen Bennett has touched thousands of children through her varied ministry experience. At age 19 God gave her a burden to impact forgotten inner-city children. She launched children's ministries in Cleveland, Tennessee, Chicago, and Atlanta. In 1989 Karen went on staff as children's pastor at Mount Paran Church of God, one of the nation's largest churches.

Now Karen focuses her vision as pastor of Metro Church, which reaches over 3,000 children, 350 adults, and 150 teenagers weekly. She and her staff equip other churches to reach those trapped in the ghettos of our country through videos and seminars.

12

The Disciplined Life

GREGORY A. HACKETT

When a person talks about a disciplined life, negative connotations often arise. Some feel a disciplined life quenches the "move of the Spirit." Others feel a disciplined life limits the "faith factor" in our walk with God.

There are many characteristics attributed to being spiritual. A disciplined life usually is not one of them. This is unfortunate. In an age of pressure and confusion we need people—especially leaders—who are disciplined. Many athletic contests have been won as a result of the discipline of the coach and the players. Likewise, many great churches and ministries have been built and continue to grow because the leaders of those ministries exercised discipline. A flower takes only a few months to grow, while an oak tree takes years. We enjoy the beauty of an oak tree in the present because of someone's discipline in the past. Likewise, many great ministries today are the result of the discipline of a previous generation.

The Bible has much to say regarding a disciplined life. Unfortunately, in a desire to be liked by people rather than approved by God, this area has not been adequately addressed in the church, even when it comes to leadership. Note the following scriptures that address self-discipline:

> Teach us to number our days aright, that we may gain a heart of wisdom—Psalm 90:12.

> Since an overseer is entrusted with God's work, he must be blameless—not overbearing, not quick-tempered, not given to drunkenness, not violent, not pursuing dishonest gain. Rather he must be hospitable, one who loves what is good, who is self-controlled, upright, holy and disciplined—Titus 1:7,8.

> Buy the truth and do not sell it; get wisdom, discipline and understanding—Proverbs 23:23.

> For God did not give us a spirit of timidity, but a spirit of power, of love and of self-discipline—2 Timothy 1:7.

These scriptures teach us that we are to be disciplined. Two questions come to mind: In what areas are we to be disciplined? How are we to be disciplined? The answers, especially important for Christian leaders, are found in the Word of God.

Two key areas in which we are to be disciplined include time management and ministry.

TIME MANAGEMENT

No matter how gifted we may be, like everyone, we have a limited amount of time. I often hear people say "time flies," but it progresses at the same pace for everyone. Others say they need to "make up time," but once time is spent there is no getting it back. The wisdom of Psalm 90:12 is ageless. We need to number our days aright, or translated, we need to watch our time. Our time *is* our life. If we make our time count, we make our life count. If we waste our time, we waste our life.

Each of us has a limited amount of resources with a limited amount of time to accomplish a limited amount of things. This is a reminder of our humanity: we are not God. As a result, we must identify time-wasters. What are time-wasters? They differ for each of us, but the results are the same: time-wasters are anything that prevent us from achieving our objectives effectively.

Since our time and resources are limited, we must use them wisely, understanding that we can't do it all. But it's not God's will that we do it all. Each of us is a *part* of the body of Christ, not the entire body of Christ. It's important to stay focused on our objectives. We need first to establish those objectives, then have a daily, weekly, or monthly plan that will help us accomplish them. We must prioritize our schedules, making sure there is time for the important things.

Here are a few suggestions for using time wisely:

1. During appointments, don't receive phone calls, notes, or other interruptions unless an emergency arises.

2. Keep your office organized, files updated, and your desk cleared so you know where things are. This prevents

you from getting side-tracked or confused with tasks and projects at hand.

3. In board meetings, staff meetings, lay leader meetings, etc., have an agenda so that time is not wasted. I've heard it said for every hour of planning, you save three hours executing the idea. Many churches and ministries need to discover the secret of planning. It doesn't prevent all crises, but it does help to eliminate many of them. In planning, you discover your objectives, which in turn, establish your priorities.

CHRISTIAN MINISTRY

Titus 1:7,8 challenges us to be disciplined in ministry, to adhere to the truth of Scripture so that others are encouraged by it and those who oppose it are silenced.

Ministers and lay-persons alike are entrusted with God's work, so this scripture applies to everyone who affiliates with the name of Christ. It addresses the need for discipline (i.e., self-control) in all areas of life. The result is that a disciplined life is a witness to everyone—the believer and the unbeliever.

GO TO THE SOURCE

Proverbs 23:23 says to gain truth, wisdom, discipline, and understanding. Notice how they are intertwined. As we gain wisdom, we gain discipline, which helps us to gain understanding.

The Greek word for *timidity,* found in 2 Timothy 1:7, refers to "battle cowardice; terror that overtakes one who is fearful in extreme difficulty."[1] This describes many pastors today who are afraid to lead; afraid because of how they may be perceived. While they are not meant to dictate, they *are* meant to lead in love, in power, and in self-discipline.

"In love" means with the right attitude, the right spirit. This is what the apostle Paul meant in 1 Corinthians 13:1: "If I speak in the tongues of men and of angels, but have not love, I am only a resounding gong or a clanging cymbal."

"In power" does not refer to physical might or political control; it refers to God's power and anointing. That does not come from the constitution and bylaws of a church or fellowship. It comes from being in close fellowship with God and following the direction He supplies. If God's Spirit rests upon you, people will sense it and respect it.

"In self-discipline" means to have direction, a sound-mindedness, a wise head, and good judgment.[2] A pastor needs to demonstrate that he knows what he's doing; he needs to prove himself. If I want people to follow, they need to have confidence in my leadership. That confidence comes as I demonstrate self-discipline. It does not come as I exercise discipline over them.

The discipline we need comes from God: through His Word and through the Holy Spirit. He is the source of everything we need to live a life that is pleasing to Him.

DISCIPLINE IN THE EARLY CHURCH

Discipline was a problem in the early church. In Acts 6:1-7 we learn the church was forced to discipline itself and reorganize because needs were being overlooked. The 12 disciples met and found a solution. It was not in the best interest of the church for them to leave their ministerial duties to perform duties of administration. Instead, they selected seven men "full of the Holy Spirit and wisdom" (Acts 6:3, NKJV) to be administrators. The result was that "the word of God spread, and the number of the disciples multiplied greatly in Jerusalem" (Acts 6:7, NKJV).

In Acts 15:1-21, the church leaders gathered together to address the issue of circumcision. They had an agenda for the meeting, the minutes of which are contained in Acts 15. Through discipline they met, expressed their views, and came up with a solution.

As Christian leaders, in tune with the Holy Spirit, they possessed the discipline to address the needs around them.

DISCIPLINE IN THE CHURCH TODAY

When I interview ministers for staff positions, I look for individuals who are self-disciplined. Would I rule out someone who was not self-disciplined, even if his qualifications were impeccable? Absolutely. Self-discipline is required by God for those in ministry. It is as important as marital fidelity, abstention from alcohol, or proper management of church monies. Discipline sets one minister apart from another; it determines whether one accomplishes great things for the kingdom of God; it dictates the character of a man.

Concerning your Christian walk, discipline yourself to stay in there for the long haul. Whether you are a pastor or a lay-person, what you do affects the whole body. There will be times of difficulty and pain, but it is in those times that self-discipline is developed. And that self-discipline will produce a life as sturdy as an oak tree.

Pastor Gregory A. Hackett, an ordained minister for the Assemblies of God, is the senior pastor of First Assembly in Lafayette, Indiana. He received his Bachelor of Arts in Biblical Studies from Evangel College in May 1983.

Pastor Hackett served on staff as youth pastor at First Assembly of God in Logansport, Indiana, before becoming youth pastor at First Assembly in Lafayette.

He has been involved with missions outreaches in England, Jordan, Israel, Egypt, Sierra Leone, Namibia, and South Africa. He has held offices for the Indiana District Chi Alpha Board, the Indiana District Youth Ministries, North Central Bible College Youth Advisory Board, and Lafayette Community Love, Inc. Board. Currently, he serves on the Indiana District Teen Challenge Board, Emerge Ministries Board, and the Advisory Board for Metro Assembly in Atlanta, Georgia.

He and his wife Lisa have three children: Tyler, Katie, and Robert C.

13

The Importance of Vision

DONALD R. SPRADLING

Where there is no revelation, the people cast off restraint.
—*Proverbs 29:18*

President Harry Truman once said, "The only thing new in the world is the history you haven't read." I can assure you the next chapter in history written by you will be the direct result of your vision. Jesus taught, "A good man produces good deeds from a good heart.... Whatever is in the heart overflows into speech" (Luke 6:45, TLB). "For out of the heart comes evil thoughts . . ." (Matthew 15:19). The passion of our heart cannot be confined—it will find expression. "As a man thinketh in his heart, so is he" (Proverbs 23:7, KJV). I am confident this is why God has taught us in His Word to make our heart accountable! "Guard above all things, guard your inner self, for so you live . . ." (Proverbs 4:23, Moffatt Translation).

AMERICA LACKS VISION

America's number one problem isn't cancer, AIDS, crime, or family breakdown; it is the lack of vision. As impacting as the above-mentioned problems are to all of us, they are only symptoms of a greater disease—no revelation, no vision. It is in this afflicted state that we begin to lose our balance and our moral energy level. We become vulnerable to every social, spiritual, philosophical, and political disease in the air. A new worldview emerges with every leader because we have traded the revelation for fashionable ideologies. Our aspirations and ambitions have turned from the source of vision and revelation—God's Word. We play a game of rhetoric; we say one thing and do another.

The Barna Report, *What Americans Believe,* has reported some astounding but paradoxical survey results:

- Two-thirds of all adults agree that America is a Christian nation.
- But, the majority of adult Americans believe their first responsibility is to themselves (57 percent).
- 63 percent say that the purpose of life is enjoyment and personal fulfillment.
- 66 percent agree that there is no such thing as absolute truth.[1]

These are hardly compatible statements! Mr. Barna goes on to report what is happening in "Christian America":

Traditional Christian beliefs are eroding too. We increasingly doubt the existence of Satan; we deny the existence of one true God; we question whether there really is a God who hears and responds to our prayers; we devalue the local church body as an instrument of God and a resource for mankind.[2]

We are removing God and the Bible from every sector of public life, and we disallow prayer in all public ceremonies and celebrations. As a nation we demand that Americans keep their practice of faith a private matter. All the while, the crime rate continues to escalate; the family breakdown continues to advance; and the moral climate of our nation continues to deteriorate. The same individuals who say they believe in the Bible as God's Word also state they believe there are few absolutes; right and wrong depends on the situation. We have forsaken the revelation. We have lost the vision.

This country was founded upon Judeo-Christian ethics and principles that guided it through its troublesome, formative years. We have succeeded as a nation because God was in the center of our national posture. Our national song, the flag salute, and our currency all reflect our faith in God; but we stand to lose the greatness we have known since the beginning of our country. Democracy will not work for long if God is left out of the equation. We have a generation that doesn't know God. It has gone after its own vision and will reap the wages of human depravity and carnal appetite.

THE CHURCH LACKS VISION

The prophetic words of Alexander Solzhenitzen, in his 1978 Harvard Commencement Address, warned the west of "spiritual exhaustion." He said our problems are not repressive enemies, but a "listless" public. Vision and revelation are missing. The people perish where there is no vision. America is committing suicide.

As a nation, we must find our way back to our roots. What made us great was our adherence to biblical principles and ethics. "Blessed is the nation whose God is the Lord" (Psalm 33:12). We were blessed because we revered God. *As a church,* we must find our way back to our roots. The church is only the church when God is present. If He is not there, it is nothing more than a gathering of people. When the church forsakes the vision and revelation, it forfeits the right to be the church. It has opted for other plans and designs, and, consequently, lost its restraint, discipline, and significance.

SPIRITUAL APATHY

Why are we, as a nation and as the church, in spiritual regression? Because we have cast off restraint. Former Secretary of Education William Bennett, speaking to the Heritage Foundation at its 20th anniversary, said, "I submit the real crisis of our time is spiritual. Specifically, our problem is what the ancients called *acedia,* the sin of sloth."[3] I agree with Mr. Bennett. We suffer from spiritual apathy and an absence of zeal for divine, eternal things. Spiritual acedia is not a new condition; it has challenged every generation and is our Philistine giant. There is only one way to slay the giant. You return to what helped you slay the bear and the lion: the revelation of God.

The late novelist Walker Percy was asked what concerned him most about the future of America. He answered, "The fear of seeing America with all of its great strength and beauty and freedom gradually subside into decay through default and be defeated, not by communism or the likes, but from within by weariness, boredom, cynicism, greed, and, in the end, helplessness before its giant problems."[4]

Leonard Ravenhill, author of *America is Too Young To Die,* said, "America can die, but it would have to be by suicide. It would be because she thinks God is dead, and because she believes that His laws, which, when broken, have felled every nation that ever lived, do not, in her hour of freedom and influence, include her."[5]

Abraham Lincoln left us a personal challenge that reflects a similar problem faced by his generation. He said, "At what point, then, is the approach of danger to be expected? If it ever reaches us, it must spring up from among us. It cannot come from abroad. If destruction be our lot, we must ourselves be its author and finisher; as a nation of free men, we must live through all time or die by suicide."[6]

There is enough evidence recorded in history to validate God's prophetic law. "Where there is no vision, the people perish" (Proverbs 29:18, KJV). We can hide behind material- istic comforts and the luxuries of high technology and say, "Look how well we live." But the fact we live well in America does not erase the fact we no longer live nobly. There must be an alarm sounded from our pulpits, our school boards, our city councils, our state and national leaders, that will clearly define the vision of the church and the nation once again.

EMBRACE THE VISION

The importance of vision is written in memorials and historical records for all humankind to behold. Every nation, people, or church that has opted to live after the principles of God's Word has had significance. Every nation, people, or church that has elected its own set of rules and government has ultimately been destroyed—usu- ally from within.

Three things happen when we embrace the vision and revelation of God, both within our churches and our nation.

1. Identification. First, vision gives identification. One of the surest ways to be nobody is to try to be everybody. A worldwide propaganda message—which comes from hell—says, "I'm okay, you're okay." It isn't *what* you believe, but *that* you believe. Right and wrong are relative. Nothing could be further from the truth. One of the major reasons Israel remains after centuries of vicious attacks from her enemies is that she knows who she is and what God has promised her. Israel's identification is clear and is taught diligently and persuasively to her children. We must never forget who we are.

America's vision was clear for nearly two centuries. Now we have allowed humanism and relativism to emerge as fashionable, acceptable philosophies that determine our values and ethics. It is commendable that our nation opens its doors to immigrants and welcomes other races and cultures. But we must not change our spiritual identity to accommodate those who come to America with other ideologies. Israel was warned not to mix with other cultures and thereby lose her distinction and identity. We can respect and appreciate one another and still remain "one nation under God."

The church is at her best when she knows who she is. Vision focuses our identity. Rick Warren and the Saddleback Church in Orange County know who they are. They know who "Saddleback Sam" is and why God has called them to reach "Sam." Bill Hybels and the Willow Creek Community Church in the suburbs of Chicago are focused as to their identity as well. Their vision is to reach un-churched Harry and unchurched Mary. These fictional characters, like Saddleback Sam, represent the "target audience" Willow Creek Church hopes to reach for the Lord. God has given them great success with a church body that exceeds 15,000 and continues to grow.

The Assemblies of God proclaimed with unwavering conviction why they were formed in 1914. They believed, "We are called and empowered to be witnesses in all the world." They are now the largest and most effective missionary force in the Protestant world.

If America is to remain among the great nations of the world, she must have an awakening of her vision and revelation. One nation under God. In God we trust. If the church in America is to be a great influence among the nations, there must be a revival of vision and revelation. We are called to be the light of the world. We must shine like never before in a dark and dying world.

2. Inspiration. The importance of vision is found in the power of inspiration. Vision is empowering. In all walks and endeavors of life vision gives inspiration. Knowing *who* you are is the first step in knowing *why* you are. That leads to the desire and commitment to fulfill the mission to which you were called.

The Allied Forces united on June 6, 1944, were willing to march through hell if need be to preserve freedom for the peoples of the world. This kind of inspiration can only be born out of a fully-embraced vision.

The great stories of the Bible are replete with men and women inspired by God-given vision and revelation to accomplish great things for the kingdom of God. If Jesus Christ is the same yesterday, today, and forever, that type of inspiration should abound today as it did then. And it does. There is a fresh stream of God's grace flowing through the church in America. Men and women are on bended knee, as Daniel of old, praying for their nation, for the restoration of Jerusalem, and for the return of God's people to a new and deeper commitment. There is new inspiration because there is new vision.

3. Incarnation. Scripture teaches that Christ was planned from the foundations of the earth. There was a vision of Christ centuries before His birth in Bethlehem. Vision needs incarnation or it will remain simply that: a vision; an idea that never came to fruition.

A vision grips the heart. It impregnates the spirit. The Bible declares, "Your life is shaped by your thoughts" (Proverbs 4:23, Good News).

Webster's definition of incarnation is "to give bodily form, to give actual form; to make real." Vision produces incarnation. Vision tells you *who* you are and *why* you are, and the natural flow out of this recognition is inspiration to *be* who you are. The moment we begin to be what we have envisioned we are, the vision is incarnated.

The Bible is a vision. It is God's vision for His people. It clearly identifies us and gives us divine distinction and purpose. But it remains merely pages of type unless we accept it as ours. God incarnated His vision to us in the Person of Jesus Christ. The vision became flesh so that we might behold Him and know Him. We, the church, are also called to be the vision incarnate to a world who may never see God otherwise.

America must return to its original vision; to being a people who say, "In God we trust"; who declare, "One nation under God"; then live as if they believe it.

The church must return to being the body of Christ. God's vision is that the church be empowered by the Holy Spirit so that we might be God's vision incarnate: the kingdom of God in man.

Inspired people are needed for this midnight hour. As the church goes, so goes the nation. May God give us people with vision; vision to look upward to know God; vision to look inward to know ourselves; vision to look outward to see a world that is lost without Christ.

The choice is ours. God help us to make the right one; to say as Joshua, ". . . as for me and my house, we will serve the Lord" (Joshua 24:15, KJV).

Donald R. Spradling is senior pastor of Christian Life Church in Long Beach, California. He graduated from East Central State College in Ada, Oklahoma, with a Bachelor's degree in math and science. He completed his master's thesis in the area of counseling and guidance. His post graduate work was conducted at the University of Oklahoma.

He has pastored five churches and has been the host of television and radio programs. Don writes for periodicals and magazines such as The Pentecostal Evangel *and* Advance. *The Reverend Spradling has also actively ministered in many places of influence: state legislature, national guard, city councils, military bases, civic groups, educational institutes, and political rallies. Don is an Executive Presbyter in the Southern California District of the Assemblies of God.*

He and his wife Kay have two children: Greg and Stephanie. Stephanie and husband Rex have two daughters: Morgan and Maddison.

14

Responding to Adversity

DR. GEORGE D. JOHNSON

Falling backward into an open fire pit is no small event. Michael, my tenderhearted, three-year-old nephew, traumatized by his burns, agonized in shock and pain. Amazingly, Michael responded cheerfully in the midst of his suffering, confounding doctors and nurses by his positive attitude.

That isn't the end of the story. Get ready for round two. An electrical explosion a few months later struck with a vengeance, scarring Michael's face. Returning to his grandparents' home from the hospital emergency ward, one question remained. How would little Michael respond this time? After entering the house, Michael seated himself under the kitchen table and began to sing:

God has a plan for my life;
God has a plan for my life;

I just can't wait to see
What's in store for me;
For God has a plan for my life.[1]

Michael does not wear a permanent halo. He is subject to feeling and expresses pain like other human beings. But he can teach us a great lesson about adversity: the manner in which we respond is directly related to the level of our commitment to God. He learned such behavior because his parents provided a home that fostered principles essential for a right response to adversity.

God does have a plan for our lives, as Michael already knows. That plan is for success, not failure. "'I know the plans I have for you,' declares the Lord, 'plans to prosper you and not to harm you, plans to give you hope and a future'" (Jeremiah 29:11).

Responding to adversity with godly discipline is vital to our future success. Reacting to adversity with ungodly attitudes sabotages God's plan for our lives. For this reason, God clearly reveals the path to success. He provides everything we need for right responses to adverse situations. God has made an incredible investment in our success. We can cooperate in His effort to make us successful children of God, regardless of how contrary the winds of life may become, or we can sabotage those efforts. The choice is ours.

"EXERCISING" OUR OPTIONS

What disciplines do we need to overcome adversity such as loss, sickness, death, slander, satanic warfare, etc.? They are what I call *dynamic response disciplines*. They include *grace encountering, thought management, walking in power,* and *mystery accepting.* Our level of commitment to these disciplines will determine our success or failure—and our fulfillment or emptiness.

As with all disciplines, we begin in small ways to exercise new patterns in our lives. Recently, my doctor put me on a treadmill. After nine minutes I was begging to get off. Mercifully, he said, "Johnson, I'll let you off, but next time I want to see a better performance."

A few months later, after 13 minutes on the treadmill, my doctor was begging me to get off. I complied, but said, "Doc, I could have kept going." Only God and I knew how close I was to collapsing. The point is, consistent exercise over a period of time paid off. It will also pay off when we exercise discipline over our response to adversity.

Before we examine the disciplines, I would like to offer a word of encouragement. I am not a novice on this subject. I have had my share of adversity and expect more in the future. As a result, these disciplines have moved outside the showroom. They have been road tested. They work. And they pay big dividends. Anyone can reap immediate benefits. Dynamic response disciplines are user-friendly.

GRACE ENCOUNTERING

Throughout my years of pastoral counseling, it has not been unusual to have a certain percentage of my counselees come from the non-churched community. I have made it a policy to require the same disciplines of them as I do the regular church members I counsel. I admonish them to attend church, pray, read the Bible, and connect with some type of small prayer-support group. Regardless of their background, those who follow my instructions cannot practice those disciplines without encountering grace. Their pain and problems are exposed to God's healing therapy, which is essential to the healing process. Such encounters with grace bring supernatural nourishment, healing, and strength. Let's examine the dynamics.

1. Church attendance. The apostle Paul had something far more exciting in mind than breaking a church attendance record when he said, "[Forsake] not the assembling of ourselves together" (Hebrews 10:25, KJV). He knew big things could happen when Christ and His people got together. If you are going through a trial, do not turn away from the body of Christ by neglecting church attendance. Hurry to the next scheduled meeting, and expect God to meet you there.

I marvel at the story of the ostracized woman with a blood disease. (See Luke 8:43-48.) Chronically ill for 12 years, she had run out of options for recovery. She was drained physically, emotionally, and financially; but she had spunk. Acting on a tip as to where she might encounter sufficient grace, she went to where Jesus had gathered a crowd. The crowd wasn't perfect, but she kept her focus on the One who is. Grace did its job. Physical and spiritual healing came her way.

Joseph Parker, the great English preacher, said, "The brokenhearted are the majority in every congregation."[2] I am thrilled to see many who are bruised and broken come to the altar each Sunday in the church where I pastor. As they stand before God, the Holy Spirit comes and ministers to them. I know it as I see tears flow down their cheeks. Jesus Christ, the Great Physician, skillfully mends their brokenness. It is common to see many of them move on to the next stage as their faces radiate with the anointing of the Holy Spirit. At times, I reflect on these moments and think, "What a tragedy it would have been for them not to have come to church; what a missed opportunity had they not responded to the altar call." Thankfully, they come and encounter grace.

2. Prayer. Personal prayer is another fundamental way in which we experience grace. I will never forget a difficult time I was going through as a teenager. After 10 days of pounding the pavement, I could not find a summer job. As day 11 dawned, my despondency grew. Would today once again end in failure? Meandering into the kitchen, I slumped into a chair at the table across from my mother. She knew exactly what was wrong.

"George, have you prayed about finding a job?" she asked.

Frozen lips betrayed that I had not.

Then she did something that startled me. She got up from the table, slid the chair into position for an altar, and said, "We are going to get right down to business and pray."

I knew what she had in mind. This would not be a half-hearted, anemic prayer, but a prayer of faith. She fell to her knees and began to pray. All I remember of that prayer were the words, "Lord, give George a job right away."

I sat glued to my chair, slightly amused at her aggressive assault on my unemployment. But I also knew Mom and God were cutting a deal. Securing a summer job was as good as done. I knew Mom had touched heaven. That afternoon I was hired over the telephone by a contractor I had never met, nor had applied to for a job.

God orchestrated a series of events in response to high-voltage prayer. A response to adversity must always include prayer. No human battle can be fought and won without it. "The prayer of a righteous man is powerful and effective" (James 5:16).

A special word to Christian leaders is important. You can expect more adversity than others because of the fact you are on the front lines of spiritual warfare. This assault becomes all the more evident when you begin to defeat demonic powers waged against your church or ministry. For this reason, prayer must be your top priority. Pray personally and recruit others to pray for you as well. Peter Wagner said, "To the degree the intercessors pray, the leaders gain protection against the fiery darts of the wicked one."[3]

3. The Word. Some years ago, I heard the story of a young man in Korea who had a powerful grace encounter with the Word of God. His repeated time in prison indicated a life not likely to change for the good. Once again imprisoned, he was given a copy of the gospel of John by the chaplain. He discovered the paper was excellent for rolling cigarettes, so each day he tore a page from the gospel. He literally inhaled most of the book of John. The day arrived when only one page remained. He reasoned, "Seeing this is the last page in this little book, I will read what it has to say before I smoke it." Can you guess what he read? "For God so loved the world that he gave his one and only Son, that whoever believes in him shall not perish but have eternal life" (John 3:16). Can you guess what happened? He encountered grace. Immediately, the convicting power of the Holy Spirit came upon him and he accepted Jesus Christ as his Savior. A few years later, when he was released from prison, he went out on the street preaching the gospel. Truly, God's Word is powerful.

Turn to it—particularly the Psalms—when you find yourself in difficulty. David is honest and vulnerable. There is no pretense, no nonsense. He speaks to God in a way that is available to all of us. Therefore, we can identify with his emotional responses to experiences, whether they be in the valley or on the hilltop. We are guaranteed to find grace when we turn to God's Word.

4. Prayer-support group. Some fellow-Christians cause us more pain than gain. The apostle John identified such a person. "Diotrephes, who loves to be first, will have nothing to do with us. So if I come, I will call attention to what he is doing, gossiping maliciously about us . . ." (3 John 9,10).

It is necessary to raise the negative aspect of church life for two reasons. One, when we are responding to an adverse situation, it is important to hang out with the right crowd. We need not expose ourselves to the so-called "grace-grower." You know, the person whose obnoxious behavior acts as sandpaper designed to remove the rough spots of our life. True, God sometimes sends this type of person our way to fulfill His purposes, but don't go looking for a Diotrephes. When times are tough, we need to associate with grace-givers, not grace-growers.

The apostle Paul mentioned this type of person in his second epistle to Timothy. "May the Lord show mercy to the household of Onesiphorus, because he often refreshed me and was not ashamed of my chains" (2 Timothy 1:16). Be selective.

The second reason I mention the negative aspect of church life is that many individuals in our churches have been deeply injured by other Christians. Regretfully, many of these wounded souls isolate their real selves from fellow believers. No longer transparent, their guard is up, and that causes them to miss the spirit of grace flowing from the community of faith. Reuben Welch beautifully illustrates this truth: "When you are burdened and weary and sad, you need Jesus, but you also need someone to be Jesus to you—someone to bring His healing presence to you."[4] Be open.

Grace encountering happens through many spiritual disciplines. The foundational ones are church attendance, prayer, the Word of God, and prayer-support groups. It is essential to be in the oasis of the gathered church, for God is present there. Prayer releases the power of God into our circumstances. The Word of God is the ointment of healing grace. And grace is experienced through the words, touch, and caring of others in the body of Christ.

THOUGHT MANAGEMENT

Grace encountering is the first step in responding to adversity. The next step is to manage our thinking. Lord Halifax said, "A man may dwell so long upon a thought that it may take him prisoner."[5] Thought patterns influence our actions, good or bad. Author Gary Collins said, "The mind can control its own thinking, and this in turn can influence behavior."[6] The monster of adversity sucks from our being the energy of hope and courage. The result is that one not only suffers from the adversity itself, but from torturous and depressive thoughts as well.

I have chosen thought management as a therapy rather than other disciplines, such as positive thinking, for two reasons. First, all thinking must pass through the grid of truth. Positive thinking is appropriate, but, taken to the extreme, develops into an evangelical Christian Science. As an example, the apostle Paul instructed individuals to think accurately about themselves, not underrated nor over-inflated. (See Romans 12:3.) An accurate cognitive assessment protects a person from journeying into the land of make-believe. Second, positive thinking should not play the leading role in the cast of theological truth. Its strength and validity are only fully realized when it grasps the hands of all other spiritual disciplines.

With this understanding, the practice of positive thinking is an appropriate response to adversity. While I am not an advocate of all Robert Schuller's methods and theology, I am convinced that a lot of good comes from his message. In a society plagued by pessimistic attitudes, believers are called to buck the tide and manage their thinking. Scripture admonishes: "Whatever is true, whatever is noble, whatever is right, whatever is pure, whatever is lovely, whatever is admirable—if anything is excellent or praiseworthy—think about such things" (Philippians 4:8).

When I counsel, I often steer my counselees toward Dr. David Burns' cognitive therapy in his book *Feeling Good*.[7] I don't endorse 100 percent of what he says, but, overall, his approach is remarkable when responding to adversity. A psychiatrist at the University of Pennsylvania, Burns has helped many individuals cope with stress, depression, guilt, hostility, and negative thinking. His principles work for non-believers, but are even more effective for Christians, because believers are exposed to numerous encounters of grace. Our battleground is the mind. Burns' therapy involves unloading distorted thoughts and replacing them with realistically positive ones. Romans 12:2 says, "Do not conform any longer to the pattern of this world, but be transformed by the renewing of your mind."

There is another dimension to thought management, which I call "delivered thinking." It is possible to carry a negative thought pattern so long that it becomes ingrained in us. This type of stronghold hinders the purposes of God. Sometimes these ungodly patterns become demonically influenced, but not always. Tom White, a leading authority on spiritual warfare, defines a stronghold as "an entrenched pattern of thought, an ideology, value, or behavior that is contrary to biblical truth and which emanates from human nature."[8] The medicine of positive thinking and cognitive therapy will not touch this ailment. Only deliverance by the Holy Spirit can bring release.

Here are some things to remember concerning thought management:

- Positive thinking is appropriate when it is balanced by grace and truth.
- Cognitive therapy, the ability to negate distorted thoughts and replace them with right ones, is a powerful remedy.
- Delivered thinking occurs when one is supernaturally delivered from an entrenched mind-set that is alien to the Word of God.

WALKING IN POWER

Walking in power is similar to thought management, but it has a deeper spiritual component. The apostle Paul presented the challenge in Ephesians 6:10: "Be strong in the Lord and in his mighty power." Paul was speaking about adversity, particularly adversity brought about by demonic forces.

Paul's admonition was not an invitation to become a muscle man or power tycoon. Our Lord Jesus Christ taught us to be poor in spirit, mournful, meek, hungering and thirsting for righteousness, merciful, pure in heart, peacemakers, and persecuted because of righteousness. (See Matthew 5.) When Paul talked about strength and power in Ephesians, he meant it in a spiritual sense. The "mighty power" he referred to deals with the anointing of God and the authority of Christ in our lives.

Adversity wants us to retreat. Fear can paralyze us when we are under spiritual attack. Our own strength may fail us at such times, causing damage to our body, soul, and spirit. I have been in such a place; perhaps you have too. You may be there right now—depleted of energy, losing hope. Like Elijah, your brook has run dry. You wonder where you should go, what you should do. I have good news for you. Scripture says, "The reason the Son of God appeared was to destroy the devil's work" (1 John 3:8). You may say, "I know that verse, and it isn't helping me. The works of the devil are destroying my life." Let me encourage you, every believer has times when he feels this way. The attack can be devastating, but God will not allow the devil to defeat us. He desires that we move beyond our destructive thoughts and walk in the authority of Christ and the anointing of the Holy Spirit.

To walk in power we must do three things:

1. We must exercise our faith in God's promises when faced with adversity. Walking in power requires us to believe God's purpose is for us to "be strong in the Lord and in his mighty power" (Ephesians 6:10). We must believe that after rain there is sunshine; after weeping there is joy. When we cling to His promises, we can face the challenge and come out singing, like my nephew, "God has a plan for my life."

2. We must have a fresh anointing of the Holy Spirit. We must make the time and do whatever is necessary to be in the presence of God; to allow that anointing to flow over us. Fresh oil from the throne of God will break the chains that bind us.

3. We must take a stand. There comes a time when self-pity has to end and determination begins. Like Gideon, we must believe, "The Lord is with you, mighty warrior" (Judges 6:12). It is time to defeat the works of the devil. We can live above our circumstances; we can stand in the face of adversity.

Walking in power is a discipline that involves three specific actions:

- believing that God wants us to be strong.
- being available for a fresh anointing of the Holy Spirit.
- taking a stand and seeing the victory of the Lord.

MYSTERY ACCEPTING

What is mystery accepting? It is surrendering to the fact there are circumstances and events that occur in the spiritual realm that we will never understand this side of heaven. The apostle Paul said, "Now we see but a poor reflection as in a mirror; then we shall see face to face" (1 Corinthians 13:12). Spending much time analyzing the mysteries of God is futile. We can leave the unanswerable questions for eternity. We are not yet living in the fully-revealed kingdom of God. Accordingly, our understanding is limited; but in the ages to come, many mysteries will be revealed.

Let's look at one example. It is a mystery that we are to be conformed to the image of Christ while living in an environment that is hostile to that image. Regarding Jesus' parable about the wheat and the weeds (see Matthew 13:3-30), Thomas Green likens the wheat to our virtues and the weeds to our weaknesses. The weeds are not to be yanked out lest the wheat be pulled up at the same time. He wrote:

> . . . some at least of our instinctual and involuntary weaknesses are likely to remain in us until the harvest time of death. The Lord leaves them in us to keep us humble, to make us realize how totally we depend on Him, and how helpless we are to do good without His grace and power. The wheat of our virtues—trust, humility, gratitude, zeal—could not come to full maturity, it seems, without the weeds of our instinctual failings.[9]

We have a glimpse into the reason for the weeds, but much remains unknown. Why this methodology? Many good theological discussions could result in this simple question. For now, I'll bask in the sunlight of the answer given to the apostle Paul, "My grace is sufficient for you" (2 Corinthians 12:9).

I would like to close this discussion with a prayer:

Lord, give us Your grace; give us Your mind. In the
power of Your Holy Spirit we take a stand against
the enemy. We lay to rest those things we cannot
understand, and we trust You. Amen.

*Dr. George D. Johnson is a graduate of Northwest College in
Seattle, Washington. He holds a Master's Degree from the California Graduate School of Theology and a Doctor of Ministry degree
from the Canadian Theological Seminary.*

*Dr. Johnson has pastored four churches: Cedar Park Assembly,
Kirkland, Washington; Richmond Tabernacle, Richmond, B.C.;
Elim Tabernacle, Saskatoon, Saskatchewan; and presently, Fraser-
view Assembly, Vancouver, B.C. Dr. Johnson is actively involved
in the Holy Spirit's renewal in today's church, especially as it
relates to pastoral leadership.*

*He and his wife Joyce have three children: Janyce, Benjamin,
and Joylene.*

15

Enduring the Call

JOHN D. BUTRIN

No man is fit to preach the gospel, seeing the whole world is set against it, save only he who is armed to suffer.
—*John Calvin*[1]

In today's success-oriented culture many in ministry face the temptation to "cut and run" when their ministry meets with less-than-great results. Perhaps their work for God has become more difficult than they anticipated, or an unexpected set of circumstances has dealt them a setback. Ministers often find themselves misunderstood by others, and the purity of their motives comes under attack. Unrealistic levels of expectation, actual and perceived, are generated until life resembles a pressure cooker about to explode. It is at this point that, for the sake of their own personal sanity and the well-being of their families, many ministers decide to find a less demanding career.

A survey of 500 pastors by Focus on the Family's pastoral ministries department revealed that spiritual burnout, family problems, and financial pressures are at a critical level for the majority of ministers today. Ninety percent admit they have been discouraged in the past three months; 70 percent of those have considered leaving the ministry.[2] When factors like these are coupled with a lack of ministry results, is it any wonder the ministry drop-out rate is approaching record proportions?

The apostle Paul's advice to Timothy to "endure hardship . . . like a good soldier of Christ Jesus" (2 Timothy 2:3) seems far removed from many who find themselves in a maelstrom of confused emotions about the call of God. They rationalize, "Surely it was intended to apply to other times and arenas of ministry, not to me." They probably aren't sure what such "hardship" might entail, but it's hard to imagine that it might apply to their own current struggle. Rather than seeing difficult circumstances as a validation of the call, it is more convenient to see them as reasons to question and ultimately abandon the call. It is much easier to see our point of despair as an exit, rather than a doorway to greater fruitfulness in our ministry.

ARRESTING EVENTS

I stared into the faces of the church board members grouped in a semicircle across the room from where I was seated next to the church's senior pastor. As their youth minister, I had been ushered in to discuss the events of the previous week when I had brought embarrassment to the pastor and a blemish to the reputation of our church. From their countenances and the tone of their questioning, it was obvious they wanted my formal resignation. Having been forewarned by the pastor, I was ready to submit it.

An avid outdoorsman since childhood, I have always had an interest in guns and hunting. When one of the young men of the church asked if I would be interested in purchasing a hunting-type handgun, I was interested. I asked where he had gotten the gun; he replied he was selling it for a friend. That, along with the low selling price, should have been enough to warn me that this deal was trouble, but I chose to believe his story. I convinced myself that our common interest in handguns could open a long-sought window of opportunity to minister to him.

A few days later the young man knocked on my door. When I answered, he said I must give him the gun to turn in to the police since it had, in fact, been stolen. He said it was one of several that had been taken from a railroad car, and if all the firearms were not turned in, everyone involved would be arrested. I handed over the gun, which his contact gave to the police the following day.

Thinking the episode over, I was surprised to receive a call at my church office from a detective inquiring as to the whereabouts of the young man. I said he was attending a nearby college and asked if this pertained to the stolen guns. After a moment of silence the detective said, "So you're the minister who's involved." I explained that I had briefly possessed one of the guns, but had taken steps to turn it in the moment I knew it was "hot." He seemed to appreciate my candor and asked if I would bring the young man with me to the police station the next day to "iron it all out."

The next morning when I arrived at the station, I was read my rights. It was not until he came to the final sentence that I understood I was being charged with possession of stolen goods.

"We came here—at your suggestion—to get this all straightened out," I said. "Nothing was ever said about bringing me up on charges."

"I'm sorry, Reverend," he said, "but there are numerous suspects in this case, all of whom had one or more of these guns in their possession. Try to understand our situation; we cannot exempt you from arrest without exempting the others as well."

I had to think of something. There had to be a way out of this. Didn't he know that I was an ordained minister of the gospel? What could I say that would change his mind? In desperation, I insisted he allow me to make one phone call. I knew I was entitled to that much. He allowed me to use the phone to contact the church's attorney who advised me to cooperate fully with the process. The process involved emptying and inventorying the contents of my pockets, taking a full set of fingerprints, posing for a mug shot, and being transported to the courthouse holding tank with 20 or more criminals.

The hours waiting for arraignment were sobering, but, always the optimist, I knew this must surely be the worst of it. If I could survive this day, it would all work out. People would ask questions and I would have to explain how I had gotten into this mess, and that would be that. It would be a hard but valuable lesson. I didn't know how hard until the evening edition of the city newspaper printed the story of my arrest on the front page under the caption: Local Cleric Arrested in Gun Thefts.

"Oh no," I groaned, "anything but this."

My consternation increased exponentially when I read the next sentence. Instead of printing my name as the person arrested, they printed the name of my senior pastor, complete with details about his excellent reputation in the city and his many years of unblemished ministry at the church.

Both the senior pastor and I tried to put the best face on the situation during the following Sunday's services, but I was definitely running in "survival mode." My actions had hurt the pastor deeply, but, ever the shepherd, he reminded me of the apostle's encouragement that ". . . our present sufferings are not worth comparing with the glory that will be revealed in us" (Romans 8:18). His words were comforting, but I needed a megadose of encouragement in order to survive this disaster.

Such encouragement proved to be in short supply. Moments after the board asked for my resignation, my footsteps echoed down the darkened halls of the church as I walked out into the cool autumn air unemployed.

I cried, "God, this is unfair. I don't deserve to get fired for making a mistake."

I had recently become engaged to the wonderful young lady who would later become my wife. Until now, our future appeared happy and bright. We looked forward to many years of ministry wherever the Lord would lead us. We certainly didn't foresee this. Was it a tactic designed by the enemy of my soul to cause me to abandon my call? Perhaps. But now, years later, I realize this episode was part of my endurance training.

Occasionally, a close friend jokingly asks if I've gotten any good deals on guns lately. Smiling, I recall the lessons I learned about the faithfulness of God to those He calls. Incidentally, I was found innocent of the charges, and the newspaper printed a small article about it on an inside page.

ANSWERING THE CALL

I love to identify with the prophet Isaiah's call to ministry as recorded in Isaiah 6. I exult in the splendor of his vision of the Lord seated on His throne, attended by angelic beings in constant worship of Him. I thrill at the thought of the smoke-filled temple being shaken while Isaiah recognizes his sinfulness, and I vicariously feel the heat of the coals from the altar as they touched his lips. In response to the appeal from the throne for a representative voice to proclaim the divine message, I answer with the prophet, "Here am I. Send me!" (Isaiah 6:8). However, I must not fail to read the specifics of the call: the message Isaiah would be required to preach and the predicted dismal response of his hearers. I would rather ignore his subsequent plea, "For how long, O Lord?" (Isaiah 6:11). One can almost hear Isaiah moan as he grimaces through tears of frustration, "Lord, this isn't exactly what I envisioned when I first heard Your call. When do I get to see Your glory and splendor in my ministry like it was when I appeared before Your throne? I never thought things could get this difficult."

The Lord's answer isn't very encouraging. "Until the cities lie ruined and without inhabitant, until the houses are left deserted and the fields ruined and ravaged, until the Lord has sent everyone far away and the land is utterly forsaken" (Isaiah 6:11,12). If most of us were to hear such a prognosis, we would pack our bags and assume we were out of God's will by ever being involved in the ministry.

E. H. Chapin said, "Not in the achievement, but in the endurance of the human soul does it show its divine grandeur and its alliance with the infinite God."[3] The path of ministry may never be glamorous nor lucrative, and learning to endure is crucial. Today's minister must take special care not to determine the validity of God's call by such external factors as numerical success, denominational recognition, or easy circumstances. We must guard against the temptation to abandon the call because our circumstances are not what we had envisioned. Discouragement often comes from being overworked, under-appreciated, and inadequately compensated; and the temptation to quit begins to grow in us. At times it seems that people and events have conspired against us, and we begin to wonder if staying in the ministry is worth it.

Later in his ministry, Isaiah discovered a marvelous fact about sticking with it and fulfilling his call: "This is what the Sovereign Lord, the Holy One of Israel, says: 'In repentance and rest is your salvation, in quietness and trust is your strength'" (Isaiah 30:15). Repentance, rest, quietness, trust: here are principles that will hold a person's ministry on a steady course amid the most turbulent of times.

PEACE THAT PASSES ALL UNDERSTANDING

I sought the serenity of the hospital chapel, hoping to find a place where I could get some answers for the turmoil in my spirit. My dad, my friend, my example and mentor in both life and ministry, was in another part of the hospital undergoing emergency surgery. A tumor, even a malignant one, would have been preferable to a surgical team trying to remove a .22 caliber bullet—self-inflicted— from the right front lobe of his brain. The surgeons did their best, but the damage was too severe. In spite of life-support systems, Dad died later that evening.

As I knelt at the chapel altar—my mind filled with conflicting thoughts and emotions—I retraced the six years of my ministry and beyond to the 25 years Dad had spent serving the Lord. To say that he was a man of God was more than a figure of speech. He epitomized all that a man of God should be. He never became famous, but he had been faithful to his call as an evangelist, and God had used him in dynamic ways. Now, two years after being diagnosed as suffering from manic depressive disorder, he had ended his own life.

In deep anguish, my mind and spirit cried out to God for answers. "These things don't happen to men of God. Oh Father, Dad trusted You wholeheartedly during his entire ministry. How could You let this happen? Suicide! Why not a heart attack or a stroke? A person could die from those causes without bringing reproach and embarrassment to Your work."

My anguish turned to self-pity and then anger. "What about the stigma? What will our friends and colleagues think? How will Mom, who served so faithfully by his side, be able to handle this? What about my sister who is just beginning her missionary career?

"God, is this the way You treat Your people? I don't think I like Your retirement plan. In fact, I don't think I want to work for You anymore."

How could quietness and trust be my strength now? I wasn't even sure God existed, let alone had a plan to bring us through such a painful experience.

"Oh God, please forgive me," I wept, "but I need to know that You are real and can get our family past this horrible nightmare."

In the midst of my prayerful sobs, I became aware that I was no longer alone in the chapel. Thinking a doctor or nurse had come to bring news about Dad's condition, I turned to see who had entered the room. I was over-whelmed by a Presence that I can only describe as two arms—invisible, but real—wrapped around me. Visibly I was alone, but now my whole being was cradled in the presence and peace of Jesus.

For the first time in my life—though I had often preached about it—I experienced firsthand the genuine peace that transcends understanding. The questions re-mained, and some of them still linger, but the peace of the Lord assured me that God's plan and call were still in effect. Once again quietness and trust prevailed. He would see us through.

In the will of God nothing happens by circumstance. God has used the pain of the memory of my father's death to deepen my empathy for people who experience emotion-al stress and trauma, especially the surviving victims of suicide. Two months following Dad's death, I was awak-ened with a call telling me the mother of a 12-year-old had just committed suicide. The daughter had heard the gun-shot and discovered her mother's body on the bedroom floor. I hurried to the home where I found a traumatized, grief-stricken girl experiencing a pain greater than one can imagine. Taking her in my arms, I felt a bond of grief as we wept together. Months later, after her own healing had begun, she told me how much it meant to have someone who could understand how she felt that fateful night.

I have often pondered the tragic event of 20 years ago. It affected family members in various ways, but I most often review them in light of my call to ministry. To say I have been affected in a positive way would seem to imply I don't fully understand the tragedy of my father's death. With that risk in mind, I am compelled to say again, through it all, God has been faithful and His call continues to be validated in my ministry.

IN JESUS

Among my most admired mentors, a former college professor stands out in my memory for his tenacious adherence to God's call whatever the crisis or source of discouragement. Robert Cummings had been a pioneer missionary to India in 1920, but in his later years he devoted himself to transplanting some of his zeal for God and missionary endeavors into his students. I will never forget his telling of the dark crisis of his life when in 1932 he suffered a nervous breakdown that threatened to undermine his calling and his faith in God. In his book, *Gethsemane,* he wrote:

> Night and day for about three months, horrible and obscene suggestions and imaginations poured in an increasing flood through my consciousness. I could not sleep, except when given sleeping potions, and as these vile powers would pour their unmentionable abominations into my mind, it was utterly impossible to resist them, though my whole being shrank in indescribable revulsion and loathing that passed far beyond the point of agony . . .[4]

He went on to describe the separation he felt from God, and his inability to pray. This condition continued for two years until a faithful saint brought the promise of Jesus: "I will never leave thee, nor forsake thee" (Hebrews 13:5, KJV). Robert Cummings had heard it before, but on this day it took hold and drove him to his knees. He prayed,

"Lord if there's anything You can do for me, won't You do it? I would pray if I could, but I can't pray. There are no words to describe what I feel. Anyway, I don't even feel. My heart is like a lump of stone."[5] Then something began deep within him:

Away down deep in my consciousness a chorus began to sing. I did not know there was anything so deep within. The Word says, "Deep calleth unto deep." God's deeps called to the deeps in me, and down in the depths of my heart He himself started the second verse of that hymn written by an infidel after he had found the Lord. The hymn was found on his desk after his death. The name of it is "In Jesus." I had not sung it for years. How could I sing, for I had lost my song? He (Jesus) began singing it within my being:

My heart is night, my soul is steel;
I cannot see, I cannot feel;
For light, for life, I must appeal
In simple faith to Jesus.

As the last word sang itself out in the silence of my heart, I knew *He* stood with me. He gathered me in His arms and brought me into a place of nearness that I had never known before. His precious blood cleansed away all the sin and stain, and all the feeling of evil, all the effect of that terrible experience. I had been under a great mountain, and that mountain, at His word, was buried in the sea. I had been bound with all the fetters of hell, but at His word, the fetters snapped and I was free. Oh, the unspeakable joy of that deliverance![6]

Again the words of Isaiah come to mind:

> I called you. I said, 'You are my servant'; I have
> chosen you and have not rejected you. So do not
> fear, for I am with you; do not be dismayed, for
> I am your God. I will strengthen you and help
> you; I will uphold you with my righteous right
> hand.... For I am the Lord, your God, who takes
> hold of your right hand and says to you, Do not
> fear; I will help you—Isaiah 41:9-13.

What could be more assuring than the Lord taking us by
the hand and telling us not to be afraid?

MID-STREAM TRAUMA

When my son was small I often took him on hikes in the
woods, sometimes making an overnight back-pack trip. On
one such trek during early spring we were crossing a
rushing mountain stream that had been fed by the melting
snow high in the mountains above us. We started across the
stream, stepping on the rocks that at first seemed spaced
evenly enough to allow us to cross without danger. I went
ahead, charting a course that I thought my son could follow
without much difficulty.

Arriving at the far bank I turned to see him stranded
mid-stream, trembling, and at the point of tears. Both of his
feet were soaked because of a near miss in reaching the
rock he was standing on. I couldn't hear his voice over the
roar of the water, but I could see the fear in his eyes. There
was no way he was going to try for the next stone. Realizing he was at the point of panic, I quickly retraced my

steps until I could reach his hand and pull him safely to my rock. From there he clung to me until we were safely on the other side.

That's exactly what God does for us during our "midstream" experiences where fear and disappointment, discouragement and loss tell us we can't make it. It is then that God rushes to our side, takes us by the hand, and says, "Do not fear; I will help you." Then He guides us safely to the other side.

SUCCESSFUL TO THE END

In his now-classic book entitled *Spiritual Leadership*, J. Oswald Sanders succinctly described the conditions under which those in ministry today must work:

> It would not be exaggeration to affirm that never in human history have leaders been confronted with such a concentration of unresolved crises and impossible situations as in our day. Consequently, if they are to survive, they must be able to thrive on difficulties and regard them as routine.[7]

Today's minister, having first affirmed the call, must adopt an attitude of total commitment to the ministry, combined with an unflagging trust that "the one who calls you is faithful and he will do it" (1 Thessalonians 5:24). If a person is sure of the call, he can endure the call.

Since earning his Bachelor of Arts degree in Bible from Central Bible College in Springfield, Missouri, John D. Butrin has served churches in Pennsylvania, Massachusetts, and California. He was the State Youth Director for the Pennsylvania-Delaware District of the Assemblies of God for six years. He also served as Presbyter of the East Bay Section of the Northern California/Nevada District. He currently serves as an Executive Presbyter of the Northern California/Nevada District, and is the senior pastor of Sequoyah Community Church in Oakland, California.

He and his wife Gayle have been married 22 years. They have three children: Joshua, Leah, and Ami.

16

Dealing with Disaster

GARY MOREFIELD

After settling into my office chair to begin some administrative work, I was interrupted by my secretary with an emergency phone call from my wife Meg. "I've been in a car accident," she said. "I'm okay, but Brian is hurt. You need to come to the hospital." Brian was our four-year-old son.

"Is he going to be all right?" I asked. Meg said yes, but I knew by the sound of her voice something was terribly wrong.

When I arrived at the hospital I learned Brian had been catapulted from our car and thrown 70 feet after another vehicle ran a red light. Although he was wearing a seat belt, the force of the impact caused him to be ejected from our car. He landed on his head.

Brian had slipped into a coma by the time we saw the doctor. He told us the next 24 hours would be critical. He also told us that with closed head injuries there was no way of knowing how long the coma would last, what the extent of the damage would be, or if he would live or die. Thus began a long, nightmarish ordeal of dealing with a disaster.

DEFINING DISASTER

No two disasters are alike; they come in all shapes and sizes. So how do you define disaster? The *American Heritage Dictionary* calls it a "great destruction, distress, or misfortune,"[1] but that definition is relative. A disaster to one person is merely a ripple in the water to someone else. A traffic ticket, for example, can be a traumatic experience to some, while to others it is just a part of driving. Simply put, a disaster is anything that negatively impacts your life to such a degree you cannot ignore it. If the situation or circumstance is such that you have to take some action to alter your lifestyle in handling this need, you have a disaster on your hands. When normal schedules and routines of life are altered, or when sleep patterns are broken, you have a problem you cannot ignore.

DO I HAVE WHAT IT TAKES?

Nothing can prepare us for the crises of life, but there are principles we can apply that help reduce the severity of disasters when they hit.

Like most of you, I watched many of the reports on TV after the Los Angeles earthquake in January 1994. Thousands were lined up at local grocery and convenience stores to buy, for the most part, two items: water and batteries. There were reports that in other cities located far from the earthquake, people were buying water and batteries. Having a good supply of these items will not save us from such a disaster when it occurs, but it can lessen the severity. I have found the following attitudes helpful in dealing with disaster:

1. Acknowledge that troubles come with life. There's no rule book that says life is going to be easy. In fact, just the opposite is true. Jesus said, "In this world you will have trouble. But take heart! I have overcome the world" (John 16:33). Jesus stated a fact: "You will have trouble." He wasn't being negative. He realized that God "sends rain on the righteous and the unrighteous" alike (Matthew 5:45).

Life brings difficulties to all; but when we fight, scream, and complain "this isn't fair," life becomes miserable for us and those around us. The sooner we accept the fact the path isn't always smooth, the sooner we learn to seek and receive the peace Jesus talked about in John 16.

Paul Brand and Philip Yancey, in an article in *Christianity Today,* accurately wrote:

> In the United States, a nation whose war for independence was fought, in part, to guarantee a right to "the pursuit of happiness," I encountered a society that seeks to avoid pain at all costs. Patients lived at a greater comfort level than any I had previously treated, but they seemed far less equipped to handle suffering and far more traumatized by it. Pain relief in the United States is now a $63 billion a year industry, and television commercials proclaim better and faster pain remedies. One ad slogan bluntly declares, "I haven't got time for the pain."[2]

Brand and Yancey said that in order to experience joy, comfort, and peace, we must know the contrasting experience of pain. The article quoted Chinese philosopher Lin Yutang as he recalls an ancient Chinese formula for happiness:

> To be dry and thirsty in a hot and dusty land and to feel great drops of rain on my bare skin—ah, is this not happiness! To have an itch in a private part of my body and finally to escape from my friends and go to a hiding place where I can scratch—ah, is this not happiness!

2. Don't be surprised. A second way to lessen the severity of a disaster is *not* to be surprised when it strikes. Jesus spent much of His time teaching the disciples to be prepared—not surprised. "They will put you out of the synagogue; in fact, a time is coming when anyone who kills you will think he is offering a service to God" (John 16:2). Concerning His second coming, Jesus said not to be surprised, but to be on the alert. (See Matthew 24:42.)

None of us are immune to the heartaches life brings our way, including Jesus. Who am I to think I should escape the difficulties of life when even the Son of God had more than His share? Jesus said, "Remember the words I spoke to you: 'No servant is greater than his master.' If they persecuted me, they will persecute you also" (John 15:20).

3. Recognize you are already prepared. The third attitude in dealing with disaster is to realize that you are already prepared for trouble when it strikes. Just as Jesus spent time preparing His disciples for things to come, He spent time preparing us. Through His Word He has given us guidelines and principles by which we can be better prepared to deal with disaster.

Many of the Psalms are prayers offered during difficult times, and they can be used to prepare us for battles. This is a great example:

> God is our refuge and strength, an ever-present help in trouble. Therefore we will not fear, though the earth give way and the mountains fall into the heart of the sea, though its water roar and foam and the mountains quake with their surging. There is a river whose streams make glad the city of God, the holy place where the Most High dwells —Psalm 46:1-4.

Twice this Psalm includes the phrase, "The Lord Almighty is with us; the God of Jacob is our fortress" (vs. 7,11).

Psalm 121 includes these verses: "I lift up my eyes to the hills—where does my help come from?... He will not let your foot slip—he who watches over you will not slumber; the Lord will watch over your coming and going both now and forevermore" (Psalm 121:1,3,8).

Recognizing that God has prepared us makes a difference when we are in the midst of battle. If we take God at His word that "the steps of a good man are ordered by the Lord" (Psalm 37:23, KJV), we can take solace in the fact we are prepared for any battle.

We must trust that God has already prepared us for this battle, as nightmarish as the trial may seem. Even though you may not see that God has prepared you, trusting in His Word can help take some of the sting out of the trial.

4. Avoid the "why" syndrome. Often, the first thing asked when tragedy occurs is "why?" There's nothing wrong with the question, but it can distract us from getting through the battle. It brings our emotions into the situation, rather than trusting in the Word of God to see us through it. Frankly, there is not always an answer. Asking why when there is no answer opens the door for two emotions that should be avoided during disaster. The first is self-pity. The second is blaming others, including God.

Asking why may lead us to believe God is punishing us for some reason. True, God often uses difficulties to bring "loving correction" to help us grow and build character. But when we're hurting because of tragedy or disaster, the last thing we need to do is torment ourselves with the feeling that God is disciplining us. He will show us at a later time if the situation was intended to bring correction. We just need strength to get through without compounding the problem with thoughts that won't help the present situation at all.

When Jesus healed the blind man in John chapter nine, the disciples wanted to know, "Who sinned, this man or his parents, that he was born blind?" Jesus said, "Neither this man nor his parents sinned . . . but this happened so that the work of God might be displayed in his life" (John 9:2,3). We need to be delivered from the need to know why —either for ourselves or others—while in the midst of a crisis. Job struggled with not knowing why, and it caused added frustration. God really does see the whole picture. We may not know the answer until we see Him face to face, but by that time it won't matter anyway.

I have a long way to go, but I have learned not to trust my emotions during a crisis. For that matter, I have learned not to trust my emotions when I am tired, like Sunday night after an exhilarating, but long, day of ministry.

Help us, Lord, to trust You to show us in Your perfect time.

5. Lean on the prayers of others. Some disasters are so devastating that we are just too numb to pray. While my son was in a coma, I was so heartsick I could not praise, just plead. I had to rely on the prayers of God's people. Friends and church members came to our aid with prayer and intercession. Relying on the prayers of others was a great source of strength and comfort.

Dr. Paul Meier and Dr. Frank Minirth in their book, *What They Didn't Teach You in Seminary,* gave helpful direction in learning to lean on others while in crisis:

> Out of shame or embarrassment, the tendency for most of us is to hide our pain. But if you yield to this, it will cut you off from those who would offer you help and support, those who would pray with you and guide you to organizations that can assist you and your family.[3]

Moses learned the importance of this principle when Aaron and Hur held up his hands until the sun went down during the Israelites' battle with the Amalekites. (See Exodus 17:8-13.) In the Garden of Gethsemane Jesus looked for the same kind of support before the disciples failed Him by falling asleep. Be willing to make your pain known to trusted friends and prayer warriors, and then lean on their prayers.

6. Take it easy on yourself. During a crisis it is easy to place demands on ourselves that are unrealistic. Attempting to maintain a level of calmness or show of spirituality can gloss over real feelings. We have to keep going, but to press on as if nothing is wrong only prolongs any grieving process that may be necessary to healing. It is okay to feel pain, hurt, or even anger. God is big enough to handle our emotions. In his letter to the Ephesians the apostle Paul said, "Be angry, and yet do not sin" (Ephesians 4:26, NAS).

Dr. Meier and Dr. Minirth gave other helpful suggestions. They said, "Don't expect to be as creative as usual, as objective or productive. Certainly keep going, but understand that when you are enduring a long period of crisis, you may not be capable of giving your top performance. Give yourself permission to adjust your pace."[4]

In other words, lighten up on yourself. Give yourself a break. You have enough to be concerned about during a disaster without compounding the problem by condemning yourself about what you are feeling or experiencing. Dr. Richard Dobbins, in his book, *Your Spiritual and Emotional Power,* wrote:

> Isn't it sad to see people focus on their sinfulness rather than on God's love for them? When I focus on my sinfulness, I feel horrible about myself. And yet, I want to be honest about my sins. I can't forget John's reminder that, "If we say that we have no sin, we deceive ourselves, and the truth is not in us." But he also adds, "If we confess our sins, He is faithful and just to forgive us our sins and to cleanse us from all unrighteousness" (1 John 1:8,9, NAS).

7. Hang on to hope. As believers, we should never be without hope. Yet, there are times when we feel we have run out of options.

I was a suicide prevention counselor for two years. Persons who are suicidal see no light at the end of the tunnel; they have run out of options. Suicide seems the only solution. Getting a suicidal individual to see other options gives enough hope to persuade them to choose an alternate solution.

Hope brings clarity of thought and purpose to life. Someone once said, "Where there is no hope in the future, there is no power in the present." As a Christian, I find hope in Jesus Christ provides me with options if I am willing to wait on Him for them. Trying to cope without hope can be terrifying. Hope allows us to hear the words of Jesus, who said, "Come to me, all you who are weary and burdened, and I will give you rest. Take my yoke upon you and learn from me, for I am gentle and humble in heart, and you will find rest for your souls. For my yoke is easy and my burden is light" (Matthew 11:28-30).

The greatest step for the believer is to know that even in death we have hope. We take our last breath in faith knowing we will soon be with our Lord.

A LONG RECOVERY

The doctors didn't offer much hope for the recovery of our son. Only time would tell if he would remain in the coma indefinitely, awaken from the coma, or slip into eternity. During the first 12 critical hours my wife and I sat by his bed and agonized over our son. Every minute seemed an eternity.

Wednesday evening's service—the highest attended Wednesday service on record—saw our church go to prayer. We received word that people all across the nation prayed with us as our son's condition was announced over Christian television. As we sat at the bedside of our son, we were too overwhelmed to pray. We needed the prayers of God's people.

Coming out of a coma induced by closed head trauma is a slow process. The longer it takes, the more severe the trauma to the brain. After seven days Brian began to slowly open his eyes and move his limbs. At that time, he began to experience focal seizures. These seizures are much like epileptic seizures, rendering one incapacitated. Though difficult, the seizures were finally controlled by medication.

By the tenth day Brian was awake but unable to talk or walk. It was only then the doctors were able to determine the extent of the head trauma. He had regressed from an active four-year-old to the mental and physical capacity of a one-year-old. Our son would have to learn to walk and talk all over again. There were no guarantees he would progress; he could possibly remain as he was.

We never lost hope in God's ability to heal Brian. We began to work very diligently along with Brian's speech and physical therapists and neurologists—and we continued in prayer. He began to progress slowly.

Sitting on my lap one day after he had begun to talk again, Brian shared that after he was thrown from the vehicle he saw Jesus. Without any solicitation he recounted the event over a period of weeks. He said Jesus picked him up in His arms and told him He loved him, and told us things our four-year-old would not have known. Brian described Jesus down to the very last detail as He is described in Revelation 1:14-16. While riding in a car one afternoon, Brian shared how in heaven the light is brighter than the sun, but you can look into it without hurting your eyes. "In heaven, God is the light," he said. We knew beyond doubt that Jesus had revealed Himself to our son.

Brian is now a normal 10-year-old, and is at grade level in most subjects. God has done a miraculous work in his life. It still requires extra work to deal with some of the deficiencies as a result of the head trauma, but we are two of the most thankful parents alive.

I have no idea why this disaster occurred in our lives. I don't expect to know the "whys" or "wherefores" until I stand face to face with Jesus. I do know that God sustained us through our traumatic ordeal. We are grateful that He spared our son, and we grieve for parents who are not so fortunate. We take every opportunity to minister to those who have experiences similar to ours.

We know life can throw some pretty bizarre curves. We are no longer surprised by them. None of us are immune to disasters, but God has prepared us for whatever comes our way, and He is faithful to stay with us to the end.

Gary Morefield, who holds a B. A. in Biblical Literature and a Master of Divinity degree, served as a youth pastor in San Diego and Sonoma County for seven years. He pioneered Green Valley Assembly of God in Henderson, Nevada, in 1983. The church now averages 700 in Sunday morning attendance. Gary has also served as presbyter of the Southern Nevada Section of the Northern California and Nevada District of the Assemblies of God for five years.

17

Winning and Keeping Friends

DAVID MCFARLAND

It was my son Matthew's first week in preschool, and my wife Marsha and I were apprehensive about it. Three days into this new venture Matthew came home, nearly in tears, and said, "I don't have any friends at school." That was 15 years ago, but I still recall the pain that pierced my heart when he said those words. Parents with children of any age undoubtedly can relate to that pain. Or perhaps they relate to the pain because of their own experiences of loneliness.

When God created us, He built into us two characteristics that have caused both joy and sorrow: free will, and the need for fellowship and social interaction with others. Based on the choices we make and the friends we spend time with, we experience blessings or heartaches.

We begin life totally dependant on our parents. We move toward independence during our teenage years and find the experience can be painful for teenager and parent alike. As we mature and become adults, we reach a balance of interdependence with the individuals God has placed around us.

The journey from dependence to interdependence is filled with many experiences, good and bad. We discover that people can be our greatest asset or our biggest liability. Often, the outcome is determined by how we manage our relationships, from the closest friend to the most casual acquaintance.

STARTING POINT

In developing relationships at any level, there is a starting point. We must know who we are, where we are, and where we are going.

1. Know who you are. It is important to know who we are, because we interact with others based on our self-image. If we were told as children—verbally or non-verbally—we were unwanted, or if we had other negative input from our parents, we will act and react accordingly. If we were loved and cared for, our actions and reactions will reflect that as well. This is directly connected to our self-esteem.

The Bible says we were wonderfully made by a loving heavenly Father. God so loved us, and wanted and appreciated us, that He sent His Son to die for our sins so we could spend eternity with Him. That tells me I am a lovable person who is wanted and appreciated. In fact, I have said many times—even in the pulpit—the better you know me, the more you will love me. According to the Bible, God created me that way.

2. Know where you are. I believe in a supernatural God whose timing is perfect. We often don't understand God's timing; in fact, we often think He is late based on our self-imposed deadlines. We live in the reality of yesterday, today, and tomorrow; past, present, and future. These are time frames to which we switch back and forth as needs or desires dictate.

Most of the time we live in the middle zone of the present. This is the *comfort zone* where we do what we know how to do. We play to our strengths and successes because this is where we have built our track record. We have the most potential in the comfort zone, because we are most familiar with it. Usually, we don't mind leaving the comfort zone—if it's our idea; but we don't like others forcing us out.

The highest zone is the *challenge zone*. This is where we try what we haven't done before. Blind faith pushes us on to deeper depths and higher heights. The time frame of the challenge zone is tomorrow. Becoming effective in this zone guarantees that we will have a place of usefulness and effectiveness in tomorrow's society. We are more uncomfortable in this zone because we are trying new things. God stretches us, and that can be painful.

The lowest zone is the *coasting zone*. It focuses on yesterday and its accomplishments. When we are in the coasting zone, we think and talk about the "good ol' days." Spending limited time in the past is useful in respect to learning from mistakes and thanking God for past victories, but you can't live in the past unless you're a history teacher.

In regard to the zones we occupy, remember several rules. First, go to the challenge zone only when you are rested, sharp, and of clear mind. We can't stay in the comfort zone all the time; we'll stagnate if we do. Nor can we stay in the coasting zone for long periods of time, lest we become boring and obsolete. A good rule of thumb is to spend 15 percent of our time in the challenge zone, 5 percent in the coasting zone, and 80 percent in our comfort zone. What is important is to allow God into every area of our lives—past, present, and future.

3. Know where you are going. A woman who had once attended my church was visiting one Sunday morning. After the service, she came to me and said, "Do you know what you said in a sermon four years ago that I remember to this day?" For a second I was worried. Had it been good or bad? She continued, "You said our walk with God is more of a direction than an individual action." I sighed in relief and asked, "Did I say that?"

Our spiritual journey is a process, not a one-time act. After we have confessed our sins and put our faith in God, our direction is established and our walk of faith begins. It is something we are involved with day in and day out, as we walk each day toward God—toward a closer relationship, toward a more disciplined life, and away from sin.

By knowing where we are going, we can spot people and things that would take us the other way. If we're smart we'll stay away from them. We might stumble, slow down, even trip, without changing direction. We simply pick ourselves up, correct the problem, and continue on our course. The truth is, either we are going toward God or away from Him.

GOLDEN RULE

After you know who you are, where you are, and where you are going, it's time to review basic friendship skills. A good place to start is with the Golden Rule: "Do to others what you would have them do to you" (Matthew 7:12).

1. Love people more than opinions. Anyone who loves his opinion more than his friends will end up with an opinion, but no friends. People who are not effective in relationships feel their opinion must be shared no matter who it hurts or offends. If people want your opinion, they will ask for it.

2. Give others the benefit of the doubt. We usually rule ourselves with our heart and others with our head. We have mercy on ourselves, but not always on others. This formula needs to be reversed if we want to build successful relationships. In dealing with ourselves we should use our head; when working with others we should use our heart. Give others the benefit of the doubt—and benefit by closer relationships.

3. Learn to be flexible. Some confuse flexibility with compromise. There is a difference, and we must learn to distinguish it. A good friend knows how to distinguish between principle and taste; he has learned to be flexible. In matters of principle, he must stand like a rock. In matters of taste, he can swim with the current. A good friend also knows when and how to back down, and say he's sorry.

4. Don't manipulate. The value we place on others determines whether we are motivators or manipulators. Manipulators function with selfish ends in mind; motivators function with mutual advantage in mind. With motivators, everybody wins; with manipulators, no one does. No one wants to be manipulated, not even by friends; but all of us can use motivation from time to time.

CHOOSING FRIENDS

"A man who has friends must himself be friendly" (Proverbs 18:24, NKJV). In other words, sowing the seeds of friendliness will reap the fruit of friends.

When I was in the seventh grade I learned a valuable lesson about friendship. "Jeff" was the class oddball and no one liked to be around him. One day he brought a set of walkie-talkies to school, and suddenly I felt it my Christian duty to be his friend. Webster defines *friend* as a "person attracted to another by respect or affection." I had neither for Jeff; I simply wanted to use his walkie-talky. We were "friends" until one of the walkie-talkies broke, at which time I immediately lost interest in Jeff. My parents observed what had occurred and pointed out how I had used him because of what he had to offer. I was ashamed of my actions, but not enough to reestablish a friendship with the class "weirdo." I have since repented and have made an effort not to repeat my actions.

TYPES OF RELATIONSHIPS

There are basically three categories of relationships in which we can become involved:

1. Draining relationships. In this type of relationship, we find ourselves opposite individuals who sap our mental, emotional, spiritual, and physical resources. These individuals never give—they only take.

2. Mutual relationships. In this relationship, both individuals give and take, bringing balance. No one keeps score; it's a mutually satisfying relationship.

3. Encouraging relationships. Here, we are in a relationship with persons we admire and respect. Often, we find ourselves on the receiving end; not because we are takers, but because the other person has more to offer, and perhaps is a discipler God has placed in our life. That brings to mind the relationship between Paul and Timothy. Paul poured his life into this young minister, who gladly soaked up the wisdom from a great man of God. In the end, Timothy had matured to the point of being a great source of support to Paul.

Usually, in the course of our lives, we will find ourselves in all three types of relationships at one time or another. The key is to keep the proper balance. Don't allow yourself to be dominated by draining relationships. They will take the very breath of life away. If you are involved in such a relationship, take steps to withdraw enough to "refill your emotional tank." With the help of God, and counsel from spiritually encouraging relationships, you can become rejuvenated. If you continue to allow yourself to be drained, you will find yourself on a course to disaster.

We must also guard against allowing ourselves to continually be the recipient in an encouraging relationship. After all, we don't want to become a drain on another individual. Like Timothy, we must grow from the wisdom we gain from an encourager to the point where we, too, are putting something into the relationship.

The mutual relationship is the one we should most often find ourselves involved in. It blesses both parties and adds to the well-being of each.

CONFRONTING FRIENDS

A true friend is worth fighting for—even if it's the friend you have to fight; for if you see a friend in a self-destructive mode, you are obligated to confront him. Confrontation must be handled with the wisdom of Solomon, the patience of Job, and the love of David. It is impossible to count the number of casualties that resulted because a friend lacked confrontational skills. It's important to remember that self-confrontation should precede that of others. Luke 6:41 speaks about removing the beam from your own eye before you remove the speck from your brother's eye.

Conflict is part of life and is almost unavoidable in confrontation. The important thing to remember is that confrontation is not to condemn or tear down, but to correct and build up. It should be fruitful and lend to the relationship, not diminish it.

There are different ways to handle conflict. Some walk away from it; some wink at it; some "white flag" it (surrender and give up). The correct way to handle conflict is to work at it. That often involves confrontation. And that can be difficult.

There are different reasons why confrontation is difficult. We fear being disliked; we don't want to create anger; we don't want to be rejected; or we may not know how to share what needs to be shared. But God has promised to give us wisdom if we ask for it.

In confronting someone, it is important to have a proper attitude—one that is developed by the Holy Spirit. That attitude is one of helpfulness, not condemnation. We often fear that confrontation will destroy trust, but when approached with the proper attitude, the individual knows we want to help. Sometimes confrontation does destroy a friendship, but remember that Jesus also lost friends along the way.

There are certain goals in confrontation that need to be established before you attempt it.

1. Confront the issue—not the individual. As difficult as it is, keep personalities out of it. Again, confront the issue, not the individual.

2. Understand the issue. Try to have a clear understanding of the situation. Many times you know only half of the story. It's impossible to successfully resolve a conflict without knowing all the facts.

3. Establish trust. Those we confront must know we are committed to their success and well-being. If we haven't established their trust and confidence, it will be difficult to confront them with positive results. We must earn the right to confront.

4. Look for a positive outcome. Perhaps the most important goal of confrontation is to bring about positive change. We can seek to correct a situation, but our motives must be proper. Only then can the outcome be positive for both parties.

HOW TO CONFRONT

Time should be spent in prayer before confrontation. Ask the Holy Spirit for the right timing, attitude, motive, and spirit. Then clear the air of misunderstandings and rumors.

When confronting someone, do it one-on-one. Phone calls and letters are less effective and should be used only as a last resort.

Confront in the right spirit. The Bible is full of scriptures in this area. They say to confront in gentleness, in meekness, humbly, without pride or self-pleasing.

Start with a positive note. Affirm the person. Don't attack his integrity or pass judgment on his motives.

Structure the confrontation and allow time to finish. List what the problem is, why it is a problem, and the consequences the problem will bring.

Share from your perspective why you feel the way you do.

Encourage a response from the other party. Expect him to feel shock, resentment, or even bitterness. Give him time to react, unload, and offer his perspective. It is important to remain calm while talking through the issue. Finally, offer a plan of action you would like him to take.

If there was a positive response to the situation, put the issue in the past and go on from there. If not, deal with the subject again after you have processed the new information.[1]

Constructive confrontation is not learned overnight. We can do all the right things, and the problem still remain unresolved. The key is to work at it with a good attitude and keep our spirit in check. We may never solve the problem; we may only manage it.

We cannot control the wind, but with God's help we can adjust our sails to reach our destination.

WINNING FRIENDS

In Dale Carnegie's classic book, *How To Win Friends and Influence People,* he lists six ways to make people like us. They are just good common sense, but important enough to mention.

- Become genuinely interested in other people.
- Smile.
- Remember that a person's name is to that person the sweetest and most important sound in any language.
- Be a good listener; encourage others to talk about themselves.
- Talk in terms of the other person's interests.
- Make the other person feel important—and do it sincerely.[2]

One of the things our loving heavenly Father plans for us to do in heaven is to enjoy the friends we made on earth. Like the song says, friends are friends forever.

David McFarland has been senior pastor of New Life Center in Rancho Cordova, California, for six years. Previously, he was senior pastor at First Assembly of God in South San Francisco, where he pastored for 10 years. While in the Bay Area he produced and directed a weekly half-hour Christian television program. The Reverend McFarland is a Bible school teacher, computer consultant, and published author. He is also founder and president of a church software company named APOD Productions located in Sacramento, California.

He and his wife Marsha have two children: Amy and Matthew.

18

Sexual Lies

HOWARD FLAHERTY

"You can't do it, Howard! You will never be allowed to go on public school campuses to speak about sexual abstinence. Administrators will not want a minister to speak to their students about such a politically charged subject."

When I began my ministry in the public school arena three years ago, several of my colleagues spoke those words to me. They didn't mean to discourage me or steal my vision; they believed it would be nearly impossible for a Christian to get on secular campuses. Over the past three years, however, I have spoken to tens of thousands of teens all over the western United States on the subject of abstinence. And I have taken a position that is clearly scriptural.

It is exciting to find that students and staff alike are enthusiastic. People want to hear a logical message that will benefit the young people of America. The average person is frustrated with the statistics regarding teens and sex, and they want an alternative to the "anything goes" philosophy taught by the world.

SEXUAL IMAGERY

Every aspect of our society uses sexual imagery to capture our attention. Film, television, music, advertisements, and talk shows all use sex in some form to sell their products.

While driving one day, I noticed two billboards advertising different brands of cigarettes. On each, an attractive, healthy-looking young model was chosen to present their product. The young man was handsome and virile, sitting atop a horse; the young woman was beautiful and seductive, draped across a couch. The Surgeon General has stated that smoking cigarettes is unhealthy, but both ads sent a message that smoking will lead to an exciting—and sexual—life.

Millions have bought the lie. Consequently, thousands of men and women in America die from lung cancer, heart disease, and other related diseases each year. Why is this happening? Because people believe the lie. The average American is not stupid or unable to discern truth, but he has not been taught to evaluate what is true from what is presented as true.

ABOUNDING MYTHS

Since the sexual revolution of the 1960s, we have been given many messages filled with lies and half-truths about sexuality. Those lies have contributed to the pandemic growth of new and dangerous forms of sexually transmitted diseases; teenage pregnancy; abortion; emotional, physical, and spiritual anguish; and the breakdown of family values.

Speaking to students in public schools, I address three of the most accepted lies from the sexual revolution.

1. Everybody is doing it. The peer group perpetrates and believes the lie that "everybody is doing it." Then it exercises tremendous control over our behavior. After all, the peer group has the power to accept or reject us, and that has tremendous bearing on what we do.

As I wait for an assembly to begin, I like to watch students as they walk to the assembly hall. Every time, I observe peer groups in action. There is always a group of girls who come in together, talking, all dressed and acting the same. They are followed by a group of "jocks"—those young men who are the school's athletes. They, too, are distinguished by the way they walk, talk, and dress.

The power of the peer group is incredible. Most of us want to belong. When the pressure is toward a positive, productive activity that encourages a healthy lifestyle, then it's good. When it encourages a lifestyle that is destructive in any sense, it is not good.

When my son Tyler was in the seventh grade he had an eighth-grade girlfriend. One day, as he was getting off the school bus, a seventh-grade girl approached him and said she had some "juicy" information about him. He gave her a bored look and asked, "What?" She replied that she had heard he was having sex with his girlfriend.

"What?" he said. "Where did you hear that?"

"Your girlfriend told me," she said.

Tyler headed straight for his girlfriend.

"You won't believe what I just heard," he said. "A girl said she heard that we were having sex."

His girlfriend giggled. "She did?"

"Yes, and she said you told her that."

"Really?"

"Did you tell her that?" Tyler asked.

"Yes," she said with a shrug.

"You're fired!" he said, and that was the end of the relationship.

When hearing from Tyler what had happened, I told him I was proud of how he had handled the situation. There was tremendous pressure to "do what everyone else was doing," but Tyler chose the better way. After I had time to think about the situation further, I wondered what kind of pressure made a young girl tell her friends she was having sex with her boyfriend—even when she wasn't.

Many have bought the lie that "everybody is doing it," but, thankfully, many have not. Statistics indicate there has been an alarming increase of sexual activity among teenagers in America, but a majority of teens in junior high and high school are abstaining.

These "non-active" teens can be broken down into two groups: those who have never engaged in sexual activity (approximately 50 percent of teens under the age of 18); and those who previously engaged in sex and now choose not to. I am excited about that. They bought into the lie, realized it was a destructive way of life, and changed their decision. Unable to undo the past, they chose "secondary virginity" as the only healthy, intelligent lifestyle.

2. You cannot control yourself. This lie says the urge to engage in sex is so strong during the teenage years that you cannot control yourself. Thousands of young people buy into it.

Several years ago, while preparing for an assembly, I spoke with a friend who works as an AIDS educator for the State of California. When I said I was preparing to present a sexual abstinence message, he replied, "Oh, you're going to tell them to 'just say no,' right?"

"Isn't that what abstinence means?" I asked.

He repeated, cynically, "You're going to tell junior and senior high school students to say no to sex?"

"Yes."

"Good luck."

Those two words spoke volumes to me about the way society views teenage sexuality. Many believe that teens lack both the will and the ability to exercise choice in this area of their lives. They view them as "animals out of control."

I observe teens regularly who exercise their power to choose in a variety of ways. They choose what clothes to wear, what hairstyles they like. Teens choose friends, activities, and whether or not to do homework. They also choose whether or not they will use drugs, and what classes they will take. Teens are perfectly capable of making decisions; they do it all the time.

Choosing to postpone sexual activity until marriage may be difficult, but it is not impossible, as many would have us believe. A growing number of young people are aggressively saying no, because it is the only sane choice. Having contemplated the pros and cons, they have opted to wait.

3. Sex is free. When I graduated from high school 23 years ago, the "free love" message prevailed, and many of my peers bought the message. In the years since, however, we have seen that sex wasn't so free after all. A heavy price tag has been attached in the way of STDs—sexually transmitted diseases.

During my senior year of high school in 1970-71, I took a sex education class. One day was set aside to discuss the topic of STDs. One day was adequate because there were really only two diseases to talk about: syphilis and gonorrhea. Today teachers are mandated by the state to spend weeks of study in this area, because there are now more than 40 known STDs. Whereas syphilis and gonorrhea respond to penicillin or sulfa drugs, many of today's sexually transmitted diseases are incurable—even deadly.

As I speak to teens across the nation, I address five of these diseases that have affected young people dramatically. I speak honestly and openly in an effort to warn them of the dangers they face if they are sexually active. Here are some statistics:

- **Genital herpes:** 500,000 new cases occur annually.[1] It is estimated that more than 25 million Americans are infected.[2]
- **Venereal warts:** 24 million cases in the U.S., with a high prevalence among teens.[3] Genital warts is the most common STD. Some types of the viruses are believed to contribute to cervical and anogenital cancers.[4]
- **Chlamydia:** 4 million cases occur annually.[5] Between 10-30 percent of 15-19 year-olds are infected.[6]
- **Gonorrhea:** 1.3 million new cases occur annually.[7] Strains have developed that are resistant to penicillin.

- ■ HIV/AIDS: The federal Centers for Disease Control estimate that there are one million cases nationwide.[8] The rate of heterosexual HIV transmission has increased 44 percent since September 1989.[9]

It is obvious that sex is not and never has been free, neither physically or emotionally.

I was in my office in Placerville, California, about 10 years ago, when a young lady from my youth group burst through the door. She dropped into a chair, buried her face in her hands, and wept uncontrollably. I sat silently for a few moments, not knowing what to say or do. Finally, she lifted her tear-stained face and began to tell me about an episode that had occurred the previous Friday night.

"I went to the football game," she said, struggling to regain her composure. "As I was making my way down to the field, I ran into a couple of guys who are friends of mine from school. I hung around with them the first half of the game. At half-time, one of them suggested we go up to the campus." She struggled again to gain control. "They both had sex with me between the rows of outside lockers."

"They raped you?" I asked, astonished.

"No," she replied. " I let them."

"Why?"

Her reply made no sense to me at all. "I just wanted to be loved."

"How do you feel now?" I asked.

She began to cry again. "That's why I had to talk to you. This week at school I was on my way to class when I noticed a group of guys standing in a circle, laughing. As I walked past them, one of the guys called me a slut, and the rest of them laughed. Later, I passed a group of girls who were laughing and having fun. As I went by, one of them called me a sleaze. I was so embarrassed, so hurt. The guys told everyone in their gym class what happened, and now the whole school knows."

She buried her face again and wept for several minutes.

She wanted to be loved, and she paid the price. Sex isn't free.

SAFE SEX?

In light of the statistics, I have been asked why I do not talk about "safe sex" practices; why I simply don't encourage teens to use condoms as a means of protection. To me, this is illogical. Not only are condoms not safe, they are not even approved by the Food and Drug Administration as a contraceptive for pregnancy. In fact, there is a name for persons who use condoms for birth control: parents. Condoms may be *safer,* but they are not safe.

The reason, however, that I do not talk to teens about condoms has more to do with my experience of the past 16 years than it does with condom efficacy as a disease or pregnancy preventative. I have yet to find a condom that protects a teenager from the emotional fallout of sexual promiscuity. I have met thousands of teenagers who have suffered with emotional, physical, and spiritual pain as a result of sexual activity before marriage.

There are three primary reasons why many teens do not wait for marriage to become sexually active: popularity, self-image, and the need to feel loved. Teens are looking for a sense of belonging, and they believe sexual activity will provide that. Using sex as a means to gain intimacy is a response to an individual's need for love. In a world where people are experiencing brokenness in every area of life, they are looking for ways to satisfy the need for loving intimacy. Not until it is too late do they understand the consequences of premarital sex.

COUNTERREVOLUTION

By believing the lies of the sexual revolution, many young people choose a course that proves to be harmful and destructive. As I speak in public school assemblies, I call them to a counterrevolution. I encourage them to adopt a lifestyle based upon truth and love, rather than deceit and selfishness.

The story of Melody Waltz, a young lady in her thirties, and a friend of mine, illustrates the power of love. More than 10 years ago, Melody told her husband she did not want to be married any more. After the divorce, she began to date several different men and was sexually intimate with one of them. After a few months, they broke off their relationship.

Melody didn't think much about him after that. But several years later, her health began to decline. She went to her doctor and was given a battery of tests to determine the cause of her ill health. The tests determined she was HIV positive—she had the precursor disease to AIDS. She kept her HIV status secret for a year. Only she and her doctor knew about her condition.

Her ex-husband had never given up on Melody. He was a good father to their son, helped Melody financially, and reminded her that he still loved her. He wanted a reconciliation and spoke of it to her on many occasions. She always rejected his overtures, but he didn't give up.

About a year after Melody had discovered she was HIV positive, she again went to her doctor. Her condition had deteriorated significantly. She was no longer simply HIV positive—she had AIDS. She left the office in tears and cried all the way home. She would finally have to tell those close to her about her condition.

When she entered her house, she found her ex-husband sitting on the sofa. He noticed her tears and puffy face and asked, "Melody, what is going on with you? Everyone in the family is worried about you. You're obviously very unhappy. Please come back to me so we can be a family again. I love you."

Melody exploded into tears. "I can never be your wife again. My life is over. I'm dying from AIDS."

Without hesitation, he said, "Now more than ever, you need me. Come home so I can take care of you."

That is radical, revolutionary love.

Melody's health continues to decline. She could die at any time from an AIDS-related illness. In the midst of the struggle and pain, she is cared for by a loving, selfless husband who knows about true love. She is a born-again Christian and excited about her newfound relationship with Jesus Christ.

I tell young people about Melody, because I want them to know that love is so much more than sexual. Love involves love-making, but the foundation of true love is choosing *to* love. That kind of love changes people. And, if enough young people choose to love unconditionally and selflessly, it will change the world.

I receive thousands of letters every year from secular, unchurched teens who are tired of the world's "anything goes" philosophy. They are ready for a change . . . a counterrevolution . . . a revolution that tells the truth . . . a revolution based upon absolute, measurable, and unchanging truth.

Howard Flaherty is president of First Class Speakers, Inc. in Vista, California. A motivational speaker who tackles tough issues such as sexual abstinence, drug and alcohol abuse, and violence, Howard speaks to thousands of public school students across America each year. He formerly served as a youth pastor, associate pastor, and senior pastor in the Northwest, Northern California/Nevada, and Southern California Districts of the Assemblies of God.

He and his wife Pamela have two children: Tyler and Kathryn.

19

Stake Your Claim

DAVID DONALDSON

Father's Day will always be a special day to me, because it was on Father's Day that my daughter was born and I became a father.

What a day that was. I received a call saying my wife had been taken to the hospital. I hurried there and entered the lobby with my heart pounding. Suddenly I was stopped by a nurse who asked if I needed help. "Yes," I gasped, "my baby's having a wife." Through her laughter she directed me to the maternity ward.

During my early adult years I received a lot of advice on parenting, but nobody enlightened me as to how a maternity ward could prepare you for fatherhood. Babies crying, women screaming, mothers-in-law lecturing, nurses totaling your bill, and fathers-to-be moving through the halls like zombies from *Night of the Living Dead*. Before you know it, you're escorted out of the hospital with your wife, your bill, dead flowers, and a live baby.

After we piled into the car, I looked in my rear-view mirror, saw an unfamiliar creature in the back seat, and said, "Wow! What happened?" Bill Cosby summed up my feelings best when he said, "The only mistake God made is giving us children with batteries included, yet the instructions are missing."[1]

When I arrived home and the numbness began to subside, I realized this baby was not part of a hospital lease program: she was not for rent; she couldn't be returned; and she was here to stay. When the reality of it all sank in, I pronounced two sobering words: "She's ours." Those are powerful words, because when a parent declares to that child and the world, "You are mine," one is staking a God-given claim.

UNCONDITIONAL LOVE

I am intrigued by suburban graffiti called bumper stickers. In a way, it's parents staking their claim. Some read, "My child is student of the month," or "My child is on the honor roll." I've designed a bumper sticker that reads, "My child is *not* student of the month. My child is *not* on the honor roll. My child is my child."

Staking our claim isn't based on what our children have or haven't done. It's based on who they are. When we stake that claim it communicates an unconditional sense of belonging, acceptance, and pride to our children; but it also communicates much to the parent. We say to ourselves we are willing to invest our reputation in how this child turns out. To some, that can be a scary proposition.

But if we don't stake our claim—if we don't choose to actively parent our children—someone else will. If we're not staking, someone else will be taking. The world is filled with claim-jumpers, parent substitutes, surrogates, all too ready to step into our role.

THE TV PARENT

One such surrogate is the TV parent, notorious for feeding our children huge portions of the wrong foods. The TV parent is hard of hearing. He won't listen to a child when she needs to express how she feels or what she's thinking. Yet, on the average, the TV parent spends more time with America's children than their parents, pastors, and teachers combined. (In our nation, 96 percent of households have television sets, while only 90 percent have indoor plumbing. Perhaps we can conclude that more waste is coming in than going out.)

THE EDUCATIONAL SYSTEM PARENT

Today's school systems tend to reason, "We hold degrees in biology and psychology. And, therefore, we should be the ones to teach your children about ethics, the origin of life, and sex." Many districts, knowingly or otherwise, exclude parents from the educational system, insisting they are more qualified to raise our children.

THE "UNCLE SAM" PARENT

Uncle Sam says to millions of parents everyday, "I've got you covered. I'll make sure your kids have enough to eat and get a proper education." Meanwhile, millions of parents do not reside with their children or are absent from their lives altogether.

THE BOYFRIEND PARENT

Several years ago a teenage boy sat in my office and told me how his girlfriend longed for love and acceptance that she wasn't getting at home. He capitalized on it by fulfilling his own selfish hormonal drive. If we don't stake our claim and be parents to our children, someone else will fill the void with their own selfish agenda.[2]

STEPS TO SUCCESS

Here are three ways to stake your God-given claim and experience the rewards of a successful family.

1. Love God. The Bible says, "Hear, O Israel: The Lord our God, the Lord is one. Love the Lord your God with all your heart and with all your soul and with all your strength. These commandments that I give you today are to be upon your hearts" (Deuteronomy 6:4-6). Here is a clear biblical mandate for parents to model their love for God. Dr. Dobson, respected author and teacher, says a child "identifies his parents with God, whether the adults want that role or not. Most children see God the way they perceive their earthly father."

Charles Barkley, controversial player for the Phoenix Suns, said, "I don't want to be a role model—so I'm not." I've got news for Mr. Barkley. He is a role model whether he wants to be or not. The same is true for parents. We are going to shape the lives of our children negatively or positively; we cannot remain a neutral force.

A mother and her son were driving down the road. The inquisitive boy asked, "Mommy, why do all the idiots come out when Daddy drives?"[3]

Perhaps you've heard the story of Timmy and his pastor. One Sunday morning after service he approached Pastor Johnson and said, "You're a boring preacher. Your messages are as dry as the desert." Just then Timmy's mother saw her young son talking with the minister. She ran over, grabbed Timmy by the arm, and said, "Pastor Johnson, don't mind him. He just repeats what he hears."

Our children are watching and listening.

Oliver Wendell Holmes said, "Pretty much all the world's truth telling is done by children."[4] As teachers we communicate knowledge to our children. As parents we reproduce who we are. Let's model our love for God.

Loving God should be followed by training our children to love God. In this same passage of Scripture we read, "Impress [the commandments] on your children. Talk about them when you sit at home and when you walk along the road, when you lie down and when you get up . . ." (Deuteronomy 6:7). The responsibility for spiritually equipping children resides primarily with the parents; all other influences are secondary.

Parents often relegate their responsibility as spiritual leaders to others because they feel inadequate. These same parents usually *send* their children to church instead of *taking* them. God has given us the mandate to "train up" our children "in the way they should go." (See Proverbs 22:6.) We must take the responsibility seriously. Our attitude toward the church should not be, "Here is my child. Use your gifts to teach him"; rather, we should say, "I'm the one called to be the primary spiritual teacher. So, therefore, please equip me so I can equip my child." Wise parents recognize the value of the church in complementing and reinforcing their teachings, but not in taking their place.

Staking your claim as the spiritual leader begins with a decision: "As for me and my house, we will serve the Lord" (Joshua 24:15, KJV). Then parenting changes from a noun to a verb as we leave the sidelines to take an active role in our child's spiritual upbringing.

How important is a father's role in his child's spiritual development? According to John Maxwell, 77 percent of children will remain in church after becoming an adult if both parents are in church, 55 percent will remain if just the father attends, 17 percent will remain if just the mother attends, and only 6 percent if neither parent attends.[5] The wisdom of Solomon still rings true: "Train a child in the way he should go, and when he is old he will not turn from it" (Proverbs 22:6).

2. Love your spouse. There are plenty of studies that document the connection between a strong marriage and a successful family. By using the acronym "SPOUSE," we will explore ways to build a strong marriage.

Servanthood. Ephesians 5:25 says, "Husbands, love your wives, just as Christ loved the church and gave himself up for her." Christ's love toward the church was both unconditional and demonstrative. We are to love our spouse in the same manner.

> If you have any encouragement from being united with Christ, if any comfort from his love, if any fellowship with the Spirit, if any tenderness and compassion, then make my joy complete by being like-minded, having the same love, being one in spirit and purpose. Do nothing out of selfish ambition or vain conceit, but in humility consider others

better than yourselves. Each of you should look not only to your own interests, but also to the interests of others. Your attitude should be the same as that of Christ Jesus—Philippians 2:1-5.

This attitude of servanthood will breed security in our children. A fourth grade girl named Tash wrote in her essay: "My dad treats my mom very nicely, which makes me feel wanted."⁶ The most effective way to love your children is to love their mother or father.

Partnership. Marriage is not a 50:50 relationship. It is a 100 percent commitment to each other and to God. It can be liberating when marriage partners realize they cannot adequately meet their spouse's needs apart from God. As husband and wife grow closer to God individually, they will grow closer to each other.

One frustrated marriage partner said, "I married you for better or for worse, not realizing it could get this much worse." When we place our expectations in a person instead of God, we give them control over our emotional and spiritual well-being. Conversely, the more freedom we have from a spouse's expectations, the more dependant we are on God to be the source of our love.

Ongoing Romance. A couple celebrating their 25th wedding anniversary was given an all-expense paid visit to a marriage counselor by their children. During the first visit the counselor could not get a word in edgewise. Frustrated, the counselor walked over to the wife and gave her a hug. Turning to the husband he said, "She needs this a minimum of three times each week." The husband pulled out his calendar and said, "OK, I'll bring her by on Monday,

Wednesday, and Friday." Needless to say, this couple had lost the romance in their marriage.

Romance in marriage usually doesn't survive because it is too closely linked to physical intimacy. "While effective romance may lead to sex, our goal in effect should not be sex. God has wonderfully crafted women with a built-in relational safety switch that won't allow a few moments of pleasure to counterfeit a meaningful relationship."[7]

Romance is not an act, it is an attitude. It is not something we do to stoke the fires of passion; rather it is an expression of affection that endures long after the wedding day. Here are some tips:

1. *Plan.* Schedule romantic activities and then give your spouse your undivided attention.

2. *Share each other's interests.* Participate in activities that especially interest your spouse—willingly, not grudgingly.

3. *Perform kind and loving deeds.* Leave love notes for one another. Send flowers or balloons on occasion—just because. Make a phone call "just to say I love you." Keep the spark alive simply by doing the things you did before you got married.

4. *Keep your words sweet.* Use endearing words when you speak to and about your spouse. Compliment each other on appearance and accomplishments. Don't take one another for granted—express your love.

Understanding. A person doesn't need a degree in psychology to know there are enormous differences between men and women—how we look, how we think, how we feel, and how we communicate. Going the extra mile to learn how we communicate is half the challenge. Here are a few guidelines to enhance one's understanding skills:

1. *Try to recognize the issue behind the issue.* What is really being said? Is the important issue being side-stepped?

2. *Restate what the other person said.* "Now let me repeat what I think you said to make sure I understand." This eliminates misunderstandings and wasted time.

3. *Stick to the issue.* Conflicts most often arise when the conversation moves from the issue to attacking the individual. Deal with the issue at hand without blame, condemnation, or any manner of verbal assault.

4. *Use word pictures.* Use word pictures or illustrations to describe how you feel. My wife employed this most effectively one day. She said, "Sometimes I feel like a plant that gets a bucket of water poured on it when you need affection. What I need is a sprinkling of meaningful conversation and touch everyday."

If there is little communication between spouses, the home environment can be unpleasant for all. On the other hand, if there is an atmosphere of love, the whole family will absorb that love.

Solitude. Every couple must make time to escape the pressures and noises of life. This can be accomplished daily by setting aside a devotional time for the couple and the family. Each week the couple should spend at least one evening together without interference. This could be a formal date or a walk in the park; but it is a time when communication can occur without interruption. Two or three times a year, a couple should get away together for a weekend. Have friends watch your children, then do the same for them.

Evaluation. A navigator charting a course must evaluate the ship's position in relationship to its destination; otherwise it is in danger of getting lost. Similarly, couples need to establish measurable goals for their marriage, then periodically evaluate their relationship. This keeps the marriage going in the right direction, with the couple on the same track.

A challenging standard, for a father in particular, is to treat his wife the way he wants his daughter to be treated by her future husband, and model how his son should treat his future wife.

3. Love your child. Finally, we stake our claim by loving our children. That must include spending time with them. Pete Rose, a former baseball player, said, "When I was married, my wife said that I spent more time at second base than at home."[8] Unfortunately, Pete isn't alone. Studies indicate parents in America spend less time with their children than any other nation. The average father spends as little as 37 seconds a day with his children. In addition, experts say that when we do spend time together, it's usually infrequent blocks of time, such as family vacations.

We often put off day-to-day involvement with the idea that we'll make up the time with some grand gesture. It's the "quality versus quantity" mentality, and it has no place in our families. In the mind of a child, quantity is quality. There are no shortcuts or substitutes.

There was a young boy who felt neglected by his dad. Influenced by today's professional athletes, he grabbed his baseball glove, went to his father, and said, "Dad, either play with me—or trade me."

MAKE TIME FOR YOUR FAMILY

A frequent question is, "How can I spend the time I need with my family when there are so many other commitments vying for my time?" Here are some suggestions:

1. Verbalize your commitment. Communicate to your children that you want to spend time with them, not because it is your duty as a parent—but because you want to.

2. Plan activities. Mark dates on the calendar, buy tickets to an event, demonstrate to your children that you will keep your promises. Broken promises create feelings of insecurity, disappointment, and anger. In the movie *Hook,* Robin Williams played a successful lawyer who was an inconsistent father. In a hard-hitting scene he turned to his son and said, "When we get back, I'll go to all the rest of your games. I promise; my word is my bond." His son, the victim of numerous broken promises, replied, "Yeah—junk bonds."

3. Let your kids know you're accessible. Let them know they have a direct line to you. This conveys that no person or project takes precedence over them.

4. Assist children with their duties. Try to meet them on their own turf. Think about the places they go and the things they do, and find ways to participate. For example, assist them with their education. It has been said, "A father is worth a hundred school masters." Meeting children in their world will speak volumes to them.

5. Be accountable to others. Tell others of your commitment to your children. Ask them to hold you to your word.

6. Take advantage of parenting events. Make a point not to miss Father's Day, Mother's Day, birthdays, open houses, baptisms, first dates, graduations, and so on. These events will be markers they will never forget.

It was "Career Day" at Johnny's fourth grade class. Student after student stood to their feet and shared what their parents did for a living. One student said, "My dad is a doctor." Another proudly declared his father was a lawyer. Finally, all the students had shared except Johnny. He stood to his feet, proudly pointed to the back of the room, and said, "My dad is here."

When we take time to participate in parenting events, we develop a relational bank account and make regular deposits in the lives of our children. The investment will pay big dividends.

Your relationship with your children is one of a kind. Proverbs 17:6 says, ". . . parents are the pride of their children." No one else can take your place. Make your presence count. Love your children.

PRESERVE YOUR HOME

As our plane landed in northern Florida, Hurricane Andrew was exiting South Florida, leaving a chilling trail of devastation. News reports showed hundreds of homes scattered like confetti across the swampy landscape. People wept as they sorted through the debris to find precious family heirlooms.

The camera zoomed in on a family gathered where their living room once stood. A reporter asked a young boy, "How do you feel now that your home is destroyed?" He grimaced at the pile of rubble and said, "My house is gone." He paused, then smiled at his family, saying, "But I still have my home."

If we model our love for God, if we unconditionally love and serve our spouse, if we unconditionally love our children, our homes will withstand the most turbulent storms of life. Under your roof is the potential for a successful family—if you stake your God-given claim.

David Donaldson is a graduate of Evangel College. He has served as senior associate of Canyon Hills Assembly of God in Bakersfield, California, and is currently national director of ChurchCare Network, Inc. He is also co-founder of LEAD Ministries, an organization committed to providing training materials for pastors and laity. He has authored numerous manuals, including Rock Solid.

He and his wife Kristy have two children: Breahn and David-Paul.

20

The Art of Motivation

MICHAEL S. FARIAS

One of the keys to "success" is motivation. Through the years there have been many gifted motivators. They are found in the history of the church, government, sports, and all walks of life. But have you ever wondered who motivates the motivator? And how does an individual generate self-motivation?

There are times in life when self-motivation comes naturally, usually when something is in a state of newness. For example, when you buy a new car, you are probably more motivated to keep it clean and regularly maintained than you were with the old one. The same kind of motivation exists in ministry. Early on, individuals are excited about where they are and what they are doing for the church. But then something happens. In time, as motivation is lost, churches begin to show signs of neglect. The paint peels, the roof leaks, broken windows need to be repaired. But people lose motivation in all areas of life—not just with their churches. A job becomes boring and routine; a marriage fails because the couple doesn't work at it anymore. Is lost motivation inevitable, regardless of where it may occur? Certainly not. Nor is it inevitable in our ministry and our relationship with God.

Not having vision for the future—the inertia—nor the drive to press forward and conquer new challenges is what causes the lives of people to become boring and unproductive. Where should that drive come from? We may find the answer by looking at the life of David:

> David left his things with the keeper of supplies, ran to the battle lines and greeted his brothers. As he was talking with them, Goliath, the Philistine champion from Gath, stepped out from his lines and shouted his usual defiance, and David heard it. When the Israelites saw the man, they all ran from him in great fear—1 Samuel 17:22-24.

This, of course, relates to the great confrontation between David and Goliath. How is it that young David was able to go up against the giant when the strong, experienced, and equipped soldiers of Israel could not? Where did David get his strength, his courage, his motivation? The simple answer would be "from God." But if God is no respecter of persons, why didn't the others respond as David did? He went forward when others could not; he overcame distressing circumstances and was victorious when others would not even try. What motivated him?

MODERN-DAY GOLIATHS

All of us, at one time or another, will be challenged by a Goliath. He is the giant obstacle that hinders us from marching to victory. He takes away our joy and happiness. He robs us of our sense of well-being and pride. He causes us to stagnate spiritually. Don't be fooled by his sudden appearance when he comes in the form of a gigantic financial dilemma, a medical malady, an emotional puzzle, or a spiritual battle. If you are not prepared, he will stop you in your tracks. He needs to be conquered. You can't live in fear of him; you can't pretend he isn't there; you can't allow him to stop your progress. You must deal with him swiftly—the way David did—with boldness, assurance, and motivation.

When faced with a Goliath, from where do you pull your strength and courage? Again, it would be easy to reply, "from God." But we know that it is easier said than done. So what do you do? Do you say, "God, I need strength," and there you have it? Do you fast and pray until you receive the motivation to press forward? Do you gain strength from listening to Christian music? Do you play a tape of your favorite preacher/teacher until your faith and motivation are restored? Do you seek advice, counsel, encouragement, and motivation from others? What works?

David found his motivation or drive from a special source. It wasn't through Christian tapes; it wasn't through his pastor's latest sermon; he didn't go home to fast and pray; he didn't consult anyone. He moved— quickly and with determination—because some of his motivation came from a built-in resource. You and I have been blessed with the same resource. It's called memory. God had delivered David in the past, and he knew his heavenly Father would be by his side.

When David heard the challenge of Goliath, he wanted to see something done. He was instantly motivated to act, and he was instantly ridiculed by his brothers. Eliab, his oldest brother, said, "Why have you come down here? And with whom did you leave those few sheep in the desert? I know how conceited you are and how wicked your heart is; you came down only to watch the battle" (1 Samuel 17:28).

PRESS ON

Has that ever happened to you? You were motivated for a good cause and felt God was going to use you, then your "brother" ridiculed you, discouraged you, threw a wet blanket on your fire? Undoubtedly, it has. Undoubtedly, it will happen again. Learn a lesson from David. In spite of his brother's ridicule, he pressed on. Regardless of how discouraging it might have been, he was motivated to conquer.

As if that weren't enough of a setback, David was questioned by the highest authority in the land. After viewing the situation, Saul, King of Israel, said, "You are not able to go out against this Philistine and fight him; you are only a boy, and he has been a fighting man from his youth" (1 Samuel 17:33). I can imagine how the argument went. "He will destroy you. You are out of your league. Why don't you take on something you can handle? Your emotions have gotten the best of you. Come to your senses. Listen to me, David. I am the authority, and I know what is best for you."

Sometimes, well-meaning individuals give us advice on how to deal with our Goliaths. It gets especially confusing when a respected authority figure is among them. Pastors, teachers, deacons, and spiritual leaders who care about our well-being can hinder us from dealing with the situation as God would have us deal with it.

I am reminded of the apostle Paul when he was preparing to go to Jerusalem. The prophet Agabus declared that Paul would be harmed, taken into custody, and delivered to the Gentiles. Luke wrote, "When we heard this, we and the people there pleaded with Paul not to go up to Jerusalem" (Acts 21:12). Because of their love for Paul they tried to persuade him to deviate from what God wanted him to do. Paul would not be moved. He knew God's will and was motivated to act, to go. He replied, "'Why are you weeping and breaking my heart? I am ready not only to be bound, but also to die in Jerusalem for the name of the Lord Jesus.' When he would not be dissuaded, we gave up and said, 'The Lord's will be done'" (Acts 21:13,14).

Some use their authority—gained by experience or position—to dissuade us from challenging our Goliaths. Others use the authority of the Word of God. They open the Scriptures and ask, "Has God said . . . ?"

OBSTACLE OR DETOUR?

It was one of the most difficult times of my life. I was facing an enormous Goliath. My wife and I had been Christians for about a year when we felt God call us into the ministry. That meant we needed to prepare for Bible school. We proceeded to take the appropriate steps: counseling, interviews, applications, prayer, etc. We closed a business, sold possessions, put our home up for sale, packed our belongings, and anxiously awaited May, when my first semester would begin. Everything was going fine, except for one thing. Our home would not sell. It had been on the market for months. We reduced the price by more than 10 percent; still no offers. It was a Goliath blocking the path to progress.

As the deadline approached I steadily became more uneasy. Had God called us or not? I needed encouragement. I needed my faith to be quickened. I went to see my pastor. He was aware of my situation, and I hoped he would have the right words for me. Instead, I was stunned by what he said. "Brother Mike, maybe now is not the time to go to Bible school." That isn't what I wanted to hear. I wanted him to tell me to go forward. Needless to say, I was disappointed and discouraged.

I learned, however, not to look for outside influences for motivation. I also learned not to allow outside influences to stop me from doing what God called me to do. I know I had heard the voice of God, and I knew I was to be obedient. My Goliath was merely an obstacle, not a change of direction.

I had to be at student orientation on Tuesday night. We spent Monday packing our station wagon and U-Haul trailer. Monday night I received a phone call from a man who had looked at our house three weeks earlier. He made an offer, and by nine o'clock Tuesday morning we were on our way to Bible school, with papers signed and deposit money in escrow. Goliath had fallen, and I learned a lesson I would never forget. That was 15 years ago, but the motivation I gained from the experience has helped me face other Goliaths, knowing without a doubt they would fall.

MEMORIES THAT MOTIVATE

David had learned the lesson as well. When Saul discouraged him from facing the giant, David assured him the giant would fall. He said:

Your servant has been keeping his father's sheep. When a lion or a bear came and carried off a sheep

from the flock, I went after it, struck it and rescued
the sheep from its mouth. When it turned on me, I
seized it by its hair, struck it and killed it. Your
servant has killed both the lion and the bear; this
uncircumcised Philistine will be like one of them,
because he has defied the armies of the living God.
The Lord who delivered me from the paw of the
lion and the paw of the bear will deliver me from
the hand of this Philistine—1 Samuel 17:34-37.

David remembered the victories God had given him, and
he knew Goliath, too, would fall by the hand of the
Almighty. No wonder he wrote years later, "I will never
forget your precepts, for by them you have preserved my
life" (Psalm 119:93).

David drew his strength, his courage, his motivation
from memory—a resource God has given all of us. We are
told, "Only be careful, and watch yourselves closely so that
you do not forget the things your eyes have seen or let
them slip from your heart as long as you live . . ." (Deuteronomy 4:9). Do not forget all God has done for you; it will
be a constant source of encouragement and motivation.

Do you remember the day of your salvation? How and
where it happened? Do you remember the specifics?
Certainly, you do. It was a life-changing event. Remember,
too, the day of answered prayer. God answered before, and
He will answer again.

I remember one of the first answers I received to a
prayer, shortly after I was saved. I was tuning up my work
truck when I was called to the telephone. A few minutes
later when I returned to my work, I discovered I had
misplaced the rotor—a small electrical component vital to
the truck's performance. Without the rotor the engine will

not run, and I had lost it. I retraced my steps from the truck to the phone and back again, frantically searching for the item. Frustration had set in when it occurred to me to pray about it. I asked God to show me where the rotor was, and before I could finish my prayer I located the rotor on the bumper of the truck.

Every answered prayer, every fallen giant, is a source of motivation that cannot be taken away. So remember the day of answered prayer; remember the lion and the bear; remember the giant lying on the ground, no longer a threat. It will motivate you like nothing else.

"Praise the Lord, O my soul, and forget not all his benefits" (Psalm 103:2).

The Reverend Michael Farias, a credentialed minister with the Northern California and Nevada District of the Assemblies of God, has a broad range of experience in ministry, business, and community involvement. His business background spans almost two decades, and he also owns his own business.

Mike currently serves as ChurchCare Network's District Director for Northern California and Nevada. His passion to see smaller churches revitalized and affecting their communities as never before can be seen in his preaching and commitment to this ministry.

Mike and his wife Cindy have three children.

21
Making Money Work

RON S. GRAVELL

Among the problems facing our nation today is the inability to control our spending and to make our financial resources work for our benefit. Integrity, wise management, and resourcefulness have all too often fallen by the wayside as we attempt to keep up with the ever-present financial crunch occurring in our homes and churches. Yet, the God we serve is the Creator and Owner of the universe. He is the One who hands out the "talents" for which we become responsible.

Robert Orben has said, "Nowadays, money is like a New Year's resolution—you make it, but you can't keep it!"[1] This chapter will explore the biblical principle of stewardship to help us get the most out of our money. We will learn how to take the resources God gives us and make them work for His kingdom, instead of holding onto them. As we look into the concept of stewardship, we find we can trust God to provide for our needs and use our God-given wisdom to watch our finances grow.

STEWARDSHIP

Stewardship is defined as "the employment or use of one's time, talents, and possessions."[2] The concept of taking what was given to you, using it to benefit others, and then receiving more in return is difficult to grasp. We take our hard-earned checks, put them in a bank, and receive very little in return for this. It seems as if many families and churches have difficulty just paying monthly bills.

As stewards of Jesus Christ, the amount of these commodities isn't important; it's how we use them. First Corinthians 4:1,2 says, "Let a man regard us in this manner, as servants of Christ, and stewards of the mysteries of God. In this case, moreover, it is required of stewards that one be found trustworthy" (NAS). Let's look at a few keys to good stewardship.

1. Promote Christ. As Christians, it is our primary thrust in life to promote Christ. In the busyness of daily schedules it is easy to forget that. We have been chosen by God to affect the world with His plan for life. We have been entrusted with the mysteries that can be understood only by having Christ alive within. We know we are servants, but we are also the voice of God's grace.

2. Be trustworthy. A steward is an individual who has been given great responsibility. That is accompanied with an obligation to be trusted with what they are given. Most believers today think they are using their faith to the utmost. Some believe they have been given great gifts by God that can result in changed lives. Yet, some are discouraged because they think being trustworthy is the bottom line. The truth is we must also trust.

3. To be trustworthy, we must ourselves trust in God. As God desires to find us trustworthy in all aspects of our lives, so must we trust Him. It isn't enough to trust in certain areas alone; we must trust Him thoroughly and completely. I find it easy to trust God for salvation and love, but at times it is difficult for me to trust that He will meet all my needs. As He proves faithful I learn to trust more, but I still have to grow in this area. Proverbs 11:28 is a perfect reminder: "He who trusts in his riches will fall, but the righteous will flourish like the green leaf" (NAS).

THE TRUST FACTOR

The principle of stewardship is wrapped in a blanket of trust: trust that God is a rewarder of those who do good; that as He gives to us, and as we put those resources to work for God's kingdom, we will see results; that as we promote Christ, He will give the wisdom we need to handle finances for our blessing and His glory.

As we listen to God He will guide us. In my own life, when I've consulted God about a decision, I've found He will close a door if it's not the one I'm to walk through. Some would have us believe that in our financial lives, we should sit back and let God pour out the blessings upon us. I don't find scriptural backing for this principle. As with Solomon, God will give us wisdom to handle every situation of life with divine insight. To narrow it down, we have been given intelligence and intellect to use in our finances. Success comes in using God's guidance to make wise choices in handling them.

START WITH A BUDGET

One of the first keys to controlling money is to budget. This isn't a new concept, but relatively few know how or take the time to do so. They try for a while, but eventually find it difficult, confining, and/or time consuming. Why didn't it work? There was a lack of discipline. It takes work to stick with a budget, but here are some ways to help.

1. Keep it simple. Don't try to budget down to the last penny. It will only frustrate you and lead to abandoning the budget. Set a few spending goals for the month, especially in areas where you tend to overspend. Beyond regular monthly obligations, try budgeting in the areas of food, clothing, entertainment, and savings.

2. Spend with your budget in mind. I look at our family budget every day to see where we are financially and how it lines up with the budget. It takes only a few minutes, but it helps me know what I can and cannot spend. I do the same with our church finances. Two or three times a week I look at where we are in light of what the church needs for the month. That helps me use church finances wisely and efficiently.

3. Have a goal for the money you save by budgeting. The goal need not be extravagant. It may be taking the family to dinner or buying something new for the house. A small reward is an incentive to continue, and the savings mount up.

CREDIT

It is sad to say, but many families are stuck in the credit trap. They find themselves so behind that they use credit cards to pay monthly bills or buy groceries, then the interest mounts and overwhelms them. If you must use credit, here are some tips for making credit work advantageously.

1. Shop for low rates and fees. Not all credit companies charge the same for using their cards. Some offer no annual fees; some offer lower rates. Some offer cash rebates on a percentage of what you spend each year. It takes only a few minutes to call, often toll-free, to inquire about credit rates.

2. Don't use credit unless you have the cash to pay for it. If you are already using credit cards to pay bills, you need to prayerfully budget with the goal of getting out of debt. This may require a great deal of discipline, but it will pay off in the long run. You must begin working toward paying off all outstanding credit cards—and not adding to them. Cut them up if necessary, but put an end to further indebtedness. If you find yourself wanting to buy that "special" item but you don't have the cash, don't buy it. Work toward paying off the smallest credit card debt you have, then apply the amount you would have paid on it toward paying off another one. Above all, don't be tempted by credit cards that come in the mailbox; throw them away.

3. Use credit—don't let it use you. It is imperative in this society to maintain a good credit rating. It is best to incur debt only for "big-ticket" items, such as homes and automobiles. If you must have a credit card, follow God's plan of stewardship and be wise about credit. If you are in serious credit debt, the following are some helpful suggestions:

- Along with your spouse, give the situation to God through prayer.
- Communicate with the credit card company and ask them to adjust your payments to a level you can afford.
- Pay obligated expenses before spending money on "fun" things each month.
- Consolidate various monthly payments into one if you can find a lower interest rate, then aggressively work to eliminate the debt.

INTEGRITY IN FINANCES

It saddens me when ministers and churches are viewed as only "out to make a buck." Good stewardship can help eliminate such a viewpoint. First and foremost we must use finances with wisdom and integrity. Do we pay our bills on time? Are we looked upon as people who fritter money away? Do we let grandiose ideas get in the way of reality?

Job 28:12 asks, "But where can wisdom be found? And where is the place of understanding?" (NAS) The answer is in verse 28: "Behold, the fear of the Lord, that is wisdom; and to depart from evil is understanding" (NAS). Money is not evil but wastefully using what God has given us is! We will be a positive witness to those around us when we combine our God-given intellect with God-given wisdom to provide for the needs of our families and our churches.

STRETCHING OUR INCOME

One of the hardest things to do is provide for the immediate needs of our families and churches, as well as maintaining a savings for the future. It seems there is always just enough for the needs of today. Billy Graham once said, "Money can't buy health, happiness, or what it did last year!"[3] The key to keeping up with inflation and providing for the future is to plan wisely. Here are a few suggestions that can help stretch the income.

1. Analyze costs and needs. Our son, James, was due to be born in June 1991. He came five weeks early. Consequently, my wife developed complications and spent 18 days in the hospital. We knew our bill was going to be expensive, but we had good insurance. Even so, I carefully examined each bill as it arrived and discovered a total of $2,500 in duplicate or mistaken charges. Statistically, 65 percent of hospital and physician statements have some sort of error on the first billing. It is not just the healthcare industry that makes mistakes. That's why it is important to do the following:

- Carefully examine every statement you receive. Compare it to your account of what was purchased or ordered. If you find a mistake, contact the billing department. If you aren't satisfied with the outcome, ask to speak to a manager. I once had to meet with the president of a company to straighten out a problem. Be nice, be informed, know your facts, and stand your ground. This has even led to an opportunity to share the gospel since people in business respect others who conduct their affairs with integrity.

- Evaluate your outlay in the area of insurance. One of the biggest expenses today is insurance. Health, auto, and home should be covered, but establish a sufficient amount of coverage then shop for the best price. Don't cut pennies that realistically would lead to your having to pay dollars. Checking deductibles and asking the company representative for ways to save can minimize insurance costs.

2. **Shop wisely.** You can always find what you are looking for at a discounted price if you are patient. Here are some tips:

- Watch for clearance sales. The typical sales item is reduced 20-25 percent. When an item is put on a clearance sale, the savings is usually 50-75 percent. By looking for such sales you can buy more for your dollar. Most stores will tell you when they are scheduled for clearance sales—if you ask them. We shop for Christmas gifts all year long using this strategy. It helps us to spend within our means and purchase great gifts as well.
- Use coupons. You can save a great deal by using coupons when you shop. Some stores offer double-coupon days, which increase your savings even more. If you find the coupons in a particular week's paper are especially suitable to your shopping needs, buy an extra paper or two and watch your savings multiply.

There are also many free items you can get by using coupons effectively.

- Purchase closeout items. Most stores have leftover seasonal items that are greatly reduced at the end of the season. That is a great time to buy. Items such as Christmas wrapping paper or decorations, or Easter supplies, can be purchased for a fraction of their original cost and stored for the following year. Or, you might turn closeout items into an investment, as we have. We purchase all the closeout merchandise from one or two stores in our area, then sell them in a variety of ways, including yard sales. Usually, we manage to double or triple our investment, and we have fun doing it.

INVEST FOR THE FUTURE

Most of us are fortunate if we make our dollars stretch to the end of the month, but by budgeting and shopping wisely it is possible to invest for the future. Here are a few suggestions:

- Monthly savings. Even putting just a little into savings each month amounts to a large savings over a period of time. Ideally, try to save 5 to 10 percent of your monthly income. If that is not possible, start with a lower percentage, but start. Persistence pays off.
- Retirement. Social Security is not going to provide a comfortable retirement. You need to discipline yourself to invest toward the future. Because of compounding interest, money grows at a giant pace when put away early in life. But it's never too late to begin.

Even if it is only $25 a month to begin with, it's taking a step in the right direction.

- Stocks, mutual funds, real estate. Stocks, bonds, points, commission—these can all be scary words, but they don't have to be. You don't have to pay big fees to invest. Real estate, a proven and sound investment, should be purchased through a broker, or someone knowledgeable with real estate. Remember, this type of investment is usually long-term, so invest accordingly. Stocks and mutual funds can be purchased without a broker. I have found that discount brokers often have many no-load (no sales charge) mutual funds. These are a good investment because a professional is managing the account and the risk is lower because of diversity. Stocks can also be purchased directly through companies by a means called DRIP (Dividend Reinvest Plan). Stocks can be purchased without commission in this manner. Bookstores sell books that teach the art of investment, so with limited study you can prepare yourself for wise investments. Whatever means you choose, get started early and watch your money work for you and your family as the years go by.

A PEACEFUL FINANCIAL PICTURE

I have found the only way to a peaceful, happy financial picture is to trust God in all things. By trusting Him, it means I don't look to others in different situations and wish I had it that easy. The grass is seldom greener on the other side. Every family has its share of financial hardship. The key is to be prepared when the hardship comes, then trust God to see you through.

I encourage you to discipline yourself financially and to ask God to bless your efforts. Malachi 3:10 says the windows of heaven will open and a blessing will come down that we cannot contain—if we obey God. Let us honor Him in our finances and those windows will open.

Ron Gravell is executive pastor at North Hollywood Assembly in North Hollywood, California. He serves with Rev. Darrell Maston, who is senior pastor. Previously, Ron was senior pastor at Fern Valley Assembly in Lake Isabella, California. He has also served as a youth pastor and associate pastor for an additional 10 years. He received his ministerial studies degree from Berean College in Springfield, Missouri. He also has been a department manager for a large, multi-million dollar company.

Ron and his wife Vicki have one son, James.

22

The Ministry of Worship

J. DUFF ROWDEN

It's been my joy over the past 20 years to lead thousands of people in worship, in a number of countries, in all kinds of circumstances. I've had people shake my hand and hug my neck as a result of the encouragement and rejuvenation they received during worship. I've seen hard-hearted non-Christians "melt" as they watched believers express their love to God in worship. I've had people offer to kill me for leading skid row down-and-outers in worship.

I enjoy watching worshipers. Some have furrowed brows of zealous intensity; some laugh as they delight in the presence of God; others enjoy a quiet and reverent peace. Regardless of the manner in which people respond, the act of worship includes every part of our being: body, soul, and spirit.

It grieves me to see individuals—or churches—refuse to allow their emotions to enter into their worship experience.

They cheat themselves and God when they view worship as nothing more than an experience in logic, complete with a "Spock-type" stoicism, and a raised eyebrow toward those who appear to enjoy themselves. As a father, nothing is more fulfilling than to see my two beautiful children laughing and enjoying life. Our heavenly Father is no different. He takes pleasure in our enjoyment of life, including the enjoyment we get from worshiping Him.

In recent years God has begun to stir His church in the area of worship. Everywhere I travel, I find people who are hungry for a fulfilling worship experience. We must become avid students of the ministry of worship, because God wants to awaken His beloved bride to a greater responsiveness than ever before. As leaders, we have the privilege to be a part of that.

In this nation and around the world people are entering into a relationship with Christ who have no understanding of spiritual things. They are truly pagan. They don't know how to pray; they don't know the Ten Commandments; they are full of questions. As ministers, our counseling efforts can't meet the demand. Only "The Comforter," the Holy Spirit, can meet their needs as they encounter God through worship.

Gone are the days when congregational singing was merely a preliminary activity to the sermon. People want to worship and will not be satisfied until we make a way for them to do so. They will change churches and even hop a denominational line in order to find fulfillment for their hungry souls. The Holy Spirit desires to declare the truth of God in a fresh way over the face of the whole earth. "Praise be to his glorious name forever; may the whole earth be filled with his glory. Amen and Amen" (Psalm 72:19).

WORSHIP IS A GIFT FROM GOD

When God created you and me, He also created a gift for each of us. That gift is so powerful that all our needs will be fulfilled from learning how to use it. God employs it to unlock all that life is meant to be. That gift is the ability to know and worship Him. As leaders, we must be keenly focused with our ministry of worship. We have to know why God gave us this gift, and what it is supposed to accomplish in the lives of His people; we must communicate this regularly to the Body of Christ, then we must lead in the kind of worship that will bless God and His church.

THREE ASPECTS OF EFFECTIVE WORSHIP

I have found three areas of worship that, if given proper attention, will help lead us into greater maturity, joy, and productivity than we ever imagined possible. They are the *goal* of worship, the *balance* of worship, and the *flow* of worship.

1. The Goal of Worship. The goal of worship is that God be honored in spirit and in truth, and that all present would see Jesus in fresh revelation by the power of the Holy Spirit.

The gift of being able to worship God is unique to each individual—as unique as the individual himself. God uses this gift of worship to do the most spectacular of all things: *to reveal Himself to us.*

None of us can understand the most elementary spiritual truth unless God, by an act of grace, reveals that truth to us. "The man without the Spirit does not accept the things that come from the Spirit of God, for they are foolishness to him, and he cannot understand them, because they are spiritually discerned" (1 Corinthians 2:14). Before I met Christ, I saw a billboard that read, "For God so loved the world that He gave His only begotten Son," and thought it was saying that God was a political environmentalist! Now I'm sure that God the Creator has a vested interest in creation, but the point is this: I missed the essential core of what the scripture was saying.

Even believers cannot understand certain spiritual truths until God specifically reveals them. Simon Peter was a believer when Christ was on the earth, but he often missed the point of Christ's teachings. He did not yet have the mind of Christ, nor had his mind been regenerated by the power of the Holy Spirit. That is why Jesus told His disciples, "I have much more to say to you, more than you can now bear" (John 16:12).

First John 3:2 says, "Dear friends, now we are children of God, and what we will be has not yet been made known. But we know that when he appears, we shall be like him, for we shall see him as he is." The thing that will change us is the total, unhindered revelation of God. In the meantime, the constant revealing of Jesus by the Holy Spirit will change us, day by day, into Christ's image.

On this earth, we receive revelation in small increments: line upon line, precept upon precept. It usually isn't terribly dramatic, but it is fulfilling. Sometimes it can be challenging and even painful. It comes when something we've read in the Bible, perhaps many times, suddenly jumps out at us with perfect understanding, or when we hear something especially relevant in the preacher's sermon; it can come on a quiet walk with God, or while in prayer.

Desire and worship. I believe God created the heart of humankind to desire the things of God. That very desire is the thing God uses in a divine act of grace to draw us to Himself. Personal desire is as individual as one's DNA structure and reflects an individual's personality. One cannot put it under a microscope to better understand it; nor can one adequately describe it to another individual, but it will often determine our vocation, our marital status, our way of dressing, the people with whom we associate, the kind of car we drive, and the music we do (or do not) listen to.

All desire, good or bad, requires cultivation. We can corrupt our good desires by cultivating bad ones. If we give in to godly desires, we enter a life of fulfillment. The Psalmist said, "You have made known to me the path of life; you will fill me with joy in your presence, with eternal pleasures at your right hand" (Psalm 16:11). Psalm 87:7 continues with the theme of fulfilled desire in God: "As they make music they will sing, 'All my fountains [source of fulfillment] are in you.'"

As Christians, we can turn the management of our desires over to God. This is called, "delighting in the Lord." Psalm 37:4 says, "Delight yourself in the Lord and he will give you the desires of your heart." Delighting in the Lord is the act of giving our entire being and personhood to Him. He in turn will give us new desires. For example, before I met Christ I hated going to church; now I love it. I used to hate being honest and transparent; now I find freedom in it.

Not only has God put wholesome desires in the hearts of His people, but He Himself has intense desires, including the desire to be close to us.

The Lord confides in those who fear him; he makes his covenant known to them—Psalm 25:14.

For the Lord's portion is his people, Jacob his allotted inheritance—Deuteronomy 32:9.

You have stolen my heart, my sister, my bride; you have stolen my heart with one glance of your eyes, with one jewel of your necklace. How delightful is your love, my sister, my bride! How much more pleasing is your love than wine, and the fragrance of your perfume than any spice!—Song of Solomon 4:9,10.

It is hard to conceive that God could love us so much, until we remember that God *is* love. It is His divine nature. He cannot be unloving, just as He cannot be unfaithful or untruthful. Love includes the expression of wholesome desire. The more our desires are brought under the lordship of Christ, the more He is apt to answer our prayers. This occurs because our desires begin to conform to the nature of Christ, seeking God's glory, not our own gratification. Matthew 6:33 says, "But seek first his kingdom and his righteousness, and all these things will be given to you as well."

The voice of God in worship. We were meant to hear and know the voice of God. Jesus said, "The watchman opens the gate for him [the shepherd], and the sheep listen to his voice. He calls his own sheep by name and leads them out. When he has brought out all his own, he goes on ahead of them, and his sheep follow him because they know his voice" (John 10:3,4). He continued in verse 27: "My sheep listen to my voice; I know them, and they follow me."

A few weeks ago I enjoyed a breathtaking scene while taking a morning walk in a beautiful green valley nestled against the southern end of the High Sierra mountain range. As the sun rose over the mountains, I watched a shepherd guide his flock of some 2,000 sheep. About 50 of the sheep had wandered away from the main flock. This wise and loving shepherd, desiring their safety, walked over to where they had begun to graze, circled around behind them and made a simple sound with his mouth. "Tsssst! Tsssst!" Immediately, the sheep moved in the right direction without so much as an upward glance. They knew that voice; they were accustomed to it; they respected it; they obeyed it.

Later that day I took my son and daughter out to that valley. I wanted to show them the flock and share what I had observed. On the fringe of the flock near a dirt road my son and I tried to mimic the sound I'd heard the shepherd make. The sheep looked up at us, but they didn't move; their ears perked, but their feet were firmly planted. They knew my voice was not their shepherd's voice.

I've met people who have audibly heard the voice of God, but I have not had the experience. Most of us won't. I think the reason is that God has a better way of communicating with us—one-on-one, Father to child, Savior to redeemed—through worship. Worship is two-way communication between the Creator and His creation. If we aren't consistently "hearing" from God in His still, small voice, then we are not attaining worship in spirit and in truth.

Worship brings revelation. There is tremendous joy, strength, and motivation in becoming mature in our spiritual desires. Furthermore, God expects us to mature and has made provision for us to do so. Luke 24:13-32 tells the story of two men on the road to Emmaus following the crucifixion of Christ. The men were dejected and without hope. "They were talking with each other about everything that had happened. As they talked and discussed these things with each other, Jesus himself came up and walked along with them; but they were kept from recognizing him" (vs. 14-16).

God was hiding Himself for the moment; He had a few questions for them. "What are you discussing together as you walk along?" He asked.

They stood still, their faces downcast. One of them, named Cleopas, asked Him, "Are you only a visitor to Jerusalem and do not know the things that have happened there in these days?"

"What things?" He asked.

"About Jesus of Nazareth," they replied. "He was a prophet, powerful in word and deed before God and all the people."

They went on with their story and told how the women had gone to the tomb, found it empty, and saw angels. Jesus explained to them about all that was written of Christ in the Scriptures, how He had to die, and so on.

But these two men still did not recognize Jesus! They were looking right at Him and did not recognize Him! I believe it was because Christ intentionally hid Himself until He saw some desire expressed on their part.

Finally, Christ gave an unspoken challenge. He had kindled a fire of desire in their hearts again, and He waited to see if they would respond by asking for more.

As they approached the village to which they were going, Jesus acted as if He were going farther. But they urged Him strongly, "Stay with us, for it is nearly evening; the day is almost over." So He went in to stay with them. When He was at the table with them, He took bread, gave thanks, broke it, and began to give it to them. Then their eyes were opened and they recognized Him, and He disappeared from their sight. They asked each other, "Were not our hearts burning within us while He talked with us on the road and opened the Scriptures to us?"

God wants us to take the initiative in showing interest in Him, "'. . . for who is he who will devote himself to be close to me?' declares the Lord" (Jeremiah 30:21).

Often, the reward is the manifest presence of God. Both Moses and David discovered this:

> Then Moses said, "Now show me your glory." And the Lord said, "I will cause all my goodness to pass in front of you, and I will proclaim my name, the Lord, in your presence. I will have mercy on whom I will have mercy, and I will have compassion on whom I will have compassion. But," he said, "you cannot see my face, for no one may see me and live."
>
> Then the Lord said, "There is a place near me where you may stand on a rock. When my glory passes by, I will put you in a cleft in the rock and cover you with my hand until I have passed by"— Exodus 33:18-22.

In reference to David, the Scriptures say, "The Lord has sought out a man after his own heart and appointed him leader of his people" (1 Samuel 13:14). David's desire to know God qualified him for leadership. His solitary years as a shepherd were the apprenticeship of what would prove to be extraordinary leadership, for during those years David learned the heart of God and he learned to express himself to God.

For both men, their worship was rewarded with revelation from God. The same holds true for the believer today: God uses worship in spirit and in truth to reveal Christ to the believer.

2. The Balance of Worship. For worship to be balanced the flock of God must receive all the spiritual ingredients necessary for Christian growth and for correct assimilation of the Word of God.

We were created with physical needs. We all need food, air, and water, and if we don't get proper amounts of each we will die. Scientists have discovered that foods contain nutrients: vitamins, minerals, proteins, water, carbohydrates, and so on—all of which play an important role in our health and well-being. As our bodies assimilate the nutrients, they put them to work to fight off disease, create new tissue growth, utilize food, and maintain organ function.

If we received all the nutrients in the vitamin category except, perhaps, vitamin C, what would be the result? Would our bodies miss it? Would the presence of other vitamins make up for the lack of vitamin C? Definitely not. The body needs vitamin C to produce collagen, which makes up our cell tissue. Since our cells die at an astonishing rate, our bodies must be regularly replenished with new cells. Without vitamin C we wouldn't get the collagen we need to replenish the cells and we'd end up with scurvy, resulting in excruciating death.

Jesus said, "Man does not live on bread alone, but on every word that comes from the mouth of God" (Matthew 4:4). Just as the physical body needs nourishment, so does the spiritual part of our being. And as our physical food contains necessary nutrients, so does our spiritual food.

Elements of worship. Worship is one such nutrient, and it contains many elements. Praise, rejoicing, thanksgiving, adoration, supplication, intercession, and consecration are all elements of worship, each as important as the next; each with a unique purpose and function. Psalm 100:4 says, "Enter his gates with thanksgiving and his courts with praise; give thanks to him and praise his name." Thanksgiving and praise take our minds off our problems and focus them onto God, preparing us for deeper worship.

Consecration is another important element of worship. It means "to dedicate; to set apart completely." A common expression of consecration is a wedding ceremony, where a man and a woman consecrate their affections and love to each other, forsaking all others, as long as they live. So, too, without consecration we cannot have a relationship with God. We cannot serve Him half-heartedly. Jesus said, "I know your deeds, that you are neither cold nor hot. I wish you were either one or the other! So, because you are lukewarm—neither hot nor cold—I am about to spit you out of my mouth" (Revelation 3:15,16).

One expression of consecration in worship is giving. We cannot say we are consecrated to God if we hold back any part of ourselves to Him, including our time, money, and talents. We should sing songs at offering time that reflect a heart of consecration, such as the great song by Francis Havergal, "Take My Life and Let it Be," or the newer chorus, "In My Life, Lord, Be Glorified."

Another element of worship is adoration, which means "to love greatly and esteem highly; to affectionately love." It reflects the deep love we have for God, as well as deep reverence. Expressing our adoration in worship is pleasing to God and beneficial to us.

Take time to examine other elements of worship to discover their meanings and their benefits.

3. The Flow of Worship. Worship services should flow together musically and spiritually in such a way as to remove anything that would detract from the person of Christ. Any professional entertainer can plan a concert that has a musical flow to it. Planning a proper worship service, however, takes more than musical preparation. It takes spiritual preparation as well in order to achieve a worship service that directs the worshipers to the throne of God.

Prayer. Prayer is vital to any worship service. The worship leader should pray over every song, that the singing of it will accomplish all God had in mind when He inspired it to be written and all He desires to do in the lives of His people.

Private worship. To lead in effective worship, we must be worshipers. We must be people who are deep in the Word of God, who spend time in the presence of God, who know and hear the voice of God. It is easy to hide spiritual weakness behind music, but if we are to achieve a successful ministry of worship we must be strong worshipers of God.

Congregational needs. Songs for the worship service should not be selected merely on the greatness of the song, but on what God has revealed to the worship leader through prayer that He wants to accomplish in the congregation. Worship is a time when God can move among His people—if we are sensitive and obedient to His direction.

Pastoral direction. For worship to flow, worship leaders must also be sensitive to what the pastor wants to see accomplished in the service. Pastors should be in regular, focused contact with their worship leaders.

Planning. For worship to flow the service should be well-planned, yet open to the leading of the Holy Spirit. New songs should be taught to key people and rehearsed with the musicians. A song sheet or overhead projector will help the congregation follow along when a song is unfamiliar.

What happens between each song is as important as the songs that are selected. Learn how to blend songs together in proper "segues." A "dead spot" can throw a wet blanket on the atmosphere achieved through worship; but a "holy hush" adds to its intensity. Learn how to tell the difference by being sensitive to the Holy Spirit.

Continued improvement. This requires a teachable spirit that can accept constructive criticism. Write it down when things go wrong—and when they go right. Think of ways to enhance your worship service, and don't be afraid to try new things.

Fellow laborers. There is always room for more when it comes to laborers in the kingdom of God. Ask Him to send you individuals who will work in the ministry of worship. Give young people an opportunity to participate, and teach them to improve their skills. After all, they are the worship leaders of tomorrow.

Recruit, recruit, recruit. A worship department that ceases to recruit is one that is doomed to a slow, painful death, and it will affect the well-being of the entire congregation.

Goal, balance, flow. Keep those words in mind in your ministry of worship. They will guide you and your congregation into true worship: worship in spirit and in truth.

J. Duff Rowden, a Bible teacher, songwriter, and recording artist, studied music at Northwest College of the Assemblies of God in Seattle, Washington.

As a missionary evangelist with Youth With a Mission, Duff organized, trained, and led mobile evangelism and worship teams in scores of street crusades, high schools, and church services in several different countries. Duff served as minister of praise and worship at Cedar Park Assembly in Seattle and Canyon Hills Assembly in Bakersfield, California. Over the years Duff's ministry has become more focused on the powerful ministry of worship and worship leading.

Duff and his wife Bonita have two children.

23

Doing Business God's Way

RICK L. SOUZA

I believe in capitalism. It works, and it motivates men to higher challenges and risk-taking than anything else I can think of. Modern communication, travel, and technology came about because someone had an idea and desired to make a profit from it. There is nothing like capitalism for motivation.

When I was in second grade I lived two blocks from a little grocery store. That store had a vast array of candy, some of which I especially liked. The clerk had the nerve to require that I pay five cents for every candy bar I wanted. That presented a problem because I usually didn't have the necessary five cents. My mother usually didn't have it either because there were six children besides me, and those nickels added up.

As I was sitting on the front porch one Saturday afternoon, listening to Duke Snyder and the Los Angeles

Dodgers, I thought of a way to acquire the nickels I needed to satisfy my sweet tooth. That afternoon I had our neighborhood's first puppet show. It would be followed by many others. Several of my friends helped put on the show after we quickly constructed a cardboard stage. Admission was ten cents; Kool-Aid and popcorn (donated by my mother) were a nickel each; and by late afternoon my friends and I had a net profit of nearly two dollars. I had discovered that ingenuity and hard work paid off.

CALLING THE SHOTS

In my adult years I have been involved in ventures less profitable than my first, but the joy of making money had taken hold of me and created within me a desire to own my own business.

There are countless thousands of Christians in America who own their own businesses. Many are motivated by the same desire that has driven me over the years: a desire to be my own boss, to be rewarded with a certain degree of independence, and, hopefully, to earn enough to do the things that are important to me.

I don't claim to have any new knowledge on the subject, but I have made a few observations in my years of being self-employed—before and after I came to know Christ—that may benefit the readers of this chapter.

SALT AND LIGHT

There is no such thing as a Christian business. A business is an entity, such as a corporation, partnership, or sole proprietorship. It has no soul; it won't live forever; and it exists primarily on paper. It will, however, take on the character of the owner, reflecting his value system by the way he conducts business.

A business can be used as a tool to accomplish more than its stated purpose. For example, the owner of a service station has the opportunity to share Christ's love in many different ways and still make a profit pumping gas or changing flat tires. Scripture says we are the "salt of the earth" and the "light of the world" (Matthew 5:13,14). We must take every opportunity, in business as well as in our personal lives, to be what God has called us to be— even if it gets in the way of making a profit.

As followers of Christ we are stewards of a business that really belongs to Him, and the transactions we make should reflect that. Nothing hampers a testimony more than to say you are a Christian and not follow biblical principles for conducting business.

Several years ago, before I became a Christian, I did some sub-contracting for a local contractor. He was a deacon at a local church and quite visible as a Christian in the community. He read his Bible in the office every morning and talked to people about Jesus every chance he could, including me on several occasions.

Business had been slow, and he was running several sales in order to generate needed cash flow. An order came in for lumber. He told an employee to deliver it—and to charge the customer full price. If the customer questioned the amount, he was to apologize and charge the sales price. The customer was an older woman who had done business with him for quite some time, and she never questioned the amount.

His instructions shocked me and tainted his testimony. In my mind, this was not how Christians were supposed to conduct business. He gained from the sale, but he lost my respect in the transaction. Fortunately, it didn't turn me off to Christianity completely, or I might never have come to know Christ.

I suppose there can be many excuses for what he did. Times were hard; business was slow. The truth is, his actions went against biblical principles and could have had an eternal impact on an observing unbeliever. Our actions speak louder than our words, and we never know who may be watching.

James 1:22 tells us to be *doers* of the Word, not just *hearers,* and a business is the perfect environment in which to do Christ's work. We need to remember that employees, customers, and the community at large are watching. Let's not allow what we do to negate what we say.

FIRST THINGS FIRST

The primary purpose of a Christian in business is to glorify God (". . . whatsoever ye do, do all to the glory of God"—1 Corinthians 10:31, KJV), which should result in the following:

- outreach to the unsaved.
- discipleship within the business.
- funding God's work.
- providing for the needs of your family.[1]

1. Outreach to the unsaved. "Whoever acknowledges me before men, I will also acknowledge him before my Father in heaven" (Matthew 10:32). That applies to everyone we do business with: employees, customers, vendors, etc.

I cannot tell you how often the opportunity has arisen for me to talk to someone about the Lord as I conduct business. Often, the relationships I establish on the job go far beyond professional dealings. You get to know someone when you work together on a concrete slab, or when you frame a house. You get to know their hurts and problems. I have prayed for many men—Christian and non-Christian—on a job site and have had the opportunity to lead some to the Lord.

I use many of the same sub-contractors on all my jobs. Some are Christians; some are not. While I prefer to do business with Christians, quality and price take priority. I have used one painting contractor for several years now who was born in a communist country, and we have become friends. He uses words in his language that I choose not to use, but his heart is good and his ethics are above board. He was never taught about God in his native land and is not a Christian. I gave him a Bible and take every opportunity I can to talk to him about the Lord, and he comes to me when he needs someone to listen. I pray for him and earnestly desire to see him come to Christ.

2. Discipleship within the business. There is nothing more effective for training workers than a good apprenticeship program. A master or qualified journeyman teaches, guides, and instructs in the elements of the trade. The apostle Paul said, "the things you have heard me say in the presence of many witnesses entrust to reliable men who will also be qualified to teach others" (2 Timothy 2:2). It would seem that Paul was a proponent of using discipleship as a function of business.

The opportunity to disciple others for Christ has no better laboratory than in our business settings. It is easy to teach those around us to worship and serve the Lord in a safe environment, such as the church or Sunday school classroom, but we should teach others to look to the Lord when the pressures of life mount by the way we conduct ourselves in the real world.

I often think no one knows a boss, pastor, or business owner quite as well as a secretary. She sees the real person, knows the real heart, and understands what really is inside by close day-to-day association. If there ever was an opportunity to disciple someone, verbally and non-verbally, it is in this relationship. Are our invoicing guidelines honest and equitable? How do we talk about customers, vendors, and competitors? Do we adhere to biblical principles— regardless . . . or only when it's convenient? Do we ask them to lie for us? Do we conduct ourselves as followers of Christ? Every business owner should ask himself or herself these questions. How they are answered determines if we can say, like Paul, "whatever you have learned or received or heard from me, or seen in me—put it into practice" (Philippians 4:9). All of us will fall short at times, but to lay aside the principles we know we should follow because of competition, stress, or economic conditions is not pleasing to God—and could well cause an employee to stumble.

As disciplers, we have an opportunity to show those around us how God answers prayer. A few years ago I was pouring concrete on a custom home I was building that was miles from town. I was nearing the end of the pour when the truck began to rattle. This meant I was nearly out of concrete, and it appeared I would run short. The north wind was blowing, and having to wait for more concrete to arrive from town would be disastrous. I hollered for my crew to gather around, and we stopped right then to pray. I needed God to extend what little concrete was left so I could finish the job. Believe it or not, we ended up with the exact amount we needed, right down to the last shovelful.

You might chuckle at such an example, but the situation was important enough for me to pray about, and it was important enough for God to answer. Everyone there heard that prayer, including the unsaved truck driver. We all saw the faithfulness of God. Who knows which of us will remember that at a critical time in our lives and be able to call out to God with belief in our hearts because of it?

3. Funding God's work. Funding the work of God should be one of the first and foremost goals of Christians in business. Proverbs 3:9,10 is as pertinent today as it was when penned under the inspiration of the Holy Spirit thousands of years ago. It says, "Honor the Lord with your wealth, with the firstfruits of all your crops; then your barns will be filled to overflowing, and your vats will brim over with new wine."

I feel strongly that it is the Christian's responsibility to return a portion of his profits to the work of the Lord. It is the most important expenditure we can make. Families like the Rockefellers, Fords, Rothchilds, Crockers, Hoovers, Gettys, and Morgans have given untold millions of dollars to foundations and charities to fund the arts, research, exploration, and to build hospitals and museums. Many of their donations have been worthwhile; but, at the same time, many of the institutions that attack Christianity the most have been funded by them.

Conversely, even though our Father owns the cattle on a thousand hills, the church seems impoverished when it comes to having enough money to fund the Lord's work around the world. I believe it is because of the misplaced priorities of Christian business owners. I have gone on missionary work projects in Mexico, the Philippines, and Africa, and have helped to raise funds for food and clothing, and the construction of churches, Bible schools, and orphanages in those countries. Seeing the need firsthand is overwhelming, yet, all too often, the needs are left unmet because there are not enough funds.

Our churches cannot bear all the expenses of spreading the gospel around the world. Most churches have budgets with more items on the "expense" side than the "income" side. Special offerings to fund missionary work can break the back of a congregation already giving as much as it can. If Christian business owners will catch the vision of Proverbs 3:9, which instructs us to "honor the Lord with your wealth, with the firstfruits of all your crops," the truth of the next verse will follow: "then your barns will be filled to overflowing, and your vats will brim over with new wine."

Since the primary purpose of our business is to glorify God, it stands to reason that the use of some of our gain should be used to glorify Him as well. If every business owner who claims to be a Christian would set aside their tithe and a portion of their profit for ministry, so much more could be accomplished for the Lord and for the furtherance of His kingdom.

I realize some businesses are small and have only a marginal profit; others are large and have more profit than they know what to do with. Regardless of the amount, God blesses the *faithfulness* of the giver and multiplies it to meet the needs. Think of a small church or a foreign missions project as you read this, and determine to do what you can to help. The blessing you become, and the rewards you receive, will only be fully understood on the other side of eternity.

I am currently working to raise funds from Christian businessmen to help finance major repairs on a church in an inner city. The church has been neglected. The exterior looks like an old warehouse. Inside, plaster has fallen off the walls, and dry rot has set in. The roof leaked terribly before we repaired it last year. It isn't the type of building that compels you to attend; but with money and hard work, we expect to bring it up to acceptable standards.

The pastor—a young man new to the work—is called of God, and, in my heart, I feel he will be used in a powerful way. We will be a part of whatever is accomplished there, and that is a tremendous feeling.

So I ask myself, if my primary purpose in business is to glorify God, should I buy new office furniture, give myself a raise, take an extra vacation—or give toward needs such as this? There are no men in the church, and it has no money. If I don't help, the work may be left undone. In the course of eternity, I could discover thousands are not in heaven because of how I decided to use my money.

That is not to say we should not buy new office furniture—if we need it; or not give ourselves a raise—if we need it; or not take a vacation. It is saying that we should prioritize, and in so doing, not forsake the work of the Lord. Some say they cannot afford it. I say we must afford it.

As it is written: "He has scattered abroad his gifts to the poor; his righteousness endures forever." Now he who supplies seed to the sower and bread for food will also supply and increase your store of seed and will enlarge the harvest of your righteousness. You will be made rich in every way *so that you can be generous on every occasion,* and through us your

generosity will result in thanksgiving to God—
2 Corinthians, 9:9-11, italics added.

My corporation is currently in the process of establishing a smaller non-profit corporation. We want to channel profit into this entity so we can select two missionary projects to work on every year; one in the United States, one overseas. Other Christians who do business with me will be encouraged to contribute to the projects. Accordingly, we have decided to maintain our office and home in a comfortable but modest style and use as much profit as possible to further the kingdom of God.

4. Providing for the needs of your family. "If anyone does not provide for his relatives, and especially for his immediate family, he has denied the faith and is worse than an unbeliever" (1 Timothy 5:8). This should be so obvious that it is unnecessary to mention, but in my observations as a businessman and minister, I have discovered the obvious isn't always obvious to everyone.

Currently, my wife and I are preparing for two weddings. Both daughters are getting married this year—within 10 weeks of each other. Our son was married two years ago, so that leaves just the two of us. In light of that, I have spent a great deal of time over the past few months reflecting on the childhood of my children and the decisions we made as parents. Did we do a good job? Would we do things differently in retrospect? We have made mistakes, of course, but I think our children would agree that Sharon and I provided for their needs. As they mature, they understand their needs were far more important than their wants, and had to come first. At times they confused the two, but we knew the difference.

Years ago, we decided to live a lifestyle that would be comfortable but not elaborate. We would forego the "toys" that many of their friends owned and establish our own set of priorities. Christian education was foremost on the list. Two months ago, at the time of this writing, we made the last of our tuition payments, which began in 1979. There were many difficult times during the 15 years we had our children in Christian schools, but next to our tithe, we consider it the most important investment we made.

We also felt it important they participate in summer camps, youth conventions, and other activities where they could experience the touch of God in their lives. Often, the bank was pressed, but God honored our commitment, and He always provided.

I encourage you to consider the needs of your family. They truly are more than food, clothing, and shelter. Those things benefit the physical being, but there are needs for the spiritual being that must be provided for as well. What are your priorities? What are their long-term benefits? Would the Lord approve? It would be the worst of tragedies to stand before the Lord, having been the most successful business person in your field, having supplied a house, car, boat, and college education for a family that never committed to the Lord. I have tried to prioritize my life so when I stand before God, my children and grandchildren will be with me. Only then can I truly be counted successful.

EXTENDED FAMILY

Employers also have a responsibility to meet the needs of their employees. Most of us are familiar with Dickens' tale of Scrooge and his treatment of Bob Cratchett's family.

We feel sorry for them and point an accusatory finger at Scrooge. Yet, I have observed similar situations in the Christian community. I see church boards who pay their pastoral staff near-poverty wages; I know of Christian employers who brag about good employees, then tell me how little they pay them. This cannot be pleasing to a bountiful God who supplies all our needs. Scripture is extremely clear on this matter:

> Look! The wages you failed to pay the workmen who mowed your fields are crying out against you. The cries of the harvesters have reached the ears of the Lord Almighty. You have lived on earth in luxury and self-indulgence. You have fattened yourselves in the day of slaughter—James 5:4,5.

First Timothy 5:18 adds, "For the Scripture says, 'Do not muzzle the ox while it is treading out the grain,' and 'The worker deserves his wages.'"

Managing and running a business can be a difficult and trying endeavor. Many laws and regulations create hardships and burdens for business owners; long hours, worry, and fatigue add to the pressures. The Golden Rule is a good bench mark to return to: "In everything, do to others what you would have them do to you, for this sums up the Law and the Prophets" (Matthew 7:12).

REAPING THE REWARDS

I love owning my own business. In spite of the trials and difficulties, I would have it no other way. As I said before, I believe in capitalism. In my opinion, so does the Lord. He allows us to invest in His kingdom and receive interest with dividends that are unparalleled on Wall Street. They are realized in both temporal and eternal benefits; they are for today as well as eternity.

If you are in business for yourself, or are considering going into business for yourself, these observations should be helpful to you. If you have been in business for yourself and have never applied these principles, or recently have forgotten to, rearrange your priorities and prove God. See if He doesn't "throw open the floodgates of heaven and pour out so much blessing that you will not have room enough for it" (Malachi 3:10).

Rick Souza is an ordained Assemblies of God minister; owner of a development company, Aerie, Inc.; and President of CFI, a lending institution for Christian ministries. He served on staff at Century Assembly in Lodi, California, for more than four years, then went into business for himself to fund his missionary work. Before entering the ministry, Rick was Vice-President of Corporate Training for American Savings & Loan.

Rick has traveled to the Philippines, Mexico, and Namibia, where he has built churches, Bible schools, and orphanages. He currently serves as Director of Church Construction Corps for the Northern California/Nevada District of the Assemblies of God.

He and his wife Sharon have three children: Brian, Mindy, and Shawn Deanne.

24

Destined to Overcome

DUANE PARRISH

My wife stood at my bedside in the intensive care unit of the hospital, anxiety in her heart. Violet looked at my swollen head resting on my shoulder, not certain she was in the right room. "Can this be my husband?" she wondered. Glancing at the name tag on my bed, she realized the seriousness of the situation. Questions filled her mind. "Will Duane ever be the same? What will happen next?"

Facing brain surgery was difficult for both of us; yet, we shared a sense of peace. After all, we trust God. We had both given our lives to the Lord and to the ministry. We pastored a wonderful church. Surely God was greater than this sickness. We did not realize we were facing the greatest difficulty of our lives.

When I awoke five days after surgery, I had full recollection of who I was. I could even identify the people in my room. I wanted to express the thoughts floating through my head, but when I opened my mouth I was speechless. Only two words came out: "Oh, God." When my doctor asked me to write my name, I could not. Overcome with fear, I reached for my Bible. I often turned to God's Word for comfort, and I knew I would find solace by reading the Scriptures now. But after opening my Bible I stared blankly at the page. I could no longer read.

Reality hit me: I had been stripped of all abilities. My wife and I stood on the threshold of agonizing change, yet in the ensuing months and years we were to learn great truths about the process of overcoming.

TRUTHS OF TRIBULATION

1. Overcoming is a process. For most, it is gradual and progressive. I had no doubt God could have restored me instantaneously, having seen instant manifestations of God's miraculous healing. He has the power to do so. Yet, the course He chose for Violet and me was to be progressive.

2. Overcoming implies difficulty, obstacles, impediments, barriers; for without difficulty, we would have nothing to overcome. Scripture even tells us to expect trials and tribulations. We read in James: "Consider it pure joy, my brothers, whenever you face trials of many kinds, because you know that the testing of your faith develops perseverance. Perseverance must finish its work so that you may be mature and complete, not lacking anything" (James 1:2-4).

James says it is not a matter of *if*, but *when*. Testing *will* come, often when we least expect it. We are to be ready and not caught off guard, for there is a purpose for each difficulty we face. It is to produce perseverance—a cheerful, constant enduring of patience—in our lives.

3. Overcoming requires us to accept God's sovereignty. Sovereignty implies God is God, and we are not. The overcoming process gains momentum when we begin to ask "what," not "why." What is God trying to show or teach me? What lesson can I learn?

In the midst of my physical, mental, and spiritual trial God gently helped me change my questions from why to what. To focus on why only kept me emotionally and spiritually paralyzed. I had to fully accept that even in difficult situations God had a plan and purpose for my life. Furthermore, my continually asking why only kept me in the problem.

Through the anguish of my testing God showed me the intense selfishness of my life. "How could a loving God punish His servant?" I asked myself. "I have given my life to the ministry, and this is what I get in return?" I learned God is more interested in my life being given to *Him* than to the ministry.

God had called me to minister, but His kingdom will be established with or without me. The weighty matters of eternity do not rest with my gifts and talents. It is not a matter of what I have done or will ever do. God is more concerned about my *being* than my *doing*. For unless *being* becomes priority, my *doing* will come from a wrong motive. God was—and is—seeking my praise and worship for who He is: the sovereign God who knows best and does all things well.

4. Overcoming reveals my total weakness. It requires God's power, not mine. Try as I might, the words would not come. For hours I agonized over simple words any two-year-old could say. Distraught and frustrated, I began to see what the apostle Paul meant when he said, "That is why, for Christ's sake, I delight in weaknesses, in insults, in hardships, in persecutions, in difficulties. For when I am weak, then I am strong" (2 Corinthians 12:10).

Often, I have seen well-meaning Christians burned out because of their effort to overcome. Desperately, they try everything. They pray harder, longer, louder; attend church more frequently; and even contribute more to the work of the Lord. All of these are good in and of themselves. But what happens when we have done all we can and the obstacle continues to stare us in the face?

God showed me in my complete weakness and helplessness that His strength was all I needed. An enormous weight was lifted when I recognized that overcoming would be accomplished by God's power working through me. It would not be because of anything I could do, but in what He would do. God wanted my cooperation, and He matched it with His power, strength, and wisdom. As a result, the glory belongs to Him.

5. Difficulty is not always a result of sin. We must remember that overcoming difficulty is part of the divine plan God has for us. Tribulation is not necessarily a sign of sin, failure, or lack of spirituality. Usually, it is an exercise in spiritual growth. As I lay in my hospital bed, a well-meaning Christian asked my wife, "What sin did Duane commit?" Evidently he believed this dreadful tragedy could only come because of sin in my life.

Jesus encountered the same attitude when He healed the man who had been blind from birth.

As he went along, he saw a man blind from birth. His disciples asked him, "Rabbi, who sinned, this man or his parents, that he was born blind?"

"Neither this man nor his parents sinned," said Jesus, "but this happened so that the work of God might be displayed in his life"—John 9:1-3.

The blindness was not the result of sin; rather, it was part of the divine plan God used to display His mighty work. Hidden within each temptation, trial, or testing is the opportunity to see God's mighty display of deliverance.

6. Overcoming demands a proper attitude toward difficulty. Scripture abounds with examples of the testing, trials, and tribulations that come to God's people. "A righteous man may have many troubles, but the Lord delivers him from them all" (Psalms 34:19). "In this world you will have trouble. But take heart! I have overcome the world" (John 16:33). "But we also rejoice in our sufferings, because we know that suffering produces perseverance; perseverance, character; and character, hope" (Romans 5:3,4).

With all the assurance of trials, we should not be surprised when they arrive at our doorstep. Instead, we should be encouraged that God has made a way for us to go through the trial and come out stronger than before.

A wise man once said, "God talks to us in our joy and shouts to us in our pain." During my painful process of overcoming, God was faithful to continually speak to me. At times His voice was only a whisper; at other times He had to shout to make me hear. Yet, through the process,

He continued to speak. He showed me three specific truths related to trouble.

First, trouble was to turn me to God. Whether I wanted to accept it or not, God was refining my life through testing. I recalled how I had told my congregation we were to praise the Lord for who He is, not just for what He would do for us. "It is God's ball game," I often said. "He has the right to call the shots in our lives, and we can rest secure in Him. After all, He always works for our betterment, not our harm." Now, God was asking me to be a player, not just a spectator.

One day, in the midst of deep depression, God spoke to me. "Duane, if I don't heal you past this present stage, will you still praise Me?" The critical test was before me.

You have got to be kidding, I thought. Boy, was I angry. *It isn't fair.* Though I could not verbalize the words, in my mind the message was loud and clear: *Is this the thanks I get for serving You since I was five years old?* My anger was intense. Violet noticed something was horribly wrong.

In my self-pity I removed myself to my office located in our home. Violet followed—upset, concerned, and determined to stay with me. I ignored her and went to the closet where I kept my gun, fully intent on taking my life. Then I heard Violet's prayer. "God, I can't stop Duane. We need Your help. Help us, please."

I was immediately convicted by the Holy Spirit. My self-pity was revealed and I was cut to the heart. Dropping on my knees, I pushed aside the gun and lifted my hands to God. Weeping, I told Him I would praise Him for who He is, regardless of whether He healed me or not.

Self-pity sees trouble as a tormenter. Faith sees trouble as a tool for our refinement. We can know how we are responding to trouble by looking honestly at our attitude. Do we resent the success of others? Do we come across short, abrupt, and hard to those who are closest to us? Are our actions cruel and careless? Do we view life through cynical eyeglasses? Or are we tender, pliable, compassionate, and useful to God? Trouble will find us. When it does, we must choose how we will respond.

Second, God showed me my trials would reap a valuable harvest. Tribulation is a word God uses in relation to His children. The derivative of tribulation is the same word "threshing." The farmer does not thresh the weeds; he threshes the wheat. Nor does he thresh it to punish the wheat, but to make it useful and beneficial.

God is more concerned about the grain of patience than He is the straw of trouble. The grains of perseverance, longsuffering, compassion, and kindness are the object of His threshing—and they cannot grow without trouble. If we resist, it may be because we do not recognize the object of the threshing process.

Third, God showed me trouble will either make me bitter or better. Only one letter distinguishes one word from the other. So close, yet miles apart. The letter "i" compared to the letter "e" changes the meaning of the word. The "i" was crucified with Christ. Our tendency is to resurrect it. Each time we do, we miss the valuable lesson that trouble can teach.

It takes a quiet heart, one stilled before God, to accept trouble as His instrument of refinement in our lives.

7. Overcoming denotes development and deliverance. In Psalm 84 we read of the Valley of Baca. Baca means "tear shrubs," or "weeping." It is not uncommon that because of the testings of life, we find ourselves in the valley of weeping. Notice what this psalm reveals: "As they pass through the Valley of Baca, they make it a place of springs; the autumn rains also cover it with pools. They go from strength to strength, till each appears before God in Zion" (Psalms 84:6,7).

We are to "pass through" the valley of weeping. Our responsibility is to make it "a place of springs." God allows the rain of His Holy Spirit to create pools to refresh us there. Those pools enable us to go from "strength to strength."

What is your attitude toward testing? What are you looking for while in the midst of your trials? Attitude is so important in times of difficulty. When you find it a struggle to hope, remember the words of David: "I am still confident of this: I will see the goodness of the Lord in the land of the living" (Psalms 27:13). No matter how difficult it becomes, the Lord has goodness in store for you.

While you may think your valley is desolate, God has prepared pools to refresh your weary spirit. They often come disguised as a word of encouragement or prophecy; sometimes in the presence of a friend. Then there are those glorious moments when God Himself ministers peace, comfort, strength, and wisdom directly to you. Even now, pools of refreshment are available to you. Look for them, for they are there.

I learned slowly that progress through the valley of testing comes one step at a time—from strength to strength. We do not receive all the strength at the beginning, but as we need it; enough for each step. That is the difference between deliverance and development. Many ask God for deliverance because they do not want to face the painful process of character development. God can deliver instantaneously; however, the normal process God chooses is deliverance from "strength to strength," allowing us to experience God's gracious development process.

God's purpose in saving us is not simply to deliver us from hell. His desire is that Christ may be formed in us. (See Galatians 4:19.) In other words, He longs to see the character of Christ developed in our lives. That process cannot be instantaneous, or we would simply become robots—mechanical objects unable to express love toward our Creator. The process of life is to conform us to the image of His Son. (See Romans 8:29.)

A professional photographer told me, "The darkroom is where the difference is made between a quality photograph and a mediocre one." He went on to explain: "When the image of the object is impressed on the film, that is just the beginning. The film then must go through the process of development. It requires the right temperature, chemicals, and time. All three elements must be carefully and accurately applied to the film. Only then will the object's image reflect the quality desired by the photographer."

At the moment of salvation, a permanent impression of the Savior is made in our hearts. It is the darkroom experience where God applies His development process, conforming us to the image of Christ.

8. Overcoming gives us a voice. Those who overcome have a voice. I am amazed at how many people I encounter who need someone to be a friend, someone who can identify with struggles, pressures, and problems. Without trials, we would not be able to feel the hurts of others. They are what make us useful to others in time of need. When we reach out to those who are hurting, we discover strength and are often reminded we don't have it so bad after all. It allows us to speak of the goodness of God, which is a testimony of God's faithfulness to all concerned.

Since the day I awoke from surgery to discover I could not speak, read, or write, Violet and I have seen God's miraculous intervention in our lives. We have also seen His power to help us move through the trial from strength to strength. Today, I have the privilege of standing in the pulpit once again, restored by the faithfulness of God. I don't speak as fluently as I once did, but that is only a reminder of how far God has brought me.

As I speak throughout North America and around the world, I see His faithfulness, new every day. Because of His never-ending faithfulness, I am compelled to share His love with those, like you, who are destined to overcome.

No matter what the trial, I can say confidently, you are destined to overcome. That is God's desire for you. He is with you each step of the way and will provide you with the refreshing rain of the Holy Spirit.

Duane Parrish has nearly four decades of ministry experience as an evangelist and a pastor. He served on the Youth Senate for the Oregon District of the Assemblies of God, and he has spoken at youth camps, camp meetings, district retreats, and missionary retreats.

Duane pastored his last church for 15 years, during which time he underwent major brain surgery. After a miraculous healing, he resigned the pastorate to begin his current ministry, Destined to Overcome. Duane now travels the world sharing what the Lord has done for him. He authored the book, A Postcard to Heaven, *distributed by New Leaf Press.*

He and his wife Violet have a burden to reach out to hurting people. They have two grown children: Mark and Patrece.

25

The Church: Haven or Hazard?

DALE A. ROBBINS

The title of this writing may seem, at first, to be rather unusual. After all, we would suppose the church to be a safe place—right? Unfortunately, the church has sometimes been a place where many have experienced wounds instead of healing. In fact, statistics show that a great percentage of persons who stop attending church do so because of some type of offense or injury to their feelings that happened there. Sometimes these occur because of the insensitivity of the church; other times, people are themselves at fault for being too touchy or sensitive to misunderstandings. In any case, it is sad that such experiences ever occur, because the church is an indispensable part of the believer's life. Not only does it provide a place for him to worship, serve, and learn about God, it is a community of believers where he can practice his love toward his brethren as the Bible requires. "But if we walk in the light, as he is in the light, we have fellowship one with another, and the blood of Jesus Christ his Son cleanseth us from all sins" (1 John 1:7, KJV).

Whatever you do, don't give up on the church. God requires you to be faithful to it and to be accountable to its spiritual leaders. (See Hebrews 10:25; 13:17.) If you have been hurt there, don't run away—equip yourself with the protection of God's Word. You may not be able to stop offensive things from happening, but by applying God's principles you can stop them from hurting you. "Great peace have they which love thy law: and nothing shall offend them" (Psalm 119:165, KJV). The following 13 steps can help believers protect themselves from getting hurt in a church.

1. Avoid developing unreasonable expectations.

My soul, wait thou only upon God; for my expectation is from him—Psalm 62:5, KJV.

The definition of disappointment is "the failure to attain one's expectations." Do not expect things from the church or the minister that they cannot deliver, or that the Bible does not teach them to do. Many expectations have to do with preconceived "traditions" that we have come to associate with a church, perhaps from another fellowship we once attended. It is a good idea to meet with the pastor and ask what you can expect of his ministry and the church.

Occasionally, people get disappointed when they find out their church cannot supply all their earthly needs. Most churches attempt to help the needy during crises and emergencies, but some expect the church to meet all their material needs or pay their bills like the early church did. Unfortunately, this just isn't possible unless everyone agrees to sell all their property and possessions and give them to the church like the early believers. (See Acts 4:34,35.) Most churches would be blessed if everyone merely paid their tithes; however, statistics show only a small percentage of churchgoers give a full tithe regularly.

Neither is it realistic to expect the pastor to spend all his time with you, to attend every social function, or for him to show you constant attention. Learn to place your expectations upon God. He will always be faithful to His promises in His Word.

2. Do not place absolute trust in people.

Thus saith the Lord; Cursed be the man that trusteth in man, and maketh flesh his arm, and whose heart departeth from the Lord—Jeremiah 17:5, KJV.

Come to terms with the fact everyone is human and will fail you at some time or another. Even the pastor will make mistakes. The only one you can trust entirely, without fail, is God.

Realizing any human can fall short, the degree of trust we place in people must be limited and will depend on their track record. The more we get to know a person's character and the history of his behavior, we can determine how trustworthy he is. This is one of the reasons why Scripture tells us to get to know our pastors and spiritual leaders—so from their godly lifestyle, we will be able to trust their leadership. "And we beseech you, brethren, to know them which labour among you, and are over you in the Lord, and admonish you" (1 Thessalonians 5:12, KJV).

There is a difference between "love" and "trust." It is possible to love and forgive someone, without placing an absolute trust in them. To illustrate, let's say there is a school bus driver who has a drinking problem. One day, while transporting a load of children, he becomes intoxicated, wrecks the bus, and kills all the children. As the lone survivor of the crash, he turns to the church to seek God's forgiveness for this horrible act of irresponsibility. If he repents of his sin, will God forgive him? Absolutely. Should the church love and forgive him as well? Of course. And what if he should then volunteer to drive the church bus? Do we trust him? Absolutely not! It would be unthinkable to put a person in the driver's seat who has shown such recent negligence. Certainly, we love and forgive him, but because of his poor track record, we could not risk the lives of our passengers. Over a long period of sobriety and safe driving, he may prove he is again reliable and capable of being trusted as a bus driver.

Remember, love and forgiveness are granted unconditionally, but trust must be earned. Trust is the acquired confidence in one's actions. We certainly can, and should, trust persons who show trustworthy behavior, but because all men have the potential for failure, we should never put an infallible sense of trust in anyone but God.

3. Focus on common ground.

Now I beseech you, brethren, by the name of our Lord Jesus Christ, that ye all speak the same thing, and that there be no divisions among you; but that ye be perfectly joined together in the same mind and in the same judgment—1 Corinthians 1:10, KJV.

Avoid becoming highly opinionated. Opinions are the interpretations and ideas of men, which if constantly pressed on other people, can cause division or promote sinful debates and quarrels. (See Romans 1:29.) Opinionated people are prone to get hurt when others disagree with them.

The Bible teaches all Christians to "speak the same thing" (1 Corinthians 1:10, KJV) so that there will be unity in the body of Christ. The only way such unity is possible is for Christians to focus on the common ground of Christ and His Word. That is, we all need to say what the Word says: to let the Bible speak for itself rather than trying to promote our opinions. In Scripture, we see that the apostle Paul instructed Timothy to "preach the word" (2 Timothy 4:2, KJV), not his opinion about the Word. A preacher is intended to be a delivery boy of God's message, not a commentator of the message. That is the Holy Spirit's job. (See 1 John 2:27.)

Similarly, at one time the news media were required to comply with a strict code of ethics. They were to report the facts of the news accurately without adding their opinion or commentary. But, as time has passed, news reporting has become less factual and more opinionated—corrupted with rumors and gossip rather than real information. Reporters have evolved into commentators who manipulate what people think about the news. Like reporters, preachers need to stick with the facts.

Naturally, every believer has his own convictions and opinions about a great many things, but if he continually tries to push that opinion on others, conflict will eventually emerge. Avoid controversy over scriptures that are vague and foster many interpretations; stand fast upon those common, basic truths—Jesus, His life, death, and resurrection—and do not add to what God's Word says. "Every word of God is pure: he is a shield unto them that put their trust in him. Add thou not unto his words, lest he reprove thee, and thou be found a liar" (Proverbs 30:5,6, KJV).

4. Do not expect any church to be perfect.

> For I know that in me (that is, in my flesh,) dwelleth no good thing: for to will is present with me; but how to perform that which is good I find not. For the good that I would I do not: but the evil which I would not, that I do—Romans 7:18,19, KJV.

It is remarkable to consider the apostle Paul confessed he was not perfect—that is, like us, he experienced struggles in his flesh. If one of the leading authors of Scripture and apostles of the early church admitted to this, it should not seem too strange if we find other brothers and sisters in the church struggling with imperfections too.

Since churches are made up of people like you and me who have imperfections, there will never be such a thing as a perfect church. Unless we understand this, we will have an unrealistic view of the church and will eventually become disillusioned and hurt.

One job of the church is to help perfect the saints—like a spiritual hospital, where people go to get well. Instead of resenting persons in the church for their flaws, be thankful they are trying to grow in Christ. Learn to love and accept people for what they are. They are not any more perfect than you are.

Just as it has been said of beauty, imperfection is in the eye of the beholder. A person with a negative attitude can find fault wherever he or she wishes. In contrast, the person with a positive outlook can always find the good and beauty in things. The well-adjusted person in the church should seek out the good and encouraging things as the Bible teaches. (See Philippians 4:8.) Those who dwell on the negative or continually find fault with the church will eventually get hurt.

5. Do not seek to promote yourself or your own agenda.

> Lift not up your horn on high: speak not with a stiff neck. For promotion cometh neither from the east, nor from the west, nor from the south. But God is the judge: he putteth down one, and setteth up another—Psalms 75:5-7, KJV.

Have a humble and meek attitude like Christ. (See Matthew 11:29; Romans 12:3.) Besides making you obnoxious, pride and arrogance will set you up for a fall. (See Proverbs 16:18.) Do not promote yourself, campaign, or strive to attain an appointed or elected position. God is the one who puts persons in such positions, and unless He does it, stay away from it. Lift up the Lord in all you say and do. Do not boast or talk about yourself. "He that speaketh of himself seeketh his own glory . . ." (John 7:18, KJV).

Avoid an attitude of competition, which creates conflict in unity. A competitive attitude compares self with others and strives to rise above that comparison. (See 2 Corinthians 10:12.) The philosophy of Christianity is not trying to outdo one another, but "submitting . . . one to another in the fear of God" (Ephesians 5:21, KJV) and lifting up one another. We are even told to "prefer" our brother above ourself. "Be kindly affectioned one to another with brotherly love; in honour preferring one another" (Romans 12:10, KJV). Competition between churches and Christians is divisive and contrary to the faith.

Do not expect to receive preferential treatment or to get your way about everything. The Bible teaches favoritism is wrong, and the church will try to make decisions and do things in the best interest of the whole congregation, not just a few. "But if ye have respect to persons, ye commit sin, and are convinced of the law as transgressors" (James 2:9, KJV). If you do things for the church or give generous offerings, do it to bring glory to God, not to bring attention to yourself or to gain influence. (See Colossians 3:17.) The Bible even says when you give offerings to help the poor, do it anonymously to gain God's approval, not man's. (See Matthew 6:1.)

Avoid the trap of presuming your opinions are divinely inspired or indisputable. Share your suggestions and ideas with church leaders, but do not push your opinions or personal agenda. You may feel your ideas come from God and attempt to add clout to your suggestions or complaints by saying, "God told me . . ." Indeed, God does speak to His children, but you will not be the exclusive source through which He reveals Himself in a matter. If your opinions really come from God, others will bear witness with it, especially His pastors and leaders. (See 2 Corinthians 13:1; 1 Corinthians 14:29). Pastors are God's representatives in His ordained chain of command, and if He wants to get something across to His church, He will bear witness with the ones in charge.

6. Avoid blaming the church for personal problems.

Thou wilt keep him in perfect peace, whose mind is stayed on thee: because he trusteth in thee—Isaiah 26:3, KJV.

When you go to church, you should try to dissociate the church from the personal problems you deal with. The majority of hurt feelings in a church result from wounds and sensitivities people carry with them. This kind of emotional distress can create distorted perceptions that may prevent you from seeing reality the same way others do. Such things as low self-esteem, abuse as a child, marital problems, personal offenses, family conflict, a root of bitterness, health problems, or job dissatisfaction can twist your interpretation of words and actions. You may imagine people don't like you or misinterpret well-intended words as an offense. Trivial problems will seem like big problems. Blame for unhappiness may be transferred to the church, its leaders, or the people. You may lash out against others or be quick to find fault with the church. Remember this: do not jump to conclusions over anything because things are usually not as bad as they seem.

7. Treat others as you wish to be treated.

Therefore all things whatsoever ye would that men should do to you, do ye even so to them: for this is the law and the prophets—Matthew 7:12, KJV.

Human beings tend to be reciprocal creatures. That is, they reflect the way they are treated. This is why Jesus gave us the Golden Rule: "Do unto others as you would have them do unto you." The way most people interact with you is a direct result of how you interact with them. If you have a frown on your face, you won't get many smiles. If you offer friendliness, it will usually be offered back. (See Proverbs 18:24.) Be gracious, encouraging, and a blessing for others to be around. If you have a negative, critical attitude toward people it will tend to generate a critical attitude toward you. "Judge not, and ye shall not be judged: condemn not, and ye shall not be condemned: forgive, and ye shall be forgiven" (Luke 6:37, KJV).

Many hurt feelings can be avoided if we realize people usually react to how we deal with them. Examine the way you say things, or even how much you talk: "A fool's voice is known by [a] multitude of words" (Ecclesiastes 5:3, KJV). Do not be rude and impolite. Make sure you are not overbearing and bossy. People will be turned off and will avoid you.

8. Have a teachable, cooperative attitude.

Obey them that have the rule over you, and submit yourselves: for they watch for your souls, as they that must give account, that they may do it with joy, and not with grief: for that is unprofitable for you—Hebrews 13:17, KJV.

The Bible teaches believers to be cooperative and submissive to their spiritual leaders—something that is not possible unless the believer is committed to a church and accountable to a local pastor. Accountability to a godly shepherd is a part of God's order for the spiritual growth of every Christian. God's Word gives the pastor authority to organize and maintain order in the church, to teach God's truth, and to correct and discipline when necessary to hold his flock accountable to biblical principles. In the apostle Paul's encouragement to ministers, he stated, "Preach the word; be instant in season, out of season; reprove, rebuke, exhort with all longsuffering and doctrine" (2 Timothy 4:2, KJV).

A lack of proper respect toward authority is a common problem today. People do not want to be told what to do or be corrected if they are wrong. This is one reason the modern church produces so many immature believers. When people hear something they don't like, or are corrected in some way, they simply pack up and go to another church. "For the time will come when they will not endure sound doctrine; but after their own lusts shall they heap to themselves teachers, having itching ears" (2 Timothy 4:3, KJV).

As long as you are part of any particular church, you must come to accept that the pastor and leaders are in charge there. Regardless of how unqualified you might think they are, God recognizes them as the authority in that body and will hold them accountable. Consequently, God holds you accountable to respect their authority, to pray for them, and to cooperate.

Always be cooperative, willing to humble yourself. If you have a rigid, inflexible attitude in the church, you will probably get hurt.

9. Do not oppose or hinder the church.

These six things doth the Lord hate: yea, seven are an abomination unto him: A proud look, a lying tongue, and hands that shed innocent blood, an heart that deviseth wicked imaginations, feet that be swift in running to mischief, a false witness that speaketh lies, and he that soweth discord among brethren—Proverbs 6:16-19, KJV.

One thing God dislikes most is someone who sows discord—who creates division and strife in the body of Christ. Do not be a gossip, a complainer, or stir up turmoil. If you are displeased with the church in some way, either try to offer your help and prayers, or, as a last resort, leave and find a church you are happy with. But never become a source of agitation or hindrance.

Do not bad-mouth a man of God; if you do, you are asking for problems. One time when the apostle Paul was being punished for preaching the gospel, he unknowingly condemned Ananias, the high priest, who then ordered the apostle be slapped on the mouth. When Paul realized who he was, he apologized for speaking against Ananias, knowing that it is forbidden to bad-mouth God's representative—despite Ananias' treatment of Paul. "Then said Paul, I wist not, brethren, that he was the high priest: for it is written, Thou shalt not speak evil of the ruler of thy people" (Acts 23:5, KJV). It is a serious matter to "touch" God's anointed—either with words or actions. Imperfect as they may be, they are His representatives. "He suffered no man to do them wrong: yea, he reproved kings for their sakes; saying, Touch not mine anointed, and do my prophets no harm" (Psalms 105:14,15, KJV).

If a minister has done you wrong in some way, do not incriminate yourself by responding in an unbiblical manner—do not lash out against him, retaliate with rumors against him, or run him down behind his back. You should go and confront him privately according to the scriptural fashion described in Matthew 18:15-17. If the first and second attempts do not bring a resolution, take the matter to the spiritual body, such as the church board or denominational overseers to whom he is accountable. Any correction or discipline should be left to them. Keep in mind, an accusation against a minister is a serious matter and will not be accepted unless the matter can be substantiated by other witnesses. (See 1 Timothy 5:19.)

When things are not as they should be in the church or with its leadership, there are honorable ways to help promote improvements or resolve inequities. However, it is unethical to oppose the church or attack its leadership, and persons who do will likely end up hurt, bitter, or worse.

10. Be committed to forthrightness and truth.

> Moreover if thy brother shall trespass against thee, go and tell him his fault between thee and him alone: if he shall hear thee, thou hast gained thy brother. But if he will not hear thee, then take with thee one or two more, that in the mouth of two or three witnesses every word may be established. And if he shall neglect to hear them, tell it unto the church: but if he neglect to hear the church, let him be unto thee as an heathen man and a publican—Matthew 18:15-17, KJV.

When someone has wronged you, Jesus says you are to first go to him and confront him privately. Most offenses in the church result from misunderstandings and could be quickly resolved if offended parties would go to the source and find out the facts. Unfortunately, some offended people will absorb the offense silently, growing bitter and resentful. It is important to God, and a matter of obedience to His Word, that such issues are confronted so that:

1. You will not become bitter and withdraw from the church.
2. The offender is held accountable to not repeat his offenses, which could harm the faith of others.
3. The offender who has perpetrated sin might be reconciled with God.

If he is uncooperative with your first private effort, you are to try a second time, taking witnesses with you. Finally, if not successful, turn it over to church leadership.

You should never take one side of a story and accept it as fact without verifying it with the other party. There are always two sides to a story. Scripture says before we believe a rumor, we are to investigate thoroughly to verify all the facts. "Then shalt thou inquire, and make search, and ask diligently; and, behold, if it be truth, and the thing certain, that such abomination is wrought among you . . ." (Deuteronomy 13:14, KJV).

It is impossible to have a relationship with a group of people without occasional misunderstandings and offenses. Unless you commit yourself to confront these issues in the way Jesus described, you will become hurt in the church.

11. Be devoted to love and forgiveness.

He that loveth his brother abideth in the light, and there is none occasion of stumbling in him—1 John 2:10, KJV.

Christians will avoid a lot of problems if they will commit themselves to an unconditional love for their brethren. The practice of loving the brethren—all the brethren, not just the lovable ones—keeps us from stumbling. Never forget that Jesus takes personally how we entreat our Christian brothers and sisters. When we love even the "least" of our brethren, Jesus accepts that love toward Himself. (See Matthew 25:40.) You cannot love the Lord any more than you love the least in the body of Christ. "If a man say, I love God, and hateth his brother, he is a liar: for he that loveth not his brother whom he hath seen, how can he love God whom he hath not seen?" (1 John 4:20, KJV).

Be quick to forgive and do not hold grudges. Unforgiveness and bitterness are some of the greatest reasons why people get hurt in the church and probably the greatest cause of apostasy—falling away. Remember, unforgiveness is one of your greatest enemies. If you refuse to forgive, it will prevent God from forgiving you and could keep you out of heaven. "For if ye forgive men their trespasses, your heavenly Father will also forgive you: but if ye forgive not men their trespasses, neither will your Father forgive your trespasses" (Matthew 6:14,15, KJV).

12. Do not get caught up in the offenses of others.

Lord, who shall abide in thy tabernacle? who shall dwell in thy holy hill? He that walketh uprightly, and worketh righteousness, and speaketh the truth in his heart. He that backbiteth not with his tongue, nor doeth evil to his neighbour, nor taketh up a reproach against his neighbour—Psalms 15:1-3, KJV.

One of the greatest characteristics of the body of Christ is to care about the burdens and sufferings of one another.

However, as we seek to console and encourage friends who have been offended, we may be tempted to take up their offense against another. In sympathy, we may tend to take their part against the pastor, the church, or whomever they blame for the offense. This is unwise and unscriptural, considering your friend may be the cause of his own offense. His hurt feelings may be caused by a misunderstanding, a difference of opinion, his own rebellious attitude, emotional instability, or immaturity. Remember, there are always two sides to a story, and only a fool develops an opinion based on one side or without all the facts.

Sometimes offended persons will seek sympathy from naive, listening ears. They go about pleading their case, pouring out their wounded heart to sincere, tender-hearted persons who will listen. Their goal is to seek out those who will coddle them, support their opinion, and take up their offense against the offending party. You should love and encourage a friend with hurt feelings, but reserve your opinion and avoid taking sides, lest you find yourself a partaker in another man's sins, or you also become offended with the church.

13. Do not personalize everything that is preached. Obviously, every pastor preaches with the hope that every person will take the message personally and apply it to his own life. However, there are always a few who think the minister is pointing his sermon specifically at them. This is a common misunderstanding that causes individuals to get hurt.

This feeling of personal focus from a sermon may occur if persons:

1. Are under conviction about a particular sin.
2. Are especially self-conscious.
3. Are under emotional distress.
4. Spend a lot of time counseling with the pastor.
5. Have previously been corrected or hurt by the pastor.

Keep in mind, a pulpit preacher does not focus his attention solely on one person. His concern is for the broad range of persons in attendance.

Occasionally, someone thinks his pastor focuses on him, the way he focuses on his pastor. When a pastor stands in front of a congregation week after week, one develops a feeling of close friendship with him, coming to know personal details of his life. However, even if the pastor knows each member of his flock, it is not possible for him to focus on each one with the same detail they focus on him. It is easy for dozens of people to know him well, but not realistic for him to know dozens of people in the same way. Consequently, some may develop the illusion the pastor focuses on them when he preaches—that he remembers their personal details in the same way they remember his. But the pastor has too many other members to consider. He counsels with many, hearing scores of similar problems and details. It is not likely he will single someone out and preach at them, while trying to minister to the entire congregation. If there is something specific the pastor needs to say only to you, he will deliver it personally, in private—not from the pulpit.

In conclusion: By applying these principles to your relationship with the church, it will help prevent many needless hurts. May God bless and prosper you in the body of Christ!

The Reverend Dale A. Robbins is senior pastor of Christian Life Center in Grass Valley, California. He has served in ministry for more than 20 years. He holds post-graduate degrees in biblical studies and has authored numerous Christian articles and publications. For many years he was producer and host of several widely seen Christian TV shows.

Dale and his wife Jerri, an accomplished vocalist and songwriter, have one daughter: Angie.

Endnotes

Chapter 1

1. Lloyd Cory, *Quotable Quotations* (Wheaton, IL: Victor Books, 1985), p. 404.
2. "Dear Abby," *Chicago Tribune*, February 2, 1991, as reported in *Parables, etc.*, vol. 13, no. 6, August 1993.

Chapter 3

1. Huldah Buntain, *Treasures in Heaven* (Springdale, PA: Whitaker House, 1989).

Chapter 4

1. On May 14, 1988, Larry Mahoney, under the influence of alcohol, drove his pickup down the wrong side of an interstate highway near Carrolton, Kentucky. He crashed head-on into a church bus bringing 67 young people and their sponsors home from a day at an amusement park. The bus belonged to First Assembly of God in Radcliff, Kentucky. Twenty-seven people died; dozens more were crippled and scarred.
2. Children's Defense Fund. Figures are daily averages based on annual figures. Some statistics are from 1988 census data. Other figures are derived from annual crime reports and other information dating from 1985 to 1988.

Chapter 5

1. Lillian Trasher, *Letters from Lillian* (Springfield, MO: Assemblies of God, Division of Foreign Missions, 1983), p. 11,12.

Chapter 6

1. Gordon MacDonald, *Restoring Your Spiritual Passion* (Nashville, TN: Thomas Nelson, 1986), p. 26.

Chapter 8

1. Stephen R. Covey, *The Seven Habits of Highly Successful People* (Fireside, Simon & Schuster Publishers, 1990), p. 146.

Chapter 10

1. *Webster's New World Dictionary of the American Language* (U.S.: World Publishing Company, 1966), p. 1455.
2. Alvin J. Lindgrin and Norman Shawchuck, *Let My People go: Empowering Laity for Ministry* (Nashville, TN: Abingdon, 1980), p. 81.
3. Lloyd M. Perry and Norman Shawchuck, *Revitalizing the 20th Century Church* (Chicago: Moody Press, 1982), p. 19-34.
4. Ibid., p. 36.
5. Ibid., p. 36-39.

Chapter 11

1. Glen Van Ekeren, 1994.

Chapter 12

1. Gordon D. Fee, *New International Biblical Commentary on 1 and 2 Timothy and Titus* (Massachusetts: Hendrickson Publishers, 1988), p. 227.
2. Ibid.

Chapter 13

1. George Barna, *The Barna Report, What Americans Believe* (Regal Books, 1991), p. 36.
2. Ibid., p. 29,30.
3. William L. Bennett, "Getting Used to Decadence," *Vital Speeches of the Day,* vol. LX, no. 9, February 15, 1994, p. 267.
4. Ibid.
5. Leonard Ravenhill, *America is Too Young to Die* (Bethany House, 1979), p. 32.
6. Ibid., p. 30.

Chapter 14

1. Psalty's Singing Tapes, Debbie & Ernie Rettino.
2. Joseph Parker, Preaching Through the Bible, vol. 14 (Grand Rapids, MI: Baker Book House, 1978), p. 33.
3. Peter C. Wagner, *Prayer Shield* (Ventura, CA: Regal Books, 1992), p. 181.
4. Reuben Welch, *We Really Do Need Each Other* (Grand Rapids, MI: Zondervan Publishing House, 1993), p. 32.
5. Jacob M. Broude, *Complete Speakers' and Toastmasters' Library* (Englewood Cliffs, NJ: Prentice Hall, Inc., 1965), p. 107.
6. Gary R. Collins, *The Magnificent Mind* (Waco, TX: Word Books, 1985), p. 19.
7. David D. Burns, *Feeling Good* (New York, NY: Avon Books, 1992).
8. Tom White, *Breaking Strongholds* (Ann Arbor, MI: Servant Publications, 1993), p. 44.
9. Thomas Green, *Weeds Among the Wheat* (Notre Dame, IN: Ave Maria Press, 1984), p. 145.

Chapter 15

1. John Calvin, quoted in *Leadership,* Fall 1993, p. 74.

2. "A Majority of American Pastors . . .", *National & International Religion Report*, April 20, 1992, p. 1.

3. Tryon Edwards, ed., *The New Dictionary of Thoughts* (New York: Standard, 1877), p. 159.

4. Robert W. Cummings, *Gethsemane* (Springfield, MO: Gospel Publishing House, 1944), p. 21.

5. Ibid., p. 24.

6. Ibid.

7. J. Oswald Sanders, *Spiritual Leadership* (Chicago, IL: Moody Press, 1986), p. 161.

Chapter 16

1. *The American Heritage Dictionary* (Houghton Mifflin Company, 1983).

2. Paul Brand and Philip Yancey, "And God Created Pain," *Christianity Today*, January 10, 1994.

3. Paul Meier and Frank Minirth, *What They Didn't Teach You in Seminary* (Nashville: Thomas Nelson Publishers, 1993), p. 138,139.

4. Ibid.

Chapter 17

1. John Maxwell, "Confrontation: The Thing No One Wants to Do," cassette tape from Enjoy Life Club, vol. 6, no. 8, February 1991.

2. Dale Carnegie, *How to Win Friends and Influence People* (New York: Pocket Books, a division of Simon & Schuster Inc.), p. 112.

Chapter 18

1. STD/HIV Prevention, Centers for Disease Control, #404/639-3, p. 13.

2. *New England Journal of Medicine*, July 6, 1989, p. 7-12.

3. Kay Stone, Sexually Transmitted Diseases Division, Centers for Disease Control, U.S. Department of Health and Human Services, telephone interview with Focus on the Family.

4. Gilead Sciences Inc., Lana Lauher and Linda Fitzpatrick, Foster City, CA, 415/573-4858.
5. STD/HIV Prevention, Centers for Disease Control, p. 13.
6. C. Kuehn and F. Judson, "How Common Are Sexually Transmitted Infections in Adolescents?" *Clinical Practice Sexuality*, p. 19-25.
7. STD/HIV Prevention, Centers for Disease Control, p. 13.
8. Pamela McConnell, Sexually Transmitted Diseases Division, Centers for Disease Control, U.S. Department of Health and Human Services, telephone interview with Focus on the Family, March 16, 1992.
9. "Heterosexual HIV Transmission Up in the U.S.," *American Medical News*, February 3, 1992, p. 35.

Chapter 19

1. James Dobson, *The Strong Willed Child* (Wheaton, IL: Tydale, 1978).
2. Ken Canfield, *Seven Habits of Highly Effective Fathers* (Nashville, TN: Tyndale, 1994).
3. David and Annette La Placa, *I Thought of It While Shaving* (Harold Shaw Publishing).
4. Ibid.
5. Heard on Joy Ministries Tape Club, John Maxwell, San Diego, CA.
6. Canfield, *Seven Habits of Highly Effective Fathers*.
7. Gary Smalley and John Trent, *Love is a Decision* (New York: Pocket Books, 1989).
8. Canfield, *Seven Habits of Highly Effective Fathers*.

Chapter 21

1. *Quotable Quotations* (Wheaton, IL: SP Publications, Inc., 1985), Robert Orben, p. 296.
2. *The Reader's Digest Great Encyclopedic Dictionary* (New York: The Reader's Digest Association, Inc., 1966).

3. *Quotable Quotations*, Billy Graham, p. 298.

Chapter 23

1. Larry Burkett, *Business by the Book* (Dahlonega, GA: Christian Financial Concepts, 1984), p. 1b.

About the Editors

Hal Donaldson is a journalism graduate of San Jose State University. He served as editor of *On Magazine* and taught at Bethany College. He is president of ChurchCare Network, an organization that sends ministries—at no cost—to smaller churches. He has authored numerous books, including *Where is the Lost Ark?*, *One Man's Compassion*, *Treasures in Heaven*, and *Downfall: Secularization of a Christian Nation*.

Kenneth M. Dobson left a successful business career to enter full-time ministry many years ago. He received his B. A. in Biblical Literature from Northwest College and his M. A. in Church Leadership from Southern California College. He formerly served with Mark and Huldah Buntain in Calcutta, India. He is the pastor of First Assembly of God in Visalia, California—a thriving congregation of more than 2,000. The Reverend Dobson's first book is entitled, *The Vow*.

For order information write:

Onward Books
P. O. Box 3237
Visalia, CA 93278.